Kiwi Air Power

Kiwi Air Power

A history of the RNZAF to the end of the Cold War

Second Edition

Matthew Wright

Published by Intruder Books, Wellington, 2019

ISBN 978-0-908318-26-1 (Intruder Books)

Publication history
First published 1998 by Reed New Zealand Ltd
Republished with minor revisions for Kindle 2015 by Intruder Books
Republished in print 2017 by Intruder Books
Republished with further revisions as a second edition in print 2019 by Intruder Books

This book is part of the New Zealand Military Series. Collect the set.

www.matthewwright.net
www.mjwrightnz.wordpress.com
www.facebook.com/MatthewWrightNZ

Contents

Foreword

Kiwi Air Power was first published in 1998, several years after I first proposed it to Reed NZ Ltd, New Zealand's oldest non-fiction publisher. It sold well in hard-cover but I did not seek a reprint.

In 2017, *Kiwi Air Power* was republished in print, as a paperback. This second edition of 2019 has been more materially revised, although I have again not updated the story into the twenty-first century. The themes I explored in the late 1990s reached their natural end around the turn of the millennium, with the transition away from Cold War priorities. The story of the RNZAF into the twenty-first century is a different tale.

Matthew Wright
May 2019

Introduction

Aircraft were in their infancy in 1909 when New Zealand's Liberal Premier Joseph Ward offered to buy a battleship for the mother country, Britain. The air services missed out, and when private enterprise donated a single aircraft to New Zealand in 1913, nobody in the military knew how to fly it. More than twenty five years passed before government was prepared to commit to a full air force.

This book takes a broad-brush approach to the history of the Royal New Zealand Air Force, which was formally made an independent service in 1937, looking to the 'how and why' that helps us understand the shapes and patterns of the past. It is not a technical history of the aircraft; the focus, primarily, is on politics and people, on the broad sweep of events that shaped New Zealand's military aviation.

In that mix, as we will explore through this book, the RNZAF's greatest asset has always been its people; not just prominent service personnel but also historically significant political figures such as John A Lee, Walter Nash and Peter Fraser. Creativity, innovation and enthusiasm have been keys to a sixty-year tradition by which the service has been achieving spectacular results, most often under adverse conditions. In 1943 RNZAF personnel discovered how to pit Lockheed Hudsons against Japanese fighters off Guadalcanal — and win. A year later, RNZAF pilots found ways of flying C-47 Dakotas further at higher weights than anybody else. Later still, it was the RNZAF that asked for — and got — an avionics fit for its Skyhawks that nobody else had considered or tried. These traditions stood the service in good stead through the lean 1990s, when shrinking budgets called for tough decisions.

One of the major shaping forces behind the RNZAF has been New Zealand's perception of its place in the world. In 1919, New Zealand considered itself an outpost of Empire. European politics were paramount; Britain was guarantor of New Zealand defence. Yet there were fears of Japanese aggression. Britain eventually shared this view, and from this emerged the 'fortress Singapore' strategy of the 1920s, with its single-minded concentration on the navy. New Zealand's military aviation suffered, but the Labour administration of 1935 took a new approach. Although ties to Britain were not weakened, the government of Michael Joseph Savage was suspicious of British ability to defend New Zealand in the face of German re-armament and Japanese militarism. Influential politician John A. Lee called for an air force as a cheap, effective, modern and practical means of self-defence. His thinking won the day, but the British — alarmed at an apparently independent New Zealand policy — managed to twist the resulting scheme towards British defence policies.

The Second World War was a rite of passage. The structure of the RNZAF expanded against the fluid movement of war, driven by men and women with little prior experience — who generally rose to the occasion. A measure of the desperation New Zealand faced as a result of pre-war indifference and the failure of the British Singapore strategy can be gauged from the fact that, in 1942, there were serious plans to pit Vickers Vildebeestes against Mitsubishi Zeroes in defence of New Zealand.

More than 50,000 New Zealand airmen and nearly 5,000 women of the WAAF saw action from Egypt to Guadalcanal, in England and over Germany. RNZAF engineers and personnel bore the brunt of the failure of British strategy in Malaya — the strategy that had strangled the development of New Zealand military aviation for twenty years. The RNZAF was in no position to send squadrons to Europe. Instead, pilots and aircrew were trained for service with the RAF. In the Pacific, the RNZAF contributed to the allied war effort; but was side-lined in early 1944 by the United States in retaliation for the Canberra Pact.

After the war, New Zealand settled back into traditional defence thinking, sending squadrons to the Middle East in support of British forces. However, the advent of the Cold War and Communist threat in South East Asia brought the focus back to the Pacific. At first this was through the lens of Commonwealth, and the RNZAF fought with British and Australian forces in Malaysia. The ANZUS link subsequently dominated New Zealand defence policies until a controversial anti-nuclear stance in 1985 prompted the United States to suspend military co-operation.

The end of the Cold War introduced further change. For the RNZAF, the late 1980s and 1990s were years of restructuring and 'tail to teeth' reforms that did not disguise the fact that the service was diminishing. Yet at the same time, there were new government demands. The fact that the RNZAF was able meet those demands was, again, testament to quality of personnel.

Matthew Wright
May 2019

CHAPTER ONE

Official indifference 1908–31

Air forces are now an essential component of all efficient defensive fighting forces... a nation thinking in three dimensions will lead and defeat a nation thinking in two, both in time of peace and war.

— Lieutenant Colonel A Vere Bettington, *Report to the New Zealand Government on the Air Defence of New Zealand*, July 1919.

The origins of the Royal New Zealand Air Force can be traced to 1908, when fifty one year old Christchurch politician and philanthropist Henry Francis Wigram visited England and was bitten by the aviation bug. The following year, in an address to the Legislative Council in Wellington, he called for a New Zealand Flying Corps. His words fell on deaf ears. This was the age of social militarism, when military action, people and hardware were socially exalted. However, New Zealand was in the grip of naval mania. The Premier, Joseph Ward, promised a 'first class dreadnought' to Britain in April, and the public went wild with enthusiasm. Ward's gift battleship was converted by British sleight of hand into a battlecruiser, and by the end of the year, a loan of more than a million pounds had been raised to pay for it.[1] Against the massive impetus and cost of this initiative, flying had to take a back seat.

Military aviation resurfaced in 1911 when New Zealand was forced to rethink its military position. First Lord of the Admiralty Winston Churchill, alarmed by revelations of German naval construction, withdrew ships intended for New Zealand waters. Despite the Anglo-Japanese alliance, both Australia and New Zealand were worried by the possibility of attack from Japan. A paper by the Committee of Imperial Defence sought to oil troubled waters. However, fears in New Zealand remained high and steps were hastily taken to organise local defence.[2] The focus remained on naval measures. Preliminary arrangements were made in 1912 to send Wallace Burn and Arthur Piper to England for pilot training, but even so, the Annual Report of the Defence Department for 1911-12 proposed no 'definite recommendations' or expenditure 'in connection with the purchase of aeroplanes... We must learn to walk before we can fly.'

Private largesse provided New Zealand's first military aircraft, a two-seat Bleriot XI monoplane, named *Britannia*, donated to the Dominion in 1913 by the Imperial Air Fleet Committee. The aircraft arrived in New Zealand in September, crated on board the *Athenic*. No military personnel had been trained to fly, but this was academic because the IAC had omitted to send the engine and propellor. The missing parts arrived in December, and the aircraft was eventually flown in January 1914 by Royal Flying Corps pilot Joseph Hammond. He was relieved of duty a few days later after illegally taking Esme McLellan for a joyride. That year Major-General Alexander Godley, commanding the New Zealand Military Forces, recommended a 'waiting policy' on the basis of the 'rapid and incessant' pace of aerial development.[3] *Britannia* was put in storage, and when the First World War broke out later that year, bundled off to Britain.

Flying at home: World War One

As fighting surged across Belgium and France, Wigram urged the government to establish flying training schools for the Royal Flying Corps. With heavy focus on providing infantry for the ground war, nothing was done to meet military aviation needs apart from donating another monoplane to the Royal Flying Corps. However, the War Office in London offered generous terms to attract New Zealand pilots. Any pilot qualifying for a Royal Aero Club certificate would be commissioned as Second Lieutenant in the Royal Flying Corps; the British also offered to pay a first-class fare from New Zealand, and refund £75 of the tuition costs.

These terms made private tuition feasible. Enthused by the successful flight of their home-built Curtiss flying boat in 1915, Auckland engineers Vivian and Leo Walsh decided to try their luck with a flying school. Government turned down their request for financial assistance, so the brothers found private backers. The Royal Aero Club agreed to issue certificates to graduates, and the New Zealand Flying School opened at Kohimarama near Auckland with three pupils. At first the only aircraft was the home-built Curtis, but the brothers later acquired a Caudron, other Curtiss aircraft, and a Boeing. Pupils included George Bolt, who founded the Canterbury Aero Club with R D Wraight and W M Angus, and in 1910 built and flew New Zealand's first glider. He later became an engineer at the Kohimarama school, and when ill health forced Vivian Walsh to stop flying in early 1918, Bolt was appointed chief instructor.

Henry Wigram matched these developments in the South Island. He was a man of his time; a successful businessman of the late Victorian mould for whom philanthropy and patriotism was a way of life.[4] Aircraft had become a private passion; and in 1916 Wigram offered to 'provide a tuition fleet, flying grounds, appliances and equipment including plant and machinery for repairing and, possibly later on, building aeroplanes to train aviators for the Royal Flying Corps of Great Britain and, after the war, for the defence of the Dominion and for every other purpose to which aviation is applicable.'[5] Like the Walsh brothers, Wigram received the cold shoulder from government, and founded his Canterbury Aviation Company privately on a capital of £30,000. The first hurdle was finding aircraft — long lead times were accentuated by the war situation. Again, Wigram's convictions drew him on, and in July 1916 he ordered two Caudron biplanes from France for £1100. In August, he spent a further £660 on a dual-control Caudron. He also secured the services of an English instructor, Cecil Hill, formerly chief pilot of the Hall Aviation School at Hendon.

Wigram asked Lieutenant J W H Scotland to find a site, and after a brief search the RFC officer recommended Sockburn, six miles out of Christchurch. By early 1917 construction was well under way. The two Caudrons arrived in April, Hill arrived the following month, and by this time, forty pupils were enrolled and thirty more had made enquiries. The stiff fee of £100 was most of a year's wage for an average worker of the day, but offset by the British promise of £75 on graduation. Teaching got under way in June. Wigram went for a ride in the dual-control Caudron delivered that month. The six pupils of the first course graduated in August after a practical flying test in front of Major James Sleeman, Director of Military Training. A larger hangar was approved in May 1918, and in July, Hill anticipated being able to train six pilots per week.[6]

World War One: New Zealanders overseas

New Zealanders fought the First World War on land, at sea and in the air. According to official figures, around 500 Kiwis were trained to fly during the First World War.[7] These were a mere handful by comparison with the 100,000-odd who served in the army during the four-plus years of fighting; but their contribution was not forgotten. Of these, some 110 were trained at the New Zealand Flying School, and 68 went on to commission in the Royal Flying Corps and its successor, the Royal Air Force. A further 170 were trained by the Canterbury Aviation Company, of whom 156 went to Europe. Most of these went first to Canada for more advanced training. Curiously, in 1933 Flight Lieutenant Arthur de Terrotte Nevill dismissed both schools as having been 'next to useless'.[8]

Many other New Zealanders learned to fly in Britain. However, some airmen whose exploits are regarded as part of New Zealand aerial tradition were only Kiwis by descent. Second Lieutenant William Rhodes-Moorhouse, though born in London and educated in Harrow, was the grandson of early colonial entrepreneur William Barnard Rhodes,[9] and won aviation's first Victoria Cross nine months into the war while assigned to No.2 Squadron at Merville. In late April 1915, Rhodes-Moorhouse was hit by ground fire while bombing Courtrai from 300 feet. Wounded in the thigh, stomach and hand, he flew back but died a day later in hospital.

Other Kiwis picked up flight skills during the war when opportunity permitted. Gallipoli veteran John Martin was in Egypt in 1918 and eagerly accepted the offer of tuition. Writing home to sisters he had not seen for four years, he reported:

Of course as you know I am now learning to fly and can fly an aeroplane by myself now and after I have had a few more hours experience I am going up with my instructor and am going to be put through all the tricks of the air such as looping, and then I will go up by myself and do them. The machine I am now on is the third different type I have learnt and I have two more still to learn but when I am done with the present machine I will be almost able to fly any machine. I was up at 4000 feet this morning doing my bombing test and I passed my test early. The highest I have been yet is 7000 feet but some machines go to 22000 feet.[10]

These efforts stood in some contrast to military aviation back in New Zealand, where efforts to obtain military aircraft for local service were minimal. Funds for six aircraft were raised by public subscription, but these were then given to the British government. More serious efforts were spurred in May 1917 by the German raider *Wolf*, which entered local waters and laid mines. The coalition government asked Britain for three 'high powered seaplanes capable of offensive tactics' but none were forthcoming and the *Wolf* went unmolested by aircraft. Pilot training ended with the Armistice in November 1918; the last pupil graduated from the CAC in February 1919. The futures of Kohimarama and Sockburn remained in the balance during these months, and after a brief flirtation with airmail services the schools were kept alive with government grants of £150 per month until air policy could be sorted out.

Post-War Developments

There was a wholesale military down-scaling at the end of the First World War; but the potential of aircraft for the future could not be ignored. Soon after the Armistice, in wake of the formation of the independent Royal Air Force in Britain, the New Zealand government requested advice on air policy. Colonel Arthur Vere Bettington arrived in March 1919 to report on the situation, but his mission was heavily overshadowed by the more influential naval report prepareed by Admiral Sir John Jellicoe, who was sent by the British to report on Dominion policy a few months later. Meanwhile, in February, the New Zealand High Commissioner in London secured delivery of six new aircraft, essentially to replace those paid for by public subscription during the war.

Bettington produced a preliminary document in June and a main report six weeks later which he called a 'continuation' of the first. His strategy was conservative. 'While it is not desired to appear unduly pessimistic or pose as a scare-monger,' he wrote, 'the Eastern political complexities and unrest should be squarely faced.'[11] This was in line with contemporary thinking both in New Zealand and Britain. Fear of Japanese military ambitions had been rife in New Zealand since the Japanese victory over Russia in 1905. Premier Joseph Ward extended these sentiments officially to the British government in 1909.[12] By 1919, the British too began to view Japan with suspicion, and Jellicoe warned the Admiralty to expect a clash.[13] Nor was Bettington's call for closer defence ties with Australia particularly innovative; Britain had considered Australia and New Zealand a single strategic unit for the entire nineteenth century.[14] Bettington's final point in his preliminary report — that New Zealand should be able to defend itself against direct attack — again reflected doctrine prevailing since before the First World War.

The problem he faced was that although the New Zealand government wanted advice on air policy, naval power remained a keystone of defence, and — as Jellicoe observed — New Zealanders were 'keenly alive to the importance... of a powerful and efficient Navy', demanding a 'strong Far Eastern Fleet... as soon as possible.'[15] Money did not stretch to an air service in the lean months after the war, nor was there much enthusiasm for expanding any of the services in wake of the struggle. Bettington was well aware of the issue. But he felt aircraft had become an essential part of any military force. 'With present types of machines in large numbers, undefended cities could be made untenable in a single day and night,' he warned:

> *Aviation provides a new and distinct striking force of tremendous potentiality. Before a formal declaration of war or expiry of an ultimatum, it may be possible for an unscrupulous neighbour to deal a paralysing blow at a vital centre.*[16]

The scheme he came up with essentially acknowledged the political realities of the post-war world. He suggested that pilots could become the nucleus of a small service based on Sockburn, which could be rapidly expanded in emergency. The scale was strictly limited; he envisaged 70 officers and 299 men by 1923, supplemented by a Territorial Air Force of 174 officers and 1090 men by 1928. Total expenditure would amount to £1,294,000 in the first four years, of which £701,250 was to be on capital works. Major A de B Brandon, one of his New Zealand assistants, looked into the suitability of various sites as air bases.

When the British government offered to give New Zealand one hundred aircraft from a large pool of war surplus machines, Bettington urged action, writing to Defence Minister Sir James Allen on 5 June that 'an early decision is necessary if you are to obtain a fair quota of this material.'[17] But Allen was lukewarm, explaining that it was 'no use accepting the machines unless New Zealand knew what to do with them' and 'nothing further would be said.'[18] Amid a clear mood of restraint, Bettington feared that Sockburn might be closed, telling Allen that 'the whole concern may languish and the directors decide to close it down.'[19] He slashed three squadrons from his scheme. However, all was overtaken by politics. New Zealand's wartime coalition government collapsed in August when Ward withdrew Liberal support. On the 27th, amid substantial political uncertainty, Cabinet decided to avoid any real expenditure on an air force. Bettington then proposed several temporary measures, including subsidising the flying schools; but his words went unheard as the country prepared for an election.

In a wider sense, although Bettington's report was caught up in the collapse of the wartime coalition, air policy in any case remained second fiddle to naval priorities. The sheer lack of enthusiasm with which Bettington's suggestions were generally received can be gauged by the fact that his report was lost by the Defence Department for several years. Jellicoe's report, delivered to the Admiralty in October 1919, was regarded as much more appropriate. From this emerged the 'main fleet to Singapore' strategy and focus on the New Zealand Naval Division. Air-minded Liberal Party leader Thomas Wilford criticised spending scarce defence dollars on the navy as 'unwarranted, unnecessary, and absolutely useless,'[20] but made no headway. The government of William Massey decided in January 1920 to accept six flying boats, twenty Avro 504's, and nine DH-9a's. But so much time had passed since the offer that the British had no DH-9a's or flying boats left. Thirty three machines were eventually shipped out, including twenty Avro 504's, nine DH-9's — which were Puma-engined aircraft markedly inferior to the Liberty-engined DH-9a — two Bristol Fighters, and two DH-4's. They arrived in early 1921 and the majority were lent to private hands. By comparison, the Australian government accepted 122 aircraft on the spot in 1919, and within two years had established the Royal Australian Air Force.

New Zealand's only positive step towards an air force came in mid-1920 when an Air Board was established under Major General Sir E W Chaytor, General Officer Commanding the New Zealand Forces. Members included Brigadier General George S Richardson, Commander T A Williams, T N Brodrick of the Lands and Survey Department, A Markman and G McNamara of the Post and Telegraph Department, and Frederick W Furkert of the Public Works Department. Aviator Thomas M Wilkes was belatedly added; he later played a great part in the development of the RNZAF.

At the end of September the Board released a cautious policy promoting civil aviation. Defence took a back seat, but the Board did recommend refresher courses for former pilots. The first was held at Sockburn under the watchful eye of Captain Leonard Isitt in 1921. The New Zealand Air Service was formed in June 1922, 'with a strength of two officers and two other ranks',[21] but the following month Massey reduced the aviation component of the defence budget to £9000. An Air Force Reserve of former RFC and RNAS pilots was formed the same year. By this time both training schools were in dire straits. Government refused to buy Sockburn, and the school ended commercial operations in March 1922, its directors even considering moving to Burnham to remain solvent. Still, the fortunes of Wigram's enterprise were better than those of the Walsh brothers. Their Kohimarama school closed in 1923, and the aircraft were burned.

An Air Force at last

The future of Sockburn entered the public arena in late 1922 as part of a general debate over military aviation. The airfield was already home of the New Zealand Aviation Corps. After slashing the defence budget that year to £317,616, the government was castigated for cutting costs to the point where New Zealand's military machine could not function. The air service came in for particular criticism, but the Minister of Defence, Robert Heaton Rhodes, fobbed the matter off with the remark that government was hampered by lack of funds, for which he blamed Parliament. The budget was accepted, but during question time a week later the member for Christchurch East, Thacker, opined that 'it was the duty of the Defence Department to see that New Zealand was represented in the Near East by pilots should the need arise.'[22]

The decisive step was finally taken by Henry Wigram, who in late March 1923 cut through the political flummery and told Massey:

> *If your Government will take over the assets and liabilities of the Company as ascertained by valuation, and will make use of the Sockburn aerodrome for the purpose for which it was formed, viz, the training of airmen and mechanics for the defence of New Zealand, I will subscribe £10,000 as a free gift in reduction of the cost of the aerodrome to the Government... If, as I hope, you are inclined to consider my proposals, I should like to have an early reply so that the necessary agreements should be prepared and signed prior to my departure for England.*[23]

Cabinet approved the offer on 16 April, Government purchased Sockburn for £21,304 and Wigram made good the difference to the company shareholders. On 14 May the government renamed the aerodrome after its patron. The New Zealand Aviation Corps was reorganised as the New Zealand Permanent Air Force (NZPAF), though it remained administratively part of the army. This took effect from 14 June. A Territorial Air Force was formed alongside the Permanent Air Force.

The NZPAF had fifteen aircraft; seven Avro 504K's, four DH9's, two DH4's, and two Bristol Fighters, based at Wigram under Isitt — now a Captain — and by the end of the year stood at four officers and five ranks. The Territorial Air Force was significantly stronger at 72 officers, all former First World War flyers. Early NZPAF work included liaison with the army during 1924 and 1925. An open day at Wigram in February 1924 proved enormously popular. Slight expansion followed in 1925 when 167 acres were purchased for a seaplane base at Hobsonville. Isitt was tipped to command and sent to England in 1926 to gain experience. The site was surveyed in 1927 and construction began the following year.

There was some enthusiasm for aerial photography during these years. The techniques had been used and refined over the trenches during the First

World War. Sleeman — still Director of Military Training — experimented with the new science over the South Island in 1918, but little further was done until 1925 when the NZPAF inaugurated aerial surveys using vertically mounted cameras, the earliest in makeshift mountings shooting through a hole cut under the seat of a Bristol F2B.

Funds remained woefully short. Defence expenditure in 1924-25 totalled just over £754,000 of which the Navy received £333,835, the Army £377,189, and the air services only £40,365. The following year the Navy was voted more than £444,000 while the air vote dropped to just £29,856.[24] By 1926 the NZPAF could no longer rely on former First World War pilots and mechanics, and most of the aircraft were worn out. Only three were on order; a DH 50 for photographic survey work, and two new Bristol Fighters.

Wigram was knighted that year for his services, and in September donated a further £2500 towards a Gloster Grebe, which arrived in February 1928. Two further Grebes were paid for by the government, along with three further Bristol Fighters delivered in 1927. The Grebes, though officially classed as interceptors, were used as high speed trainers and even personal transports. However, the worn-out Avro 504K's with their unreliable Monosoupape engines were taken out of service. Meanwhile, the first training course was held at Wigram, four months of intense effort for ten cadets beginning in November 1927. It was over-subscribed; the NZPAF fielded more than 300 applications.

In some ways, Government indifference to military aviation was explicable. In the 1920s the world had just emerged from a 'war to end all wars'. In Europe there was little thought of further fighting, and in the Pacific the Washington Treaty of 1922 halted the Sino-American naval arms race. Japanese Prime Minister Kato Takaaki cut the army, introduced modest social reforms and reduced intervention in Chinese affairs.

Money was also short, and New Zealand had to face the realities of a depressed post-war economy. The wartime prosperity bubble burst in 1921, and despite a marginal upturn in the middle of the decade, New Zealand's economic health was not good. The so-called 'jazz Premier', J Gordon Coates, who led the Reform party to victory in 1925, did not regard defence as a priority. Spending on the air services peaked at £46,368 in 1923-24, then fell steadily, bottoming in 1925-26 at £30,011 and only rising slightly until the last year of Coates' administration in 1927-28, when it stood at £33,206. However, the expenditure rose dramatically in the election year of 1928 to £44,136. That year, one-time Reformist A E Davy formed a break-away United party under the ageing former Liberal Sir Joseph Ward. They received enough votes to form a minority government.

In late September 1928, while the country was abuzz with Ward's election promise to borrow £70 million to cure the national economic ills, RAF Air Marshal Sir John Salmond proposed increasing the NZPAF to 26 officers and 192 ranks, with associated costs of £348,000 and an annual cost of £168,000. He also proposed new squadrons at a capital cost of £1,233,000 with ongoing annual costs of £418,050. A year earlier, these suggestions would have fallen on deaf ears, but Ward was aware of the value of strong defence forces, and appointed long-time air power exponent Thomas Wilford as defence minister. The aviation budget for 1929-30 rose to £60,397. Royal Air Force ranks were introduced in December 1929, replacing Army ranks, and five months later the introduction of RAF pay codes virtually doubled the daily pay of some servicemen.

Despite Wilford's enthusiasm, the decade-long focus on naval policy was highlighted by the NZPAF's first active service in January 1930. When the Samoan League or Mau rebelled in Western Samoa, a New Zealand mandated territory, HMS *Dunedin* of the New Zealand Naval Division was despatched to provide assistance to the authorities. The cruiser carried a DH-60 Moth float-plane and thirty one year old Flight Lieutenant Sidney Wallingford. The Moth was virtually unarmed; there were mounts for a Lewis gun on each side of the cockpit, but the gun had to be aimed and fired with one hand while the pilot flew with the other.

Wallingford and his crew were billeted ashore, where the aircraft was also stored on a makeshift ramp, under armed guard. Naval armourers turned a treacle tin into a bomb containing 3 lb of gun cotton, which Wallingford dropped near a missionary boat that he mistook for a vessel taking Mau rebels between islands. The bomb did not go off, and there was a formal complaint later. Wallingford flew 90 hours during the two months the cruiser was stationed in Samoan waters, mostly reconnaissance and ground-co-operation.

Plans were implemented later in 1930 to establish the Territorial Air Force on a more permanent basis. As reorganised, the TAF was led by thirty five year old Wing Commander Keith Caldwell. The TAF relied completely on the NZPAF for equipment and facilities. Four Hawker Tomtits were acquired in February 1931 as advanced trainers. However, facilities were generally insufficient for both services and plans for a large territorial air force had to be reduced.

The same month, NZPAF aircraft brought emergency supplies to Hawke's Bay in wake of the disastrous Napier earthquake. A complete chlorination plant was flown into Hastings on 4 February, and the NZPAF provided mail services even after land links were restored.

CHAPTER TWO
Uncertain Times 1931–40

'From a Defence point of view the state of the NZ air force does not permit the formulation of any Air Policy'

— Wing Commander S. Grant Dalton, Director of Air Services, 1930.

The 1920s had been lean for New Zealand military aviation, and it seemed likely the future would be worse. Salmond had shown the way, but Director of Air Services S Grant Dalton reported gloomily in 1930 that the only worthwhile aircraft in service were two Fairey IIF's and the three Gloster Grebes:

> *Such a force is totally incapable of either sustained co-operation with the Army or Navy or of acting independently in defence against air attack or as a deterrent to seaborne raid attack... Before the New Zealand Air Force can undertake the normal role of aircraft in war, considerable development along the lines suggested by Air Marshal Sir John Salmond... must take place.*[1]

The direction of the NZPAF during these years reflected a decisive shift away from fighters towards long-range bombers. The thinking behind this can be traced partially to Salmond but more particularly to a report issued by the London-based Committee of Imperial Defence in 1931. Called simply CID Memorandum 358-C, this paper recommended significant expansion of the NZPAF. Army co-operation units, fighting aircraft, torpedo bombers and flying boats were to form the nucleus of a new force that could also contribute to Imperial defence. This style of thinking was well entrenched already at service level. Junior officers — among them Flight Lieutenants A Nevill and Wallingford — produced treatises on the likely expansion of the air service, heavily influenced by prevailing thinking about air power, but adding their own slant.

Their vigorous intellectualism stood the RNZAF in good stead; the same men later rose to command the service in war. However, little was done to implement either their recommendations or even those of the CID. New Zealand was hard-hit by worldwide depression in 1931, and Coates, as Finance Minister in the coalition government led by George Forbes, argued that government books had to be balanced at any cost. State wages were slashed 20 percent between 1931 and 1932, pensions were cut thirty percent, public works expenditure by three quarters, and hospitals were plunged into a deep funding crisis.[2] The National Expenditure Commission established by Treasury in 1932 also looked at defence spending. Territorial Air Force training was reduced, and the NZPAF limped into the early 1930s in very low-key fashion. Wigram again provided private support, purchasing 81 acres adjacent to Wigram airfield from the Canterbury Park Trotting Club in 1932, which he donated to the government. Forbes gratefully acknowledged the gift as a 'valuable addition to the Air Station.'[3] The same year, three DH Moths and a Hawker Tomtit were damaged during exercises, accidents put down officially to 'lack of continuity in flying training.'[4]

Despite these cutbacks, defence spending as not slashed as heavily as it could have been. The annual grant towards the Singapore naval base was cut from £125,000 to £100,000, but no further, and plans to cut one of the two cruisers in New Zealand waters were abandoned. The reason was Asia, which again loomed large in New Zealand security thinking. Civil war raged in China during these years. Japan stood by during the Kuomintang expeditions of 1926 and 1927, but intervened at Shantung in 1927 and 1928. Hamaguchi Osachi became Prime Minister in 1929 and seemed more moderate, joining other world powers at the 1930 London Naval Conference with a variety of concessions to disarmament. But he could not halt the tide. Devastated by depression and racked with food shortages, Japan was ripe for revolt, and military expansion was widely viewed as a solution. Hamaguchi was assassinated in 1930; the following year a coup was abandoned only at the last minute. When a Japanese railway in Manchuria was bombed that year, the Japanese army used the event as a pretext to occupy the province without political authorisation from Tokyo.

Decisive change: the RNZAF emerges

Fears of Japanese ambition in the Pacific were further underlined in 1933 when Japan withdrew from the League of Nations. A New Zealand Committee of Imperial Defence was formed under Major-General William Sinclair-Burgess to co-ordinate national response. This included implementing some of Salmond's 1928 recommendations for the NZPAF. By and large, the committee concurred with both Salmond and the CID. 'The role of the New Zealand Air Force in local defences is fulfilled by the provision of aircraft... at the two defended ports — Auckland and Wellington... at the focal points of trade in New Zealand waters.' Trade protection required 'flying boats working in conjunction with bomber aircraft', but aircraft were not part of a wider scheme to despatch military force from New Zealand 'immediately on mobilisation to reinforce the garrison of parts menaced by attack, in particular Singapore or Hong Kong.' The committee expected aircraft stationed in New Zealand during peacetime would remain there in war, and that 'New Zealand's efforts for co-operation in Imperial Defence should be confined to the supply of trained personnel only for overseas units.'[5]

These plans came to partial fruition the following year, when Coates initiated major funding increases and ordered Vickers Vildebeestes to replace the worn-out Grebes and Bristol Fighters. To some extent Coates' initiative reflected plans announced that year for the RAF, but the style of re-equipment underlined the more fundamental policy shift towards bombers first identified by Salmond. The Grebes and 'Brisfits' were tactical aircraft, but the Vildebeestes replacing them were long-range torpedo-bombers. Expenditure in 1933–34 totalled only £38,548, but rose the following year to £132,230 from a budget of £197,934. This dramatic under-expenditure came about because the Vildebeestes could not be delivered at short notice, and base construction only got under way in the latter half of the year.

In February 1934 the NZPAF changed its name, with due protocols and Royal assent, to the Royal New Zealand Air Force: the RNZAF. It was an aesthetic shift — the service remained administratively part of the army — but underlined a steady improvement in the political fortunes of military aviation.

The Vildebeestes were delivered in March 1935 amid considerable controversy. The massive single-engined biplanes were obsolescent at a time when the first stressed-skin monoplanes were being deployed elsewhere. To save money, they were also delivered without either torpedoes or launching equipment. Coates later criticised the Vildebeestes as being 'out of date before they landed here.'[6] Former First World War officer and politician James Hargest was even more explicit. The Awarua MP flew in one to Wellington and told the House he was:

> *satisfied that in the event of war no person could possibly use that machine to fight successfully. Though we kept quite low down, both the pilot and I were nearly frozen, and no person could fight a machine under such circumstances.*[7]

Still, Vildebeestes represented a quantum leap over anything previously fielded. At a service level there was no doubt they were the way to go. 'It would appear wiser to concentrate on the bomber and reconnaissance aircraft units than to diversify the types of service aircraft,' Nevill wrote in a 1936 paper.[8] Six Vildebeestes were stationed at Wigram and six at Hobsonville. New structures at Hobsonville included two hangars, stores shops, a garage, barracks and administration offices. The RNZAF also ordered four Avro 626 advanced trainers. They arrived in 1936 and were put into service with A-flight of the Flying Training School at Wigram.

The Vildebeestes had an operating ceiling of 16,500 feet, which offered new opportunities for aerial mapping, but aircrews found the cold at this altitude almost unbearable, and the electric camera heaters did not extend to the crews. Pilot visibility was hampered by the radial engine, and some found they could best navigate by removing a trapdoor between their feet and looking at the ground. Nonetheless, Air Force photo mosaics were used for flood protection, a geological survey of the Southern Alps, an irrigation scheme in Central Otago, and road siting in Westland. In the end, the government left it to private enterprise to make the first real inroads into the field. In 1935, Hastings-based aviator and photographer Piet van Asch established New Zealand Aerial Mapping. He began official aerial photographic work in 1937 and established a close relationship with the RNZAF.

An independent air force and John A Lee

New Zealand's military aviation came of age in the late 1930s, when Coates' modest policy was given new momentum by the Labour government of Michael Joseph Savage which swept to power on a wave of public enthusiasm in 1935. Prime mover behind the shift was John Alfred Alexander Lee, MP for Grey Lynn and self-appointed Under Secretary to the Prime Minister. In January 1936, two months after the election, he submitted a report calling for an independent air force and demanding a defence council. He followed this in March with a call for the expansion of an independent RNZAF. Naval estimates that year looked set to rise, largely due to the acquisition of new light cruisers and the cost of establishing the Devonport Naval base. Warning of enormous future increases if both naval and air policies were pursued, Lee attacked naval policy as being merely subservient to the British whim of the day. New Zealand faced no direct threat, certainly no risk of invasion. The country was isolated by ocean, he argued; and even disruption of trade would affect the economy but not 'afflict us with hunger.'[9]

This was untrue. New Zealand had motorised with alacrity during the 1920s and by the mid-1930s was reliant on imported fuel, without which the farms could not operate or get their produce to the cities. However, Lee's strategic concept was sound. Distance was a powerful defence against direct invasion. To Lee the real solution to New Zealand's defence problems was air power, which he regarded as the arbiter of future wars. In this he reflected prevailing orthodoxy. German raids over southeast England and British raids over the Ruhr during the First World War, though small scale by later standards, were nevertheless shocking for the time and had disproportionate moral effect. By the 1930s, substantial advances in air technology coupled with the influence of air-minded strategists such as Hugh Trenchard and

Guilio Douhet had built a pervasive image of relentless destruction from the skies. British Prime Minister Stanley Baldwin warned that the bomber would 'always get through' as early as 1932. Lee was in no doubt as to the implication, either. To reduce defence spending, air defence would have to grow at the expense of army and navy. This would also suit Britain; he envisaged strong local defences able to fly to the aid of a beleaguered Empire.[10]

Lee produced a list of suggestions for Cabinet, arguing that at least one third of the defence vote should be for military aviation and for parity between air, sea and land arms. He also recommended that a British officer should develop and guide air policy until local expertise had developed. These ideas were discussed by Cabinet in May. Here the decision was taken to limit defence spending to £1.1 million, but Lee's ideas fell on fertile ground. There was even talk of concentrating all spending on the air forces. This was tempered by existing naval obligations, but the air force vote was nevertheless increased at the expense of the army.

This kind of approach was not surprising. Labour came to power on a platform of reform; and a vigorous air policy was a shift away from the conservative pro-Navy approaches of previous administrations. The socialist ideal of disarmament — which Labour had championed when in opposition — also played a part. However, the Savage administration never seriously entertained the idea of turning New Zealand's rusty defence swords into ploughshares. To simply impose theory on a complex real society was certain to create problems, and there was a substantial degree of realism in the party approach to defence. Members such as Lee had served in the First World War and understood what combat was about.

From their perspective the key practical issues were inadequate British preparation for war in the Pacific, coupled with new and worrying developments in Europe. The prospect of an unbridled Japanese military free of political control was almost too frightening to contemplate. An unsuccessful coup in Tokyo in February 1936 underlined the instability of the situation, while in Europe, Nazi Germany also became a significant threat. While discussing the prospect of the RNZAF as a separate service, Savage told the House that 'the general European situation is not one to make us feel that we can afford to be indifferent to defence matters.'[11] The principal appeal and selling point of an air sevice was that, at a time when money remained short and the government had social policies in mind, air power, with all its potential, was a means of containing defence expenditure without reducing capability. To politicians such as Lee, Savage and Nash, such a move struck a balance between their ideals of disarmament, and the practical necessity of their age.

Such a view was also unsurprising. During the 1920s, New Zealand operated short-range tactical aircraft capable of little more than limited coastal defence. Long-range power projection was still the province of warships. However, the advent of stressed-skin monoplanes and more powerful engines changed the calculation. By the late 1930s, aircraft were emerging with the affordability, range and performance needed for Pacific operations, able to carry ordinance over unprecedented distances. Such developments made it possible — for the first time — for aircraft based in New Zealand to operate effectively into the Pacific. Spectacular flights by aviators such as Charles Kingsford Smith, Jean Batten, Wiley Post and Amelia Earhart — though militarily of little value — drew attention to the latest revolution in air technology. Public interest in aircraft had never been higher; it was the 'golden age' of aviation, and as height, weight, speed and distance records fell, the expectations of what the military could deliver from the air rose sharply.

By mid–1936, then, there was no doubt that an air force would be developed. amd Labour were openly toying with the concept of diminishing army and navy in favour of an increased air force. Exactly how to proceed, however, was another matter. Lee envisaged a British advisor, but local expertise seemed easier to procure. In June, Wing Commander Thomas Martin Wilkes, Director of Air Services, was asked to develop schemes for an air force that could undertake 'its full share in the scheme of local defence of the Dominion' — with and without the planned light cruisers. And for comparison, Wilkes was also asked to look into an air force able to undertake 'the whole responsibility of Dominion defence.'[12]

The key issue was the anticipated role in local defence; to the Labour government this was the real function of an expanded RNZAF. It would be at the expense of the naval contribution to wider Imperial policies but, as Lee had already observed, Imperial defence would be a secondary role for the new air services. This priority derived from a perception of British military weakness, and from a considerable scepticism towards the CID's projected scale of attack on New Zealand. Their ideas had essentially not changed in thirty years, but Wilkes believed that 'the previously accepted scale... can no longer be regarded as a maximum.' Warning that Singapore reinforcements might have to come via the Cape of Good Hope if the Mediterranean situation deteriorated, he argued that a 'fairly strong naval force' might overwhelm local defence, destroy local shipping, bombard the main centres, and even occupy Auckland. Six months might elapse before such invaders could be repelled.[13]

To defeat such an attack Wilkes recommended two bomber reconnaissance and two bomber squadrons, two spotter flights and one flying training school. He thought it could be achieved in four years with capital costs of £1,082,500 and annual costs of £338,300.[14] A secret appendix — 'The case for a Japanese invasion of New Zealand' — argued that British preparations to defend the Pacific proved there was real risk. The Shanghai incident suggested that Japan could 'launch a limited overseas attack without warning' and the strength of Singapore might force Japanese planners to seek targets further south.[15]

Tantalised by the prospect of a real expansion programme, other RNZAF officers began flexing their intellectual muscle. Nevill evaluated possible new aircraft in July. He also rejected CID memorandum 358-C, which was 'too wide to be of value to the Dominion at present' and suggested it was wiser 'to concentrate on the bomber and reconnaissance units than to diversify the types of service aircraft.' Cost was a consideration which limited Nevill to relatively obsolete RAF types such as Bristol Bulldogs, Hawker Harts, Fairey Gordons and Avro Ansons. He came down in favour of modified Blenheims for the reconnaissance role. An associated conceptual study, planning an attack on New Zealand from a Japanese perspective, suggested that Japan could take Auckland with a relatively small fleet backed by no more than a few dozen aircraft. The whole country could be held by three squadrons of Japanese bombers based at Blenheim.[16]

There was no question within New Zealand that a scheme to expand national military air power would have to be developed. Opposition leader George Forbes promised unity on the issue, and the only real dissent in the house came from Hargest, who hinted that more effective local defence would come from expanding and mechanising the army.[17] However, there was more definite opposition from the Cabinet Defence Committee, which came down in favour of an expanded navy. The reality, at the time, was that New Zealand could not afford to do all of them.

Alarmed by the prospect of a New Zealand air policy that was incompatible with their own plans, the British took advantage of this opening to seize the initiative, citing increases in British naval expenditure as evidence of commitment to imperial defence, and downplaying the likely severity of attack on New Zealand. In a letter to the Governor General of 5 August 1936, the Secretary of State for Dominion Affairs argued that the 'relatively few' aircraft that could be maintained for the same cost as the two light cruisers would 'not affect the ultimate issue of a conflict with Japan.' In the same letter he extended an offer to send an officer to report on the New Zealand air defence situation.[18] The move was a brilliant compromise; it gave the British an opportunity to impose air strategy on New Zealand, but also became a convenient 'out' for the New Zealand cabinet, which got around the recommendation of the Cabinet Defence Committee by deciding to take no decisions until the British officer had made his report.

The expansion of the RNZAF 1936–39

The man the British had in mind was Wing Commander Ralph Alexander Cochrane. He was a relatively junior officer for the job, and had served with the Royal Navy until 1915, when he transferred to the Royal Naval Air Service. He was commissioned into the RAF in 1919. Since then he had served on a number of overseas bases including the Middle East, Palestine, Iraq and Aden, and when sent to New Zealand had just completed a course at the Imperial Defence College.

Cochrane remains a service legend and is often regarded as the founder of the RNZAF. A brief manuscript history written by RNZAF officers after the war made it sound as if he had created the whole pro-air policy himself, which was then accepted by government.[19] This was an exaggeration. An air service operating bombers had already been envisaged by the New Zealand government before Cochrane arrived. What Cochrane actually did was perhaps even more fundamental. Lee had envisaged an expanded air force able to meet local defence with a secondary role in imperial affairs. Cochrane reversed these priorities, sold the reversed concept to government, and then made the concept a reality — building a modern air force in every detail virtually from scratch. It was a monumental task given the resources and time at his disposal. His December 1936 'Report on the Air Aspect of the Defence Problems of New Zealand' laid out the shape of service development in the years to the outbreak of the Second World War.

The basic strategy he adopted was enduring. As a nation isolated by ocean and reliant on trade through or with South East Asia, New Zealand's interests could only be served by an air force able to project power across substantial distances, both for local defence and to protect trading interests further afield. Because the strategic situation at this level did not change over time, the same concept provided the basis for immediate post-war planning and remained inspiration for the RNZAF into the 1990s.

However, the specific details of Cochrane's scheme were tailored to the late 1930s. He had been sent to reconcile the Labour government's independent air commitment with British defence policies towards Singapore. In this he was brilliantly successful. There was no question of compromising British needs; Cochrane actually wrote his report during the journey to New Zealand — a clear indication he had little intention of acknowledging local requirements. Nor did he diverge from the official British position. On the basis of the CID's 1931 report, Cochrane identified three defence priorities; small-scale local defence; defending vital shipping routes; and supporting the United Kingdom. Rejecting New Zealand government thinking, he argued that New Zealand could not afford the forces to defeat a determined attack, and — predictably — that British weakness was illusory. 'The rapid strengthening of the defences of Singapore and the decision of the United Kingdom government to press forward with its programme of rearmament promises an increasing measure of security.'[20] Nor was there to be any change in naval policy. While an air force could provide defence against raids, it would do so in conjunction with 'the general naval dispositions' and 'local forces and defences'.[21]

The core of his new air force comprised two long-range bomber squadrons comprising twenty four aircraft and six reserves, with enough range 'for a flight from New Zealand to the Pacific Islands, or to Singapore, stopping only on British territory.'[22] The same force would also provide a 'reserve of personnel of great value in Imperial Defence.'[23] Perhaps in a sop to sell the scheme to the Labour government, Cochrane also envisaged a regional role and noted that the British government should help New Zealand set up facilities to operate aircraft around the Pacific islands. 'Should it be found possible to build up a force of the size suggested it will lead to a welcome strengthening of the defence position in the Southern Pacific.'

Cochrane had significant concerns over how an air force might be implemented. This was going to have to be done virtually from scratch, and he suggested concentrating resources in Christchurch to train the 100 officers and 900 men he envisaged as a first step. The service also needed a personnel reserve and an army liaison group. Territorial squadrons could wait, but civil air operations and aero clubs were to be encouraged. Capital costs came to £1,100,000 — a significant sum by New Zealand air standards, but not by comparison with what New Zealand had spent on the navy since the First World War. Cochrane calculated that annual expenditure would amount to £435,000.[24]

Cochrane's efforts to sell the scheme were assisted partially by his political intuition, partially by the Cabinet decision to wait on his report — which gave it automatic value — and partially by the New Zealand period attitude that domestic advice was inferior. Lee had certainly recommended a British officer at the outset. Wilkes remained conspicuously quiet, probably because he realised that advice 'from outside' was likely to have greater credibility. Nor, in execution, was Cochrane's force markedly different from what Wilkes himself wanted; the issue boiled down to a divergence of perception over the specific threat to New Zealand shores, and the bombers theoretically met both requirements. Cabinet accepted the report on 1 March.

On 1 April 1937 the RNZAF was made a separate organisation in anticipation of formal legislation,[25] and Cochrane was invited to implement the envisaged three year scheme. Promoted to Group Captain, he became New Zealand's first Chief of Air Staff, and a member of an Air Board chaired by Minister of Defence Frederick Jones. Isitt, now a Wing Commander, and Nevill were also appointed to the Board. A flying training school was organised at Wigram to teach forty pilots a year, both for the RNZAF and the RAF. This last role was a belated introduction. The British had suggested that pilots might be trained in New Zealand in 1934, but facilities were unavailable — and even in 1936, Wilkes conservatively thought only 10 pilots a month were sustainable in the longer term.[26] In fact, the sustainable rate was even less and only 133 pilots were trained between 1937 and 1939 under a short-service scheme by which the RAF paid the New Zealand government £1550 for each fully trained pilot.[27] During this time the RAF was also accepting

New Zealanders prepared to privately travel to Britain — provided they met rigorous RAF requirements when they got there. To reduce the rejection rate, the British agreed to accept candidates already screened in New Zealand. Some 104 candidates crossed to Britain under this scheme in 1937-38 and a further 144 in 1938-39.[28]

New air stations were established at Whenuapai near Hobsonville, and at Ohakea near Bulls. Cochrane had great difficulty finding a site in Auckland, complaining that the landscape was covered with a 'particularly vicious form of pug-clay' unsuitable for runways or hangars.[29] Thirty Vickers-Armstrong Wellingtons were also ordered for delivery in 1939. These twin-engined aircraft were new in 1937 and among the fastest and heaviest bombers of their day. They were also unique. At a time when most designers were swinging towards stressed-skin monocoque construction, the Wellingtons introduced a system of crossed diagonal frames, brain child of talented designer Barnes Wallis. This 'geodetic' system was immensely strong for its weight and more resistant to battle damage than conventional structures, which could fail if vital spars were shot through. Five Airspeed Oxfords were ordered to supplement the force, four as advanced trainers for the bomber crews and one for aerial mapping. A number of Vickers Vincent bombers — virtually identical to the Vildebeestes — were ordered as trainers.

A Territorial Air Force was developed on a shoestring budget. To cut costs, squadrons were equipped with obsolete British aircraft. Lee had been a great advocate of this approach, and when Cabinet authorised a territorial squadron in the capital in July 1937, twelve Blackburn Baffins were ordered at the bargain basement price of £2400 the lot. Some 29 of these old carrier-based torpedo bombers were eventually procured, and further cost savings were made by again eliminating their torpedoes and launching gear. The TAF was nevertheless considered likely to have a useful coast defence role.

Flight training began at Wigram in June. There was enough capacity to train forty eight men per annum, later rising to eighty. Aircraft included four Vildebeestes, three Hawker Tomtits and three Avro 626 trainers. Twelve officers and ninety six men manned the station under Squadron Leader E G Olson. A school for flight riggers was established at the railway workshops.

Enthusiasm for the independent RNZAF remained high. When the Air Force Bill came up for its second reading in October 1937, Jones summed up the whole situation with the comment that government:

> *recognised the enormous advance that was taking place in military aviation in various countries of the world, and realised that we in New Zealand could not afford to ignore that advance. ... At one time the government forgot that it had an aviation plan, and if it had not broken down on that plan we might have had more aircraft here today.*[30]

Hargest — still favouring the army — was concerned that the air services might absorb resources at the expense of the other armed forces. 'I hope that the Government will not be carried away to the extent of giving undue importance to aircraft,' he told the House. Citing Japanese experience in China he added: 'Battles cannot be won by aircraft alone.'[31] The Air Force Bill was read for the third time in early November and enacted on the 6th, though its provisions were deemed to have retroactively come into force on 1 April.[32] Simultaneously, an Air Department Act created a new government department to administer military and civilian air activity. The law made concrete a reality that had been in existence for most of the year.

Pre-war expansion

International tensions did not diminish during 1938. Japan prosecuted a ferocious war against China, while in Europe, Hitler entered Czechoslovakia and Austria. There was general unease in New Zealand and the Labour government considered improving local defence. In April the New Zealand Chiefs of Staff completed a five-year plan recommending expansion of all three services, hoping the army would receive attention. Instead, government implemented only Air Force recommendations, including a scheme for air defence north of Fiji. This had originated in the Imperial Defence Conference of 1937. As developed by Cochrane the plan called for air surveillance from Fiji to the Gilbert Islands, northeast as far as Christmas Island, and east to Rarotonga. It was approved by Cabinet in early 1938 and presented to the British in May, despite criticism that it would create an invasion route. Savage then requested a conference with the British on Pacific defence, though this was not held for eleven months.

Other initiatives in 1938 included more buildings at Hobsonville and a new regular squadron at Blenheim. The Christchurch and Auckland squadrons of the Territorial Air Force were confirmed in January, and the Dunedin squadron in February. Recruiting began in Christchurch in April. The Auckland squadron was put together in June under Squadron Leader David M Allan. More territorial units were planned at New Plymouth, Invercargill and Hastings.

The Munich crisis in September that year prompted further alarm in New Zealand, and there were separate fears of a surprise Japanese aircraft carrier-based attack. Cochrane was sceptical, writing to his successor: 'Personally I regard it as exceedingly unlikely and this view is shared by the Navy.'[33] That did not quell public fears; the spectre of a surprise Japanese raid or invasion had been bubbling along since the Russo-Japanese war of 1904-05, and at popular level the latest 'flap' seemed all too credible. Enrolment forms for volunteers from trades useful to the RNZAF were distributed to Post Office branches on 20 December and, despite the Christmas period, 3845 applications were received by mid-January 1939.

Cochrane left for Britain in early 1939 and was replaced by another officer borrowed from the RAF, Group Captain Hugh W L Saunders. The Pacific Defence Conference held in Wellington in April that year was attended by representatives from Britain, Australia and New Zealand. By this time there were serious doubts in New Zealand official circles about the Singapore strategy, despite Cochrane's assurances. Although the base had been completed the previous year, there was growing evidence that British ships might not be available. Amid fears that Japanese possession of Pacific islands might allow them to mount other attacks, New Zealand again proposed a base in Fiji, the hub of a defensive line extending into the Pacific islands. After extensive discussion it was agreed to build an air base and two landing fields, splitting the cost between Britain and New Zealand.

During the conference the British pressed New Zealand for more pilot training facilities and a commitment to send aircraft to Singapore. In the end it was agreed New Zealand would provide 650 pilots, 300 observers and 350 air gunners annually for the RAF, and the RNZAF underwent further development as a result. Blenheim Air Force Station became a flying training school with annual output of one hundred and forty pilots; government purchased additional aircraft and equipment to operate the two schools. Arrangements were concluded to build training aircraft locally. De Havilland established a subsidiary factory in March 1939 at Rongotai. Tiger Moth production began early the following year.[34] However, the real impact of the conference on New Zealand defence policy was a separate arrangement to add 6000 men to the Territorial forces.

The outbreak of war

All the major industrial nations were rearming by 1939 amid an atmosphere of mutual distrust. Britain and France guaranteed Polish security in March. Hitler nevertheless did not expect the war that followed his invasion in September. Nobody had completed any long-term rearmament programmes, and the Germans were in no immediate position to fight anything other than the campaign in Poland.

By 1939 the RNZAF's Vickers Wellingtons were approaching completion, but a scheme to fly them to New Zealand was dogged with problems. There were difficulties finding experienced pilots to make the delivery flight, and ongoing teething troubles suggested the aircraft might not be flown out in any case. Cochrane was still hopeful; the Wellington's mechanical woes had surfaced when it entered RAF service in 1938, and in December he told Saunders not to be too pessimistic simply 'because the first few aircraft are giving trouble,' though he had hoped 'the worst of the faults would have been shaken out' before the type joined the RNZAF.[35] Six of the RNZAF's aircraft were thought likely to be ready to make the flight by August 1939, and several New Zealand aircrews reached Britain in February to train and prepare the aircraft for the journey, forming the New Zealand Flight officially from 1 June. Other New Zealanders joined the unit in small numbers for the next month, but in July — as tensions in Europe climbed — the New Zealand government made the six aircraft and their crews available to the British. RAF personnel in New Zealand were in turn absorbed into the RNZAF. The remaining 24 Wellingtons were delivered to the RAF as they were completed and joined the New Zealand Flight. This was led by forty four year old Squadron Leader Maurice Buckley, who had been with the RNZAF since 1926. Other members included Squadron Leader Cyril Kay, Flight Lieutenant C C Hunter, Flying Officers J Adams, F J 'Popeye' Lucas and Aubrey A N Breckon.

By August 1939 the RNZAF was some way off its planned strength. Little progress had been made towards the base in Fiji. There were territorial squadrons in Auckland, Wellington and Christchurch, and an Aero Club organisation with sixty basic training aircraft, mostly Tiger Moths. The No.1 Flying Training School at Wigram was virtually finished, and the No.2 Flying Training School at Blenheim about half ready. Of the operational bases, Ohakea air station was three quarters complete, while the Whenuapai landing field had been prepared and some buildings started. The depot at Hobsonville was incomplete. The Dunedin Territorial flight was gathering; those at Hastings, Invercargill and New Plymouth had not commenced recruiting. The Railway Workshops schemes for training flight mechanics and riggers had only just entered operation. There were no modern aircraft in the country, but on a more positive note, the service estimated it had enough bombs for twelve months operations 'at maximum scale'[36] — one aspect of Cochrane's scheme that had been completed. These were mostly 250 lb weapons, supplemented by 40 lb general purpose and 20 lb fragmentation devices.

The European crisis deepened during August, and a precautionary alert was ordered on the 24th. Three days later, all service personnel were recalled from leave. Air Force and Territorial mobilisation orders were issued on 28 August, and on 1 September — when the Germans rolled into Poland — the Governor General issued a formal proclamation of emergency. Reserve units were transferred to the regular air force, and the Territorials were called up for continuous service. Britain declared war on 3 September after Germany failed to respond to an ultimatum. New Zealand followed.

CHAPTER THREE
European War 1939–45

The story of the RNZAF in the Second World War divides — like the war itself — essentially into two parts. Until 1942, New Zealand's primary focus was on the European war, and that theatre remained important for New Zealand until the end of the war in 1945. More than ten thousand RNZAF aviators served in the Royal Air Force (RAF) during the war, and New Zealanders had flown in most European theatres by 1945. Some 3190 lost their lives — 1680 of them with Bomber Command — and 570 were taken prisoner.[1] Other New Zealanders, who joined the RAF via pre-war short-service schemes, are also regarded as being part of the New Zealand war effort.

Expansion and development at home 1939–42

The main issue the RNZAF faced in 1939 was that it was essentially brand new and now had to implement plans that had only relatively recently been developed. The further rapid expansion to meet war requirements highlighted desperate shortages of equipment, manpower and administrative support. This was one cost of long neglect during the inter-war period. Men with little experience found themselves improvising administrative structures, working with home-made equipment, and trying to create an effective service within these constraints to meet the war emergency. The fact that so much was accomplished so quickly under these circumstances is a credit to the men and women who volunteered their skills, and to the solid basis that Cochrane had been able to establish during the last years of peace.

Even so, the war came before any of the pre-war schemes could be brought to completion. There is no question that in September 1939 the service was unable to meet even the training requirement of the previous April. Aircraft were still being delivered to meet the earlier scheme. Fifty Vickers Vincents had originally been earmarked for transfer from RAF squadrons in the Middle East, but some were retained in theatre and not all arrived. Worse, the RNZAF discovered to its dismay that the Vincents and Fairey Gordons arriving from the Middle East were in poor condition, largely because of their tropical service. Spares procurement was hampered by the war situation, and there were not enough machine tools to fabricate parts locally. Even uniforms were not readily available because a decision had been made to meet army needs first. A Defence Purchasing Committee was formed to exploit local resources, and material was ordered from London, but wartime stringencies made the work difficult.

Some aircraft were impressed from civilian ownership to help fill the gaps. Most arrived during the late months of 1939. In September and October the RNZAF acquired various de Havilland airliners, a number of Miles light aircraft, a Porterfield 35W from the Hawke's Bay and East Coast Aero Club, and a Percival Vega Gull among others. Two De Havilland Moth Minors were impressed in early 1940 and several Rearwin 9000 Sportsters in October 1942. There were also plans to use the Short S-30 Empire flying boats of Tasman Empire Air Limited (TEAL) in a military role. This prospect had been discussed by the RNZAF as early as July 1939 in consequence of the Pacific Defence Conference, and was formally raised in October with the government.[2]

The RNZAF's administrative development matched the expansion of its operational forces. The office of the Chief of Air Staff was dramatically enlarged, while the Equipment Branch went in two months from two officers and three clerks to seven officers and thirty clerks. An idea of the speed of development can be gauged from the fact that at the outbreak of war the RNZAF stood at 756 men. By the end of March 1940 this had risen to 3876 including 355 officers. A year later the service stood at 8359, but this was smaller percentage increase than in the first six months of the war. A good deal of early expansion was driven by the need to train men for RAF service.

Initial operations from New Zealand were initially limited by the RNZAF's equipment. Patrols in September 1939 to look for a suspected German submarine were fruitless. In January 1940, RNZAF aircraft reconnoitred a fifty mile radius around Wellington and Lyttleton before the first troops departed in a convoy of six liners. Two months later, a General Reconnaissance Squadron was formed, located at Whenuapai partly because the base had hangar space. However, the squadron had no modern aircraft, and the German raider *Orion* under Kurt Weyher — well briefed by garrulous New Zealand civilian radio — mined the Hauraki Gulf with impunity in June 1940, sinking the *Niagara*. Twenty survivors were picked up by the RNZAF's high-speed launch 'W1'. Two months later, the *Orion* sank the *Turakina* in the Tasman. Patrols by De Havilland Dragons and flying boats from Ohakea failed to find the Germans, nor did Vickers Vincents despatched to Waipapakauri in Northland. More sinkings in November by the *Orion*, *Pinguin* and *Komet* were outside the range of RNZAF aircraft.

These events prompted further efforts to obtain modern aircraft from Britain. In May, Britain agreed to send 18 Hudsons if Japan entered the war. New Zealand's need was more immediate, but efforts to get the aircraft were rebuffed until the end of the year, when government finally pointed out that the RNZAF had no aircraft able to operate against raiders. New Zealand was the only Dominion in this position, and had been put there by voluntarily giving away the Wellingtons. Churchill relented. Six Lockheed Hudson Mk V bombers were deducted from American orders and shipped to New Zealand. The Hudsons arrived in April 1941, disassembled and minus turrets, bomb racks, dinghies, radio and navigation equipment. By mid-July they had been put together and joined No.1 G.R. squadron at Whenuapai. Meanwhile, the New Zealand government requested a further 36 Hudsons for prompt delivery with 24 more, plus attrition reserves, to follow in 1942. The British at first were reluctant to release them, but in July agreed to issue six a month. The first of thirty Mk III's arrived in October, and a further batch of Mk IIIa's were delivered unassembled between April and June 1942. Equipment shortages again delayed their entry into service. All this took time, and efforts were made to militarise the two TEAL Short S-30 Empire flying boats, the only long-range aircraft in the country. These aircraft had already been used for reconnaissance, but in the event the conversion took many months and the need had passed before they were ready.

Despite the difficulty fielding reciprocal support from Britain, New Zealand contribution to RAF manpower continued unabated, and the British also asked for — and received - a fully manned New Zealand fighter squadron and the world's first aircraft construction unit in Malaya. Britain, of course, had immediate defence priorities; the Battle of Britain was fought and won during the period. But the moral effect in New Zealand was not good.

Work began on the Fijian bases in September 1939 and 117 acres was purchased at Nandi on which to build an airfield. The job was let to the privately owned Southern Cross Construction Company, which had virtually finished the task by March 1940, and moved on to repeat the task in Tonga. An RNZAF detachment was despatched to Lautoka in November under Squadron Leader Donald Baird, though the base was not completed until the following March. He established a Headquarters group in the grounds of the Government Buildings in Suva.

The unit was equipped with four DH-89 Dragon Rapides and one DH-60 Moth, which flew dawn-and-dusk patrols from the New Hebrides to Tonga. Trouble quickly beset the small group. A tropical hurricane destroyed two Rapides in February 1941, and a few days later a third was written off when it hit a truck during a low pass over the airfield. Two DH-86's had to be sent from New Zealand to keep the unit operational. The RNZAF was reluctant to deploy Vincents, because the single-engined aircraft were thought to be at risk of forced landing in the sea, but needs forced a re-think and in August 1941 six were sent to Fiji for short-range work. The unit was renamed No.4 (General Reconnaissance) squadron in October. A de Havilland DH-84 Dragon Mk II was also sent to Fiji in August, with the Nausori Communications Flight, but had to be written off after less than a year because the tropical climate rotted the airframe.

Fears of Japanese aggression after the Russian entry into the war prompted the United States to ask for major extensions to Nandi airfield in mid-1941. They promised extensive assistance. This never transpired, but in November, the No.2 Aerodrome Construction Squadron of the RNZAF and a large contingent of public works engineers began the work, which was largely completed by April the following year.

Longer range flying boats were also required for work in Fiji. The New Zealand government had begun discussions with Fiji and Britain during 1940. At the end of the year Prime Minister Peter Fraser requested Catalinas to equip the RNZAF unit planned for the islands, but Britain had none to spare — they were going to re-equip squadrons at Singapore. Instead, Britain offered as a gift the obsolete Short Singapore III biplane flying boats which the Catalinas were replacing in the Malayan theatre. Fraser accepted the offer in February 1941, but initial reports from Singapore indicated that all the boats required major repairs. The RNZAF despatched 26 personnel to Singapore in June 1941 to help prepare the flying boats, and Baird was appointed to command a new Singapore Flight to bring them back to Fiji. In September work began on a flying boat base at Lauthala bay to operate the aircraft. The first two Short Singapores began their delivery voyage in October, but mechanical problems extended the flight to a month. Three other Short Singapores also intended for Fiji were not ready to leave until early December and were embroiled in the initial stages of the war with Japan before finally departing the combat zone on 13 December.[3] In Fiji these aircraft formed No.5 (GR) Squadron.

Training to operate the seaplanes remained ad-hoc for much of the war. New Zealand naval aviators had experience with the Supermarine Walrus amphibian equipping the light cruisers *Leander* and *Achilles*, and in August 1941 a reserve Walrus was made available for the RNZAF to train five pilots for the Short Singapores. This was lost in October 1942, but the RNZAF acquired the six remaining RNZN Walruses and formed a Seaplane Training Flight in early 1943, though this remained outside RNZAF structure until November 1944. A more substantial consequence of flying boat operations was the rapid development of the RNZAF's marine section. A small number of boats had been operated from Hobsonville before the war to support floatplanes — though by late 1938 this was down to a motor boat and two dinghies. Several new boats were acquired at the end of 1938, and before the war broke out the service also took delivery of a 64-foot high speed launch (HSL) capable of 38 knots. This was intended for target towing, and when war broke out was fitted with an Oxford turret and two Lewis guns, along with racks for small depth charges. However, the expansion and development of flying boat activities prompted the acquisition of a number of small boats as tenders. Others were purpose-built for the service during the war.[4]

Civilian organisations made a valuable contribution to the war effort. One of the most active was New Zealand Aerial Mapping, founded in 1935 by Piet van Asch, flying his General Aviation ST-25 Jubilee Monospar. He had enjoyed a close relationship with the Air Force since before the war because he offered the only effective aerial mapping service in the country. The RNZAF had dabbled with the task of mapping New Zealand to modern standards during the 1920s, but by the late 1930s were fully occupied with the training scheme and Cochrane looked to van Asch for help. Van Asch recxalled the moment on interview, years later. 'You can't chase blue skies in a hurry if you are bundled in red tape,' Cochrane explained. 'Stay in mufti and we'll give you as much assistance as we can.'[5] Air Force refuelling facilities, accommodation and airfields proved invaluable to van Asch as he and his crew flew the length and breadth of New Zealand.

Once, surveying the Mataura river to Foveaux Strait, they discovered what southern winds could do. It was a blustery day; Van Asch and navigator Peter Marshall completed the run, and van Asch throttled back as they turned to follow the coast. Van Asch recalled: 'we were heading for Invercargill when I asked him to take a drift and the answer came back "Hell, we're going backwards!"' Another incident in the far north was more serious. 'After mapping Great Barrier Island we returned to Bill Hyslop's paddock opposite the Cavelli Islands at the same time that the *Rangitane* was sunk 300 miles east of Poverty Bay. The Monospar was mistaken for a German raider, causing a policeman to call on Hyslop that afternoon.'[6]

Although the Monospar put up faultless service, van Asch decided a higher performance aircraft was needed for wartime work. In 1943, NZAM took delivery of an AT-11 Beechcraft, imported for him by the RNZAF. It arrived complete with Norden bomb-sight, then on the secret list, which had to be removed and returned to the Defence department.

The Commonwealth Air Training Plan

During the early years of the war the RNZAF principally focussed on training men for RAF service. Numbers had been steadily increasing since 1938, when the 1937 short-service scheme was extended to provide up to 200 pilots annually. The British air mission at the Pacific Defence Conference the following year discussed the issue again; from this emerged a new arrangement for 1000 trained airmen per annum. This was subsequently raised further to 650 pilots and 650 observers and air gunners. A secret 1943 report on the RNZAF dryly noted:

To implement this obligation, a war training organisation was designed, including one recruit depot, one initial training school, one flying instructors' school, three elementary flying training schools, one observers' school, and three service flying training schools. Arrangements were also made for the training of technical personnel.[7]

The components of this scheme were not complete when war broke out in September, and it was quickly overtaken by wartime events. The British had a total requirement for 20,000 pilots and 30,000 aircrew annually for war purposes, and in the early weeks of September implemented a plan to use Commonwealth resources to train five-ninths of them. The scheme required twenty five advanced training stations in Canada, attended by pilots who had been given elementary training elsewhere in the Commonwealth. Discussions in Ottawa determined the specifics; from this the New Zealand government agreed to provide 880 fully trained pilots direct to Britain annually, supplemented by 590 pilots, 546 observers and 936 air gunners who would receive advanced training in Canada.

This Commonwealth Air Training Scheme was a very substantial increase over the April 1939 figures, and stretched New Zealand's facilities to the limit. The only way such numbers could be attained was by expanding the three existing elementary flying training schools (EFTS) and adding another. Under a rapid re-organisation, the third EFTS went up at Harewood — opening in May 1940 under Wing Commander Sir Robert Clark-Hall — and the fourth was formed at Whenuapai. A school to train instructors also opened at Mangere.

This was only the beginning; the entire system was not finally in place until May 1941.[8] A 1943 report noted that:

> *This consisted of an educational service for the training of men prior to entry into the RNZAF, an initial training wing, four elementary flying training schools, three service flying training schools, a flying instructors' school, a technical school of training, various units for home defence, aircraft repair depots, and several schools for specialist technical training.*[9]

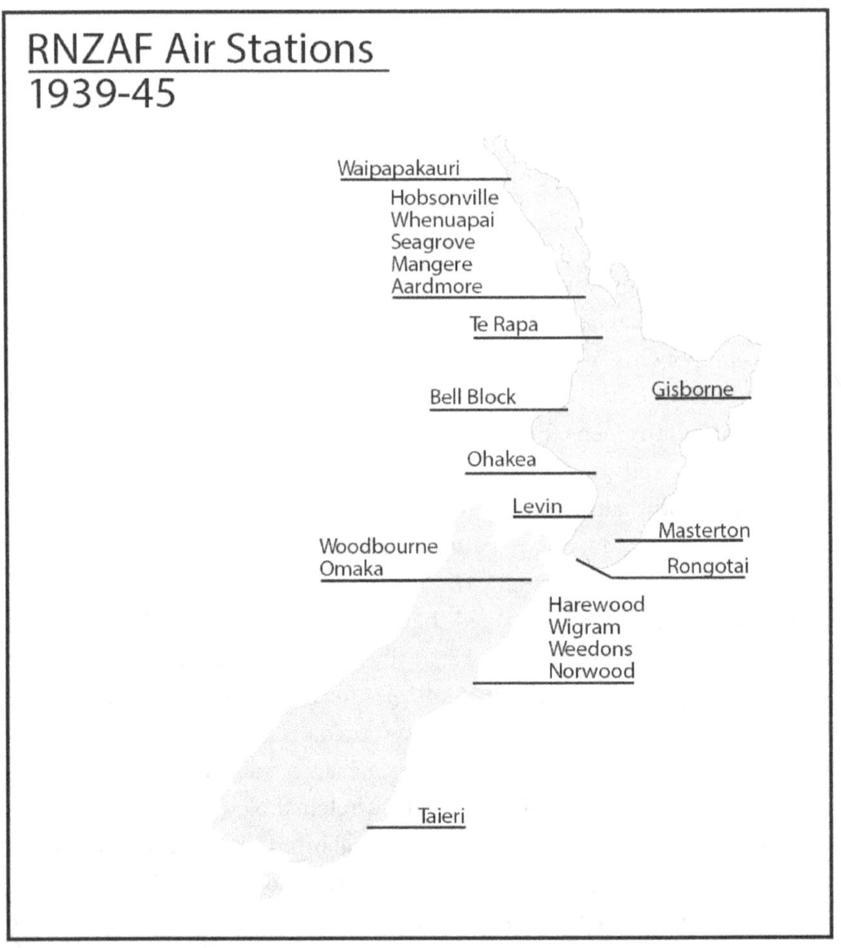

Bases were located all over New Zealand. A Recruit Training Wing was established at Ohakea, but subsequently moved to Levin. A technical training school opened at Hobsonville, and another followed at Wigram, followed by a third in August 1940 at Rongotai.

The system — when finally implemented — could train 3,896 individuals per annum, including 1,530 fully trained pilots. It was an impressive achievement in such a short time, but had been managed only through a variety of expediencies. In September 1940, for example, each stage was slashed from eight weeks to six, and the pupil-teacher ratio was increased by a quarter. The Initial Training Wing in Levin had to accept a raised intake in November, but these changes tightened the whole process too much and in December 1940, initial training was extended from four weeks to six. A sixty percent increase in numbers was hoped for. However, only two months later, the British requested a reduction to five weeks. This was rejected for a variety of reasons, including equipment shortage. Courses were then extended to eight weeks in February 1942, including sixty hours flight per pupil at each stage. Further changes had to be made to meet the new demands of the Pacific war that year.[10]

Many New Zealanders were eager to join the service during the early years of the war. Bill Houghton went to Gisborne to volunteer and was posted to Levin by July 1940. Michael von Dadelszen of Havelock North applied for the RNZAF in November 1939, and was enlisted in the Initial Training Wing at Levin on 29 September 1940. He departed in early November on board the *Awatea* for further training in Canada.[11] Some pilots were men who had taken up an earlier government offer of 40 hours free flying training. Desmond Scott was among them. Reminded by the Air Department of what he later described as a 'small clause' in his contract,[12] he left the cavalry to join the RNZAF and was sent to Britain in August 1940 after training on Fairey Gordons.

Most new entrants went to the initial training wing at Levin where they were inducted into military life — uniforms, rifle drills, the discipline and culture of a military service. A basic air training school was usually the next destination. Allan McLeod went from Levin to the Elementary Flying Training school at Taieri, near Dunedin, in September 1940. A 'splendid breakfast' impressed him from the start — the food was apparently better than it had been in Levin. Work was intense, a pressure to perform and produce results that was given all the more impetus by the war emergency. Their day was divided between lectures and a two-hour flying session.

> *It is a great feeling to be soaring alone high above the plains free from all earthly worries. Two of us share cosy little rooms and I am most fortunate in having Bill Miller as my room mate ...all the other airmen on the station are much more friendly towards us.*[13]

Leading Aircraftsman E Fancy, writing of life at Taieri in March 1942, found the morning devoted to flying and the afternoon to lectures.

> *these so far are not very arduous, the main trouble being an extremely strong tendency to fall asleep during them! The flying is a great thrill too much so at times, especially when we are introduced to aerobatics. Some mornings the boys eat a conspicuously small breakfast — a sure sign they are soon being introduced to such things as spins or loops. It's necessary to do spins before flying solo. Its a very queer sensation to see the earth apparently gone mad, spinning round and round. However, the first was the worst, after a while you almost enjoying them... The worst thing to put up with is a devilish gadget called a Link trainer, to teach instrument flying. You are shut up in a model cockpit & "fly" by a bewildering mass of dials which refuse to point to the correct place. The only solace is that one can't crash in it...*[14]

Elsewhere discipline was tighter. Fancy discovered a change when he went to Rotorua. Here, Fancy noted, 'the discipline was tightened up far too much — had very little freedom during our stay and too much pinpricking and red tape.'[15]

Nolan Wynn joined the RNZAF after a medical examination and an interview:

> *I was posted to Harewood air base Christchurch where I was given a drill and discipline course, small arms training, gas drills, live grenade throwing, marching etc. My new home was an eight man army hut with no heating and in the winter was very cold. 6AM reveille followed by ablutions where you were lucky to find even warm water in the showers, then a scramble to fold all your blankets into a neat pack and all your gear tidy and stowed away ready for inspection.... After some months at Harewood I was posted to a flying training station at Woodbourne Blenheim where the air was full of Tiger Moths with rookie pilots under training. Here I was daily indoctrinated in a classroom where I found it was difficult to concentrate owing to the continuous roar of aero engines which almost seemed to come through the windows. I was only one of a long line of personnel who had been in this situation. At this air station my accommodation improved dramatically with dormitories complete with good beds, sheets, pillowcases etc which I had not seen since leaving Nelson.*[16]

Experienced pilots were in high demand. Arthur John Bradshaw had run his own airline in Southland during the 1930s and joined the Air Force in 1941 with a three-year seniority. He feared that the transition might prove difficult after being his own boss; but had little trouble and went to Werearoa where he found 'a very full programme' of lectures and exams, along with 'a certain amount of soldiering and physical examinations.' With his piloting experience he was posted directly to the No.2 Service Flying School at Woodbourne, where he went through the No. 1C course with airmen pilots. 'This was exceedingly good for me as my experience was very limited on twin engined aircraft and such exercises as bombing and aerial gunning were quite foreign.' From here, he was sent to an Advanced Training Squadron at Woodbourne as an instructor, and assigned to advanced navigation testing. This involved two daily flights of about three and a half hours, each with two pupils and a wireless operator, typically from Woodbourne as far as Cape Egmont.[17]

Woodbourne-based instructors were required to fly dawn patrols with the Ansons. These supplemented night patrols with Vincents armed with depth charges and bombs, which were widely regarded as ineffective by the pilots, as they could not even find the Wellington-Lyttleton ferry 'whose position we knew'. After four hours or more in the air the men would return 'very cold and with sore bottoms and with very little satisfaction of having done a useful job.'[18]

The Canadian experience

The advanced training schools in Canada were the next destination for many airmen emerging from the New Zealand schools. By December 1943, some 6453 New Zealanders had gone across the Pacific. Of these, 579 returned to New Zealand, but 3910 went on to join the Royal Air Force. Some 3307 others also went direct to Britain, joining the 507 serving with the RAF at the outbreak of the war. Tragically, 2537 New Zealanders had become casualties by then, and 59 had died in Canada — though training casualties were far lower than during the First World War.

Shipboard life on the journey over was a sharp contrast to life on the training bases in New Zealand. For some, embarkation brought home the fact that they were not going to see their families for some time. James Martin told his parents:

> *It was pretty rough too but I had a stiff brandy plus a good dinner... Its certainly a big wrench to leave loved ones behind. Ones who have always been everything to me. However being a true Martin I was soon asleep and did not know anything till 6 AM... Up and showered and then into Breakfast. It was still blowing and tossing about and just after I had ordered breakfast a dirty big swell got the upper hand so the breakfast was not eaten by yours truly.... Conditions for most of us are really good and meals are excellent — really they are what one would expect in peace time on an ocean cruise.... We have watch duty to do and I do an hour every 19 — commenced at 1 am Saturday second — 10 pm Sunday 3 pm Monday and 8 am this morning. Tomorrow I go on at 3 am, so you see there is always something for us.*[19]

Lessons and lectures continued during the sea passage at first, but the RNZAF later had to rely on American transports, which were 'extremely crowded and totally lacking in suitable accommodation for organised classes.' Reporting on the matter in a secret 1943 minute, Wing Commander Campbell dryly added: 'I very much doubt if RAAF personnel are travelling under the same conditions.'[20]

Some New Zealanders, overseas for the first time, took the opportunity to experience the sights, sounds and people of a foreign country during the journey over. James Martin's ship landed him in San Francisco, and he travelled 2500 miles overland through America to Ottawa. 'The gem of the trip was Jasper — the centre of the Canadian National Park a pretty little tourist resort no bigger than Cambridge but what a delightfully refreshing place it was — nestled in the hills and looking so clean.'[21]

In Canada, the New Zealanders were taught by some of their fellow countrymen, among them Wing Commander Francis Seavill of Auckland who had joined the RAF in 1937, and was transferred to Canada in early 1940. Another was Wing Commander Graeme McDonald of Wainui. Work was intense. 'Gosh! This flying makes you tired — if we go up in the morning, most of the class is asleep during afternoon lectures,' William Vesey wrote back to friends in Levin.[22] Allan McLeod was thrilled on arriving at his station near Ottawa to find men from Levin. 'Our course here involves navigating by the heavenly bodies, a branch of navigation which is extremely interesting. We would fly at night high above the clouds and then 'shoot' stars with a sextant to obtain fixes. Sometimes we would never look out the plane's window — it was great fun.'[23] Sick with chickenpox, he fell behind and had to join another class, lamenting his friends who had moved on. 'The work although hard is very interesting & the English instructors who have actually been on operations are grand chaps with a wonderful sense of humour.'[24] Adrian Wedding could:

> *say little about the course here beyond the fact that it is long and hard enough, it has been quite interesting, to me at least. We have been flying, usually several times a week, often at night, or in the very early morning arriving back for an early breakfast. Our school is, I understand, one of the best of its kind in this country — or perhaps we have been lucky.*[25]

Off duty, the men played tourist and explored the local entertainment opportunities. Alan McLeod and his friends once borrowed skates to try out the station ice-rink. 'We were all nearly sick with laughter spending more time on the ground than over it.' The Canadians welcomed the New Zealanders. William Vesey found 'the people are very good to us and do what they can for us when we're away from camp. My cobber and I have been going to a French Canadian Doctors' place and we've had some great times.' But socialising had a cost. 'During this 14 days we can't go to bed early either, because we have to report to the guard house at 6.30 pm 7.30 pm 8.30 pm 9.30 & 10.30. Lights out at 10.30 so we have to have a shower & go to bed in the dark — not worth it!!'[26]

Adrian Wedding was another New Zealander entranced by Canadian people and scenery. He spent a glorious fortnight in September 1942 on leave with 'some friends at a little village 25 miles from Winnipeg' and could not speak too highly of the people he met. 'they have been most kind in every way. In a few days I hope to see the harvesting in progress — it is too damp at present for threshing, but a few days may make all the difference.'[27]

Other destinations beckoned. Granted two days leave, McLeod and several friends made a lightning trip to New York where they tried to see New Zealand actress Nola Luxford.

The Apollo theatre in Harlem (Negro quarter) was our next port of call. There we saw champion sewing bands, expert trap dancing, Henry Armstrong, boxer, crooned 'south of the border' much to the amusement of the large audience present. Miss Logan told the audience she had 4 boys from NZ who had only been in New York 4 hours on a 48 hour leave. She said 'I told them they had not seen New York until they had seen Harlem.' Thereupon she took us on to the stage and kissed us each. The sea of black faces went mad cheering for several minutes.[28]

On brief leave after an exam in September, McLeod travelled through the Canadian countryside shooting game. 'It was beautiful driving through the bush with occasional peeps of lakes. The trees were all turning a golden colour so you can imagine how pretty it really looked. We called at a trapper's place to hire a boat to go duck shooting on Lake Montreal. It was cold and at first the ducks were pretty wild but we shot several.'[29]

Some found romance, and by June 1943, sixty New Zealand airmen had married Canadian women. Arrangements were made to send the women and their children to New Zealand at Canadian government expense, but shipping was not available. Group Captain Trevor W 'Tiny' White, RNZAF liaison officer in Ottawa, thought that 'they will probably have to wait until the cessation of hostilities.'[30] It was twelve months before any women could be moved; in June 1944, nineteen women and four children were escorted to New York. White hoped there might be funds to 'alleviate the financial distress caused' by any war-related delays during their journey.[31]

The Canadian winter got to James Martin. 'Within 10 days I will have my wing up so that will be something achieved,' he wrote home in December 1942. 'We will all be glad to leave this place as it is the world's worst station. We all have heavy colds as a result of living in class rooms that are not heated — temperature at zero.'[32]

Changing war fortunes had a significant effect on morale. White attributed improved performance after 1943 to the fact that the threat of invasion in New Zealand had passed. But as the war dragged on, some students found their enthusiasm to learn steadily dropping. One airman at the Lethbridge Alberta No. 8 school in mid-1944 was very worried over his meteorology exam and admitted to 'some careless mistakes too as I found out later. Too bad.' He passed and was awarded his wings. 'Don't know whether to laugh or cry,' he confided. He was 'nervous as the Devil' when he went up to get his wings at the graduation ceremony.[33]

From Canada the New Zealanders were flown or sailed to Britain — another new destination for many. Bill Houghton was one of the early pilots to make the Atlantic crossing. A fully qualified pilot when he left New Zealand, he passed through Canada with only a brief pause in early 1941 and embarked on the liner *Georgic* for a lightning ocean passage escorted by the *Prince of Wales* and *Repulse*. The Battle of the Atlantic was at its height and the ships relied on speed for protection — pushing ahead regardless of weather.

> *They pointed at Scotland and opened the taps. Half the time we couldn't see the warships, they were submarining. We stopped for nothing until we got into Gourock. It was a remarkable sight to see these two warships on either side... When we left Halifax, I was a sprog PO and the first day when we pushed out of Halifax harbour, my name was put up on the noticeboard. I was duty officer — I had to report to the senior officer and see that the tough Montreal regiment blokes were getting their proper food — whether they had any complaints or not. That was my introduction to a different side of the whole story.*[34]

Other New Zealanders were flown across. Alan McLeod told friends that:

> *Our trip across the Atlantic was quite fun but as we were kept busy the time soon passed away. It was a thrill watching the sun set, moon set and then the sun rise again, but our greatest excitement was seeing the green lands of Great Britain. Everything over here is quite similar to NZ except farms, fields, herds of stock are smaller and buildings generally present a very old appearance... we have had a wonderful time although prices are high and travel facilities bad.*[35]

He had fourteen days leave and went to London, where he visited Westminster Abbey, the Houses of Parliament and Admiralty Arch, and fed pigeons in Trafalgar square. Other national sights drew his attention as he went north to his station. The Firth of Forth Bridge was a 'really magnificent structure':

I was privileged to be billeted with Sir Michael and Lady Nairn in their magnificent mansion. Two more charming and hospitable people I have yet to meet and as they had travelled all over NZ and their daughter was the fire of one of Governor General Galway's aide [de] camps they could talk freely of our wonderful country. My room had a black marble bath with huge Queen Anne 4 poster bed complete with ceiling, curtains, tassels etc. Imagine me in that![36]

Desmond Scott, though longing for the hills of Canterbury, found himself irresistibly drawn to London and had a regular circuit with friends through the West End. Some Kiwis found themselves comparing the English countryside and park-like forests with the rugged landscapes of the antipodes. James Martin found idyllic scenery when he arrived in February 1943. 'Here I am safely in the South of England,' he wrote home,

and enjoying mild weather with plenty of greenery all around. It's a beautiful spot and reminds me very much of home. This place is a famous summer resort and we are living in hotels just the same as we did in Rotorua. On Monday we go on 16 days leave and I intend going to London for a few days and then will probably go into the country... Censorship is pretty strict here and we cannot say much... Things are so peaceful in these parts that you wouldn't know there's a war on except for the military uniforms.[37]

Although the training scheme was expanded to meet wartime needs, there were bottlenecks even in Canada. By late 1943 prospective navigators and bomber crews were being re-deployed at the training stations, 'pending commencement of their training course.'[38] Money became an issue the following year. New Zealand had agreed to pay for twelve percent of the training scheme. A mutual aid agreement signed with Canada in August 1944 was not retrospective, and the government was billed $11,939,937 for pre-1944 training costs. Intense diplomatic efforts followed and White reported in May 1945 that the Canadians had 'agreed to reconsider the matter.'[39]

The Pacific war forced major changes to the scheme. A proportion of the pilots sent to Canada were re-deployed to the Pacific as the war there intensified, and these numbers increased as deployments to Europe were run down; in March 1944, the quota of trained Warrant Officer Air Gunners sent to the Pacific theatre went up to twenty every six weeks. By the middle of the year there were significant surpluses of trained airmen, and in August 1944 the decision was taken to wind down the scheme altogether.[40] At that stage it was intended that all pilots in training were to return to New Zealand when their courses ended, and some 287 who had not yet begun their courses were sent home immediately.

In fact airmen continued to drift to Britain; a batch of 200 air gunners was accepted in Britain towards the end of the year, but the balance returned to New Zealand, along with 40 bomber crew. Numbers continued to fall as the last intake passed through the system, and in March 1945, White reported that only 128 New Zealand airmen in total had embarked from Canada, 73 of them returning to New Zealand.[41]

War service with the RAF 1939–41

It took some time for airmen trained through the Commonwealth Air Training scheme to reach the RAF, but more than 500 New Zealanders were already serving with the RAF when war broke out, largely a result of the 1937 short-service scheme, and fought for the British during the 'phoney war' and dark days of 1940. These men included Flying Officer E J 'Cobber' Kain, who shot down a Dornier Do-17 with his Hurricane over France in November 1939. Another was M V 'Mindy' Blake, an Eketahuna-born mathematician who had been the 1936 New Zealand pole vault champion. He left his position as physics lecturer in Canterbury university to join the RAF in 1937, flying Gloster Gauntlets until Hurricanes arrived the following year. Surviving a nasty crash at the outbreak of war — caused by hay blocking the air intake — he fought in the Battle of Britain and shot down three aircraft.

The New Zealand Flight spent the early months of the war working up their Wellingtons. After several months at Marham and Stradishall, the flight moved in early 1940 to RAF Feltwell in Norfolk. First operational sorties took place in March, so-called 'Nickel' leaflet-dropping raids over Germany. These were characteristic of RAF operations at the time, which prohibited attacks on civilian targets and were partly a function of the 'phoney war' that followed the fall of Poland. The Germans had made no move, the French had not invaded Germany, and there were hopes for negotiated peace. Propaganda was part of the strategy, and by April 1940 the British had dropped 65,000,000 leaflets over Germany. On 27 March, three New Zealand Flight Wellingtons led by Squadron Leader Kay dropped propaganda over Hamburg. Another raid followed on 6 April. That week — after a good deal of bureaucratic wrangling — the group became officially the New Zealand Flight of 75 Squadron. This squadron dated back to the First World War, and had been re-formed in 1937 as part of the RAF's expansion scheme.

The 'phoney war' ended in early April when the Germans invaded Denmark and Norway. On 12 April, a 75 Squadron crew under Flight Lieutenant Aubrey Breckon went to Wick, where they were given Wellington L4387 and ordered on an extended reconnaissance flight to the Lofoten Islands, Vest Fijord and Narvik. The aircraft was fitted with auxiliary tanks and they carried naval officer Lieutenant Commander F O Howie as observer, returning after more than fourteen hours in the air with 72 photographs. Meanwhile, four 75 Squadron Wellingtons took off from Feltwell with eight aircraft of 37 Squadron to look for the battlecruisers *Scharnhorst* and *Gniesenau* off the coast of Norway, but found nothing.

During May, additional men and equipment brought 75 Squadron up to full strength. There was extensive action that month for all the New Zealanders serving with the RAF. On 10 May the Germans attacked Holland. Three 75 Squadron aircraft attacked German troop concentrations at Waalhaven that day. Two nights later, three Wellingtons struck supply dumps behind the rapidly advancing front line. On the front itself, seventy fighter-bombers attacked advancing German columns near Sedan. Three New Zealanders became casualties, including Pilot Officer V A Cunningham, killed while machine-gunning a bridgehead.

Six 75 Squadron Wellingtons joined 93 other aircraft from Bomber Command to attack the Ruhr on the night of 15 May, but poor weather blanketed the area and none of the squadron aircraft found the target. Further action followed in France. On 18 May, Pilot Officer R D Yule, of Invercargill, was piloting one of three Hurricanes that intercepted a dozen Heinkel He-111 bombers; Yule shot down his target. On 22 May, 75 Squadron lost an aircraft piloted by Flying Officer Collins. The Wellington was hit by flak while lining up for a bombing run over Dinant, in Belgium, and the starboard engine was set alight. Collins turned for friendly territory, but fire engulfed the wing and he was forced to order the crew to bale out. He stayed with the aircraft as it went down to give them a chance, and was killed along with the second pilot. The three who escaped were captured.

By the middle of 1940, the first fully qualified graduates of the New Zealand training scheme were reaching Britain. One was Henry Miller, who sailed for Britain in June. 'We will clean up Hitler and his b---- army,' [sic] he wrote to his family 'I will be home again soon.' Like the Great War volunteers of a generation before, Miller played tourist during the journey out and was entranced by his first sight of foreign land. Bermuda was an island paradise filled with Americans. 'The Americans think a terrible lot of us and are always wishing they could do anything for us,' he wrote. The airmen took turns at submarine watch. When he got to England he had time to see London, a 'dirty place and very smelly,' though Miller thought it would be 'wonderful during peacetime when there would be no blackout.' The next few days were a blur. He thought he would not do any fighting initially, because he had a conversion course, but wrote home that 'they seem to be rushing us through our training so as to get us on to operations as soon as possible.'[42] He was proud to be the first of 'our crowd' to solo and admitted he was 'rather pleased' with himself.

Miller was killed before the course ended when his Blenheim suffered low-altitude engine failure. He was rescued alive, but died in hospital and was buried with full military honours in a quiet churchyard in Caversham. Family friend and 'adopted sister' Hilda Appleby, then an exchange teacher in England, followed the formal letters of notification with a few words of her own to 'my dear New Zealand mother.' She could not bear the thought of the grief Miller's family faced and the misery of waiting two months for information. 'And yet perhaps,' she wrote 'by the time this reaches you, something of the first shock will have worn off.'[43] More than three thousand New Zealand airmen died in Europe during the war, but the numbers did not lessen the tragedy or reduce the pain of loss to their families and friends at home. A J Bradshaw lamented that 'it seemed no time from when they were pupils to the time that their names were appearing in the newspapers as casualties. This made very sad reading...They were probably the pick of the youth of New Zealand.'[44]

New Zealanders fought prominently with the RAF during the Battle of Britain — including Thames-born Air Vice-Marshal Keith Park, who had been with the RAF since 1919 and was in command of No.11 Fighter Group, covering southeast England. He was a 'hands-on' commander whose tactical decisions made a substantial contribution to the eventual victory. Other New Zealand commanders in the battle included Blake, Squadron Leader P G Jameson, Squadron Leader T G Lovell-Gregg, and Squadron Leader H D McGregor.

Alan Deere was involved in extensive action before and during the Battle of Britain, narrowly missing death on 9 July when his Spitfire collided with a Messerschmitt. Trapped by a jammed hood, he fought the aircraft down into a cornfield, escaping with only minor injuries. Six weeks later, in early September, he escaped unhurt after crashing into a plum tree while engaging German aircraft over his home base of Manston. Three days after that, he was taking off from Hornchurch when the airfield was attacked by the Luftwaffe. The blast of a nearby bomb sent his Spitfire skidding upside down over the airfield. He was rescued by another pilot who had suffered a similar fate — and then his rescuer collapsed and was carried to safety by Deere.

Another high-scoring New Zealand pilot during the battle was Colin Gray, who had failed his medical examination in New Zealand in 1936 and spent the next two years working on a farm to improve his health before trying again in 1939 and being accepted into the RAF. Posted to No. 54 Squadron, he shot down seven enemy aircraft in the first two weeks of August 1940, cheating death twice in the process. Another high-scorer was Brian Carbury, who joined the RAF in the 1937 intake, and won a DFC and bar during the battle. Posted to No. 603 Squadron, he shot down eight enemy aircraft in his first ten days of combat.

New Zealand RAF Squadrons 1941–44

Many Kiwi airmen arriving in Britain during the war were sent to the seven New Zealand squadrons. The political decision to develop these units was taken at the insistence of the New Zealand government, largely in recognition of the fact that the RNZAF could not send complete units, but that full squadrons could be formed within the RAF. The benefits to morale in particular were enormous, both within the squadrons and back in New Zealand. However, there was strenuous British opposition, and the squadrons were never fully 'Kiwified' by contrast with similar units developed for the Canadians and Australians — whose governments had much greater influence on British thinking.

The second 'New Zealand' squadron after No. 75 was established in March 1941, when No. 485 — otherwise known as the New Zealand Spitfire Squadron — formed at RAF Driffield in Yorkshire under Squadron Leader M W B Knight. Flying the 'glamour' fighter of the war, the squadron attracted great interest back in New Zealand where some £126,000 was raised to buy aircraft. Spitfire VB's subsequently supplied to the squadron were named after New Zealand provinces.

Whanganui schoolteacher Sergeant James A Ward won New Zealand's first aerial VC of the war. He was second pilot in a 75 Squadron Wellington commanded by Squadron Leader R P 'Ben' Widdowson that took part in a raid over Munster in July 1941. Returning over Holland, the Wellington was intercepted by an Me-110 which set the starboard engine on fire — and was then shot down itself by the rear gunner, Sergeant Allan Box. However, the Wellington did not seem to have long to fly and it was only a matter of time before the fire ignited the wing tanks. Desperate efforts to extinguish the blaze by cutting the fabric over the wing root and pointing extinguishers through the gap failed. Ward — against the advice of his colleagues — decided to climb on to the wing. He wore his parachute and had a rope around his waist, but there was every chance he would be blown off the wing with no prospect of being reeled back in. Carrying a canvas sheet previously used as an extra cushion by the pilot, he scrambled through the astrodome and into the 180 mph slipstream, punching through the fabric to grip the geodetic structure beneath. He reached the engine after an exhausting struggle and pushed the canvas into the fire, ignoring the pain. The slipstream tore at the sheet, so he pushed it harder into the gap, only to have it ripped completely away when he let go. But he had partially extinguished the blaze, and made his way to the relative safety of the fuselage.

Widdowson nursed the aircraft back and landed at Newmarket without brakes or flaps. The aircraft came to a halt in the barbed wire perimeter fence with half the rudder blown away and most of its covering burnt off. One of the crew who saw the aircraft afterwards reflected that if they had known the extent of the damage, they would have baled out. Ward was recommended for the Victoria Cross, and it was approved on 5 August.

That month No. 489 'New Zealand' squadron formed at RAF Leuchars in Scotland, initially equipped with Beauforts. This unit did not become operational until early 1942, when the aircraft were changed for Handley Page Hampdens. In March 1942, No. 486 Squadron formed at RAF Kirton-in-Lindsey, a Lincolnshire air base. Initially equipped with Hawker Hurricanes, the squadron re-equipped with Hawker Typhoon 1B's in July, and moved several times before transferring to RAF Tangmere in October for daylight operations over the Channel.

A further New Zealand squadron, No. 488, also formed in March 1942 after being withdrawn from the Far East, where it had also been manned largely by New Zealanders. Based at Church Fenton in Yorkshire, the reformed squadron was equipped with Beaufighters under twenty one year old Wing Commander R M Trousdale. Other New Zealanders with the squadron included Flying Officer F W Davison, who joined the RNZAF in February 1941, and Pilot Officer A S Cutfield, who had been with the RNZAF since March 1940. The squadron faced serious problems at first because a shortfall in maintenance staff reduced aircraft availability. The squadron moved to Ayr in Scotland in October, by which time personnel included twenty one New Zealanders, eighteen of them pilots. In August 1942, No. 487 Squadron formed with New Zealanders at Feltwell, under Wing Commander Francis Cecil Seavill. When he was killed a few months later, he was replaced by Captain R L Kippenberger. The squadron was equipped with Lockheed Venturas.[45]

Not all New Zealanders were posted to these squadrons. Bill Houghton initially went to No. 408 (Canadian) squadron, flying about five operations with them. 'It was a new squadron, they hadn't any aircraft, so they posted a few of us to 83 Squadron.' He went on to fly Handley Page Hampdens, another twin-engined 'geodetic' design. 'A wonderful aircraft, you could do anything with it.'[46] The only weakness was that the pilot was isolated from the rest of the crew. 'If the poor old pilot copped it that was curtains, you couldn't get at him. You flew it like a single engined aircraft.' Houghton was one New Zealander saved by an early night-navigation system. Electronic navigation was in its infancy at that stage, and getting lost in the dark was a real hazard. However, pilots returning at night from a raid could take advantage of an optical alternative known to the men as 'darkie, darkie' after the radio call. 'In those days we were feeling our way,' Houghton later recalled. 'We didn't have much in the way of electronic stuff. "Darkie darkie" was an early attempt to get us back to home base."[47] Pilots broadcasting this message could expect to be picked up by searchlights, which would point a direction, and they could fly along the beam until they were picked up by the next light. Aircraft were passed from light to light in this way and eventually brought back to their own airfield.

Michael von Dadelszen arrived in Canada in late November 1940, and by February 1941 had progressed to the No.4 Bombing and Gunnery School at Fingal, Ontario. On 30 March he went to the No.1 Advanced Navigation School near Manitoba, gaining his Air Navigators Badge in May. After further training in Scotland with 19 Operational Training Unit, he was posted to RAF No.10 Squadron at Leeming, Yorkshire, flying Whitleys and Halifaxes. Over the next few months he took part in eight flights over Germany and France, notching up 248 hours over Berlin, Mannheim, Hamburg, Nurnberg, Brest and Boulogne. One evening in November 1941 he watched a raid take off and wrote that he was 'much moved by the whole business.'

> *The evening I was looking on was fine, with the sun just setting in a wintry, yellow glow and half the sky a remove blue and the other half banked high with dense shining cloud. One by one the motors were started up all around the airfield and run until they were at working temperature. Their steady drumming was constantly punctuated by the short staccato roar of the four gun turrets being tested, earth spurting from the ground where the bullets converged. Then, as the time of takeoff approached, all these great, black machines started moving in two long lines towards the leeward end of the runway, looking rather like good natured, clumsy beetles. The first machine took off, the rest following at short regular intervals and all taking the full length of the runway before getting airborne, being heavy with a full load of bombs and petrol. They cleared the boundary fence with the great, full-throated roar of motors wide open and climbed over the aerodrome in wide circles before setting course for the distant target area. A heavy bomber taking off gives a tremendous impression of power just as it clears the end of the runway, and quite often your body picks up the vibrations caused by the airscrews...I watched until the last plane was in the air, and the last wave of good luck had been given by the boys on the ground, and walked slowly*

away in a very thoughtful mood. I knew where they were going and it was a long trip and rather a difficult one, and I wanted more than anything that all those blokes should get back in good time for their egg and bacon nine hours later. I looked out to the east and there I saw standing in relief against the cloud bank a great line of our bombers reaching away down towards the horizon, each a little smaller than the one behind it. From where I was the sun had set but it still gleamed warmly on the rear turrets of those planes heading east.[48]

Tragically, von Dadelszen was killed in January 1942 when his Halifax crashed over Yorkshire while returning from a raid.[49]

As Wing Leader with 234 Squadron, Blake led Spitfires over occupied France during 1941. In July he was shot down after the wing was 'bounced' while escorting bombers over Cherbourg. He shot down two of his attackers, but his own aircraft was so badly damaged he was forced to ditch in the Channel. Afloat in his survival dinghy he paddled through the night, helped by favourable winds, and was picked up by the British two miles off the Isle of Wight. In August the following year he shot down a Focke-Wulf Fw-190, but his aircraft was so badly damaged he again ended up dinghy-borne in the Channel. Despite serious injuries he again paddled for England, and was within five miles of Dover when he was intercepted by a German launch. Back in France, he tried to escape — injuring himself again in the process — but was recaptured.

Being shot down was not something to be taken lightly. Bill Houghton and his crew narrowly cheated death on the night of 8 November 1941:

We were bombing Essen right in the heart of the Ruhr — what we called 'Happy Valley' — but there were a few aircraft, Wimpys, bombing Berlin at the same time. That night we lost 41 aircraft, a lot of them came down in the North Sea. As I understand it there were 200 aircrew lost, ten percent of which reached prisoner of war camp... At that stage they were coning us in searchlights; there was a blue master searchlight — once that picked you up, surrounding searchlights coned you and then they either filled the cone up with flak or vectored a night fighter into the centre of the cone. We'd heard about this and I'd been coned several times before but it was always flak that came up. On this particular night I was picked up in a cone just as we were leaving the Ruhr valley. I was waiting for the flak to start, but it suddenly occurred to me that there was a fighter on his way in somewhere behind me, so I went down the cone as fast as I could, shooting all the time, trying to shoot out the master searchlight. Then an Me-110 followed me down, of course I couldn't see him. And he shot the living daylights out of me.

My two gunners were firing everything they had. He shot out my port engine, and half my tail. I managed to get some control by using the hydraulics. There was no way I could get at my crew, the intercom was shot up, so I had to get it down to the ground by good luck. In fact I managed to get it straightened and sailed into a mighty big tree, tore everything off, and almost crashed into the side of a German barracks. The only casualty among any of us was my navigator, who broke his leg. Next thing there was a lot of yelling and shouting, and the first thing I heard was "For you, the war is over."'[50]

No. 75 Squadron and the thousand bomber raids

All the 'New Zealand' squadrons saw extensive action during 1943. The main British air strategy during this period was guided by Air Marshal Sir Arthur Harris. He had been appointed commander of RAF Bomber Command in February 1942 and his policy was very simple; massive bombing to smash German industries, wreck their transport systems, and unhouse German industrial workers. Over time, he argued, this would bring the Germans to their knees. This approach met strong opposition from the United States, which even in 1942 favoured putting scarce resources into direct invasion of the continent the following year, Operation 'Round Up.' US General George C Marshall was particularly opposed to bombing.[51] However, he was unable to prevail in a complex debate coloured by the Dieppe raid, which ended up in favour of Winston Churchill's plan to attack North-West Africa. Meanwhile, Harris received the resources he needed.

The key was strength and persistence as far as Harris was concerned, but achieving the thousand aircraft selected for propaganda purposes was difficult. Harris had only 470 night bombers in February; and attrition was a particular problem as the German air defence system developed. Casualties were very high and — despite putting on a brave face — the psychological strain immense. To put this into perspective, the 1680 New Zealanders killed while serving with Bomber Command during the Second World War made up forty seven percent of all the fatalities suffered by the RNZAF worldwide and fifty two percent of the service's casualties in the European, Middle Eastern and South East Asian theatres.[52]

Preparations for the first 'thousand bomber' raid began in early May 1942. All squadrons were exhorted to maximum effort. Even the operational training units put aircraft into the air to bring numbers up, including one flown by Sergeant Terry Kearns of Reefton, who later joined 75 Squadron. For 75 Squadron the month meant intensive training in new electronic navigation aids such as 'Gee', while maintaining ordinary operations against Stuttgart, Essen and Mannheim. On the night of 30 May, 602 Wellingtons took off for Cologne, including 23 from 75 Squadron. They were joined by 131 Halifaxes, 73 Avro Lancasters and 88 Short Stirlings among others for a total of 1047 aircraft, although only a minority were four-engined 'heavies'. Most of the 75 Squadron aircraft carried four-pound incendiaries. Forty two bombers were lost from the raid, including one 75 Squadron Wellington piloted by D M Johnson.

Two nights later, a 'thousand bomber' raid of 956 aircraft flew against Essen, including 20 aircraft from 75 Squadron. This was followed next night by an ordinary raid of 195 aircraft, including sixteen Wellingtons from 75 Squadron. One Wellington was shot down and its crew taken prisoner. The squadron now began regular heavy raids, which became riskier in the face of ground-directed interceptors, '*Wilde sau*' (Wild Boar) roving night fighters and, ultimately, '*schrage musik*' ('slanted' or 'jazz' music) — cannons mounted at an acute angle in Ju-88s and Me-110s, which enabled the pilot to under-fly the bomber and attack from beneath. Ultimately the Germans were even able to home in on signals from British navigation aids, such as the H2S radar sets.

The emotional strain was tremendous. It was heart-rending for the aircrews to wake for a meal and see empty places at the table. Some men had strategies for facing death. One aviator wrote a letter to his wife before each raid, leaving it unsealed. When he returned, he would add a number to the bottom before posting, indicating he had survived another mission. Thoughts were often dominated by the magic number — thirty operational flights to end a tour. High-jinks to relieve the stress were often encouraged. When F J 'Popeye' Lucas left footprints on the ceiling at one base, the commanding officer ordered them left there.[53] On another occasion in 1943, the day after four 75 squadron crews were lost over the Baltic, the men were ordered to play football as a morale-booster. It worked; they came off the field arm-in-arm and spent the evening at the local bar. Nobody under the rank of sergeant was allowed to pay for their own drink.

The Wellingtons gave excellent service and were modified on the back of war experience. The 1000 lb ventral turrets were removed early on. Later the bomb bays were modified to let the aircraft carry 4000 lb 'cookies'. However, the type was not as capable as a four-engined aircraft, and the squadron re-equipped with four-engined Short Stirlings in late 1942. The Stirling was the first modern four-engined bomber to enter British service, a stressed-skin monoplane that first flew in 1939. However, the advantage of the larger aircraft was offset by its relatively low service ceiling of 17,000 feet, caused by a low aspect-ratio wing — a limitation enforced by an Air Ministry requirement that the bomber had to fit through all existing hangar doors. Stirlings were very vulnerable to flak as a result. The squadron also received the obsolescent Mk 1 version, which they were not able to exchange for the more capable Mk III until early 1943. The last Wellington sorties were flown on 25/26 October 1942, after which the squadron completed a move to RAF Newmarket and the conversion to Stirlings.

Newmarket was an odd base, built in and around a racecourse which remained in operation despite the war. Some of the men were billeted in the grandstands, which had been converted to barracks; others lived in Sefton Lodge, on the other side of Newmarket township, or the Jockey Club in the centre of town. The aircraft actually flew from the Rowley Mile racetrack.

The aerial effort accelerated when the 'battle of the Ruhr' began in March 1943. This was the start of what Harris called his 'main offensive', an all-out effort to destroy German industrial power in the Ruhr valley. This campaign was characterised by new electronic navigation systems such as H2S and Oboe, and by new German counter-measures such as the deadly *Schrage Musik* system. For 75 Squadron these months were difficult. Eleven aircraft and ten crews were lost in April, during which the squadron flew over the Ruhr and mined the Frisian Islands and Kiel. The attractions of Newmarket town proved too much for some aircrew, and Wing Commander Michael

Wyatt was finally appointed to sort the squadron out. He organised a move to RAF Mepal, a better established base with fewer distractions.

Another New Zealand VC was won in 1943 by Squadron Leader Len H Trent of No. 487 Squadron, a Nelsonian who had joined the RNZAF in the 1930s and moved on to the RAF in 1938. He flew Fairey Battles and Bristol Blenheims in France during 1939-40, and by 1942 had been posted as commander of B-Flight of 487 (NZ) Squadron at RAF Methwold, leading eleven Venturas to bomb a power station in Amsterdam on 3 May 1943. The attack was part of a diversion to allow Bostons to attack another power station at Ijmuiden, but did not go well. Two Spitfire squadrons providing cover flew high, alerting German defences, and 70 German fighters swooped to attack. Trent ordered the Venturas to fly on at top speed, but the bombers were progressively shot down. Only Trent's aircraft reached the target, causing blast damage; then he too was shot down. He and the navigator survived to become prisoners of war, and he later became involved in the so-called 'Great Escape' from Stalag Luft III. He received the VC in 1946 for his actions.

Eight Stirlings of 75 Squadron and seven crews were lost during two raids over Berlin in August 1943. By this time the Germans were using fighter versions of the Junkers Ju-88 medium bomber against British bomber streams, equipped with the *schrage musik* system — high-angle cannons that enabled the Germans to attack the vulnerable underside of the bomber. One was shot down by Stirling rear gunner Sergeant Iwi Teaika of Christchurch during a raid over Hannover in September 1943. To let Teaika get the shot, pilot Des Horgan stood the Stirling on its tail and the big bomber fell out of the sky. Horgan recovered only 200 feet above the streets of Hannover after a maximum-G pullout that caused massive damage to the aircraft — but he managed to nurse his aircraft back to England. Horgan's Stirling was not the only one that kept flying after heavy damage, as 75 Squadron pilot H A Williamson discovered during a raid over Germany with Stirling B-Beer:

> *We made our way across the lowlands of Holland at 50 feet and at times under it, and once just went under some high tension cables which were strung between steel pylons. Flying really low with the moonlight visibility almost as good as day... and with the little side window open,. we hedge and telephone wire hopped our way across Holland and were soon over the border into Germany.*[54]

During this raid, Williamson's Stirling struck a tree. Branches slammed into the forward gunner's position and ripped half the tailplane away, but Williamson somehow managed to keep the bomber in the air and returned to England — where he was awarded the DFC.

Flying Officer Lloyd Trigg posthumously won New Zealand's third aerial VC of the war the same month. Kaitaia-born Trigg was posted to No. 200 Squadron RAF in West Africa in January 1943, stationed there to hunt U-boats in the South Atlantic. Trigg distinguished himself in an attack on two U-boats in March. The unit subsequently re-quipped with Liberators and on 11 August, Trigg and his crew took off for one of the first operational sorties with the type. They found U-468, which had been patrolling the area for a month. The submarine was heavily armed with 20-mm cannons, and Oberleutnant zur see Schamong decided to fight. Trigg flew into a cone of fire, but did not deviate from his attack run and dropped six depth charges. A few seconds later the Liberator, on fire and out of control, slammed into the sea. The depth charges destroyed the U-boat. Schamong and six men survived to be captured next day, and Trigg was awarded the VC on the basis of Schamong's account.

Squadron Leader Johnny Checketts was involved in intense action during the middle of 1943. Commanding No. 485 (NZ) Squadron based at Biggin Hill, he shot down a Focke-Wulf 190 on 15 July, two more on 27 July, and at the end of the month destroyed a Bf-109G. In early August he led an offensive sweep over St Pol and engaged eight Bf-109's; the squadron shot down three, and Checketts damaged two others. He was awarded the DFC. A few days later his unit was involved in a battle with a mixed force of Focke-Wulf 190s and Bf-109s, and Checketts scored a 'probable'. But his luck ran out at the beginning of September, when he was shot down while flying cover for a raid on the Serquex marshalling yards — after scoring yet another Focke-Wulf 190. Injured, he bailed out and was rescued by a French family who tended his wounds. Helped by the French Resistance, he joined a group of escaped prisoners and was smuggled across the Channel at the end of October.

Another New Zealander who escaped occupied France was Flight Sergeant L S M 'Chalky' White, also of 485 Squadron. During a strike on a German airfield in France, his unit was 'bounced' by eighty German fighters. White shot down one, but the odds were against him and he escaped the dogfight only with serious damage to the cooling system. The engine seized before he could leave occupied territory and he made a belly-landing in a field. Although briefly captured by German forces occupying the village of Bolbec, White escaped and made his way across Occupied and Vichy France into Spain. Reaching the British Consulate in Barcelona, he was promptly taken to be a spy. Finally he returned to Britain, much to the surprise of his squadron mates who had long since thought he was dead.[55]

No. 75 Squadron spent most of the rest of 1943 minelaying, and continued this task into 1944. By this time the Stirlings were being phased out, and in March, the squadron began converting to the Avro Lancaster Mk III. Not all managed it. James Martin's crew was too close to completing its tour. 'I have now done 25,' he wrote home:

> *so there is only five more to do at the most. All have had some changes on the station and the Stirlings have been replaced by Lancasters. However I don't think our crew will change over as we are nearly finished. It's all in the air at present and the next few weeks will tell just what is what. I'm quite easy and wouldn't mind doing some trips in Lancs. It would mean Berlin and such places but it's all something to look back on. However before you get this I expect you will have had word that we have finished.*[56]

By this time the RNZAF had sent some 7300 personnel to serve in the RAF, 3300 directly and 4000 by way of Canada, to which could be added the 500 New Zealanders who had been serving with the RAF under the pre-war Short Service Commission scheme. By the end of 1943, 900 New Zealanders had transferred to other countries, 600 had returned to New Zealand, and 2500 had become casualties. Almost all of the New Zealanders in the RAF by this time were aircrew, there were very few technical service personnel. At home there was no doubt as to their contribution. 'New Zealanders have earned the reputation of taking part in every operation worthwhile on every fighting front where the RAF operates.'[57]

The Normandy Campaign

Fighting in unfamiliar skies twelve thousand miles from home, New Zealand airmen with the Royal Air Force played a key role in the air battles raging over France before and during the Normandy campaign. Out of 3900 RAF personnel involved, 500 were New Zealanders; and some 1500 New Zealand personnel in all were involved in the air campaign from April to August 1944.

Allied air superiority was the key to victory; and a New Zealander, Air Marshal Sir Arthur ('Mary') Coningham,[58] commanded the Second Tactical Air Force which played a lead role in establishing that superiority during the crucial early stage. Preparations included a controversial effort to smash the French railway system from the air. Not all analysts were convinced this was worth diverting forces from operations against the German heartland. The crews of 75 Squadron nevertheless made a superlative effort. By this time they had completely converted to Lancasters. During one raid against rail yards at Louvain on 11 May, the squadron put up 24 aircraft and shot down a Junkers Ju-88. In another raid on 19 May over the rail yards at Le Mans the aircraft of squadron Master Bomber, Wing Commander J F Barron, collided with his deputy over the target. A further raid over Duisberg on 23 May involved 500 Lancasters, of which 25 came from 75 Squadron. Some 25 aircraft was lost, including one from the squadron. By this time air operations over northern France had reached a climax; even tactical aircraft were involved.

The invasion took place two weeks later, landing 156,000 troops on 6 June alone. That morning, twenty six 75 Squadron Lancasters took off to bomb a gun battery at Lisieux, their wings painted in black-and-white 'invasion stripes' on the wings and fuselage. In poor weather they saw no sign of the 5000 invasion vessels crossing the Channel, though there had been rumours that landing in France was imminent. Other squadron Lancasters bombed Ouisterham. A further 24 squadron aircraft flew that night. Some 200 heavy bombers were directed against each of the coastal batteries around the invasion area.

New Zealand pilot Johnny Houlton shot down the first German aircraft of D-day. Houlton was leading his section in their third sortie, south of 'Omaha' Beach, when he glimpsed a Junkers Ju-88 to the south. Climbing through a cloud, he opened fire at the extreme range of 500 yards. His three-second burst struck the right hand engine and destroyed it. As the stricken aircraft plunged towards the ground, two of the crew bailed out. Houlton watched the German bomber explode on impact.

Fighter and fighter-bomber squadrons were also involved. Johnsonville-born Lloyd Mason took on a Focke-Wulf 190 on one sortie, set it alight, then turned to attack a Messerschmitt, which blew up. In another incident during July, G E 'Jamie' Jameson of 488 Squadron downed four German bombers in twenty minutes. Jameson went on by the end of August to score 11 'kills', making him New Zealand's highest scoring night fighter ace of the war.

William Judson had a narrow escape. His Mosquito was hit over the Loire, and he was seriously wounded. Semi-conscious and half-blinded with blood from a head injury, he steered his crippled aircraft for American lines, but was forced to bail out when the aircraft became uncontrollable. He hid in a hedge for the rest of the day, found food and shelter in a nearby farmhouse, and then trekked north for ten days. His injuries were attended to by the French, and he reached Allied lines a full month after being shot down.

Not every Kiwi could participate in the opening moves. Max Collett, with the RAF's No. 485 Squadron, was in hospital in England on the day of the invasion; a fall getting out of his Spitfire a few days before left him with a broken ankle. He rejoined his squadron on 31 August when they moved to Carpiquet airfield in France. By this time the squadron was under command of thirty two year old Johnny Checketts. Another highly-ranked New Zealander during the campaign was Desmond Scott, by then a Wing Commander, appointed to command a mobile wing of four squadrons. Later he became — at 25 — the youngest Group Captain in the RAF, and the most decorated New Zealand fighter pilot of the war, ultimately being awarded the Distinguished Service order, Distinguished Flying Cross and Bar, Order of the British Empire, two separate Croix de Guerre and Palms from France and Belgium, and Commander of the Order of Orange Nassau, a Dutch honour.

Another aerial 'first' of the campaign was also scored by a New Zealander. By this time N A Williamson had become a flight commander with 75 Squadron, and was leading his Lancasters over Normandy when his aircraft was hit and flight engineer P W McDevett seriously wounded:

> *He was in great distress requiring immediate medical attention. As soon as we had completed our bombing run, I decided to risk an emergency landing on the fighter airstrip near the beach head.... The landing had to be made downwind as the circuit was over enemy lines, but fortunately was made without mishap and McDevett was very soon... on the way to medical care... for the takeoff an extra high run was made into a wheat field and not realising the danger from swing during takeoff,*

Army vehicles of all shapes and sizes had lined the strip... to wave us an enthusiastic farewell... good luck took us off without mishap and not having our engineer I hoped I had turned all the petrol cocks on correctly.[59]

Williamson returned to Mepal to discover they had been reported missing after being seen to dive away sharply from the target. The unscheduled landing was the first by a heavy bomber in Europe since the fall of France.

By the end of the Normandy campaign in September 1944 some 2,000,000 men, 3,000,000 tons of supplies and 500,000 vehicles had been put ashore. With complete command of the air, the Allies smashed German divisions as they were brought up to the beaches. On 13 June Hitler ordered his V-1 flying bombs against London. Initial strikes were desultory, though over a nine-month campaign, over 8000 flying bombs were launched and many hundreds of people killed or wounded. No. 486 Squadron, commanded by Desmond Scott, switched overnight from supporting the landings to air defence against the bombs — only their Hawker Tempests were fast enough for effective operations against the pulse-jets, but it was dangerous work because the attacking aircraft could be damaged or destroyed when the target exploded. Dunedin's G L Bonham destroyed several bombs in a row without firing a shot by tipping them up with his wing to knock them out of control — an equally hazardous manoeuver — and the squadron tally came to 223 bombs in all.

During June, 75 Squadron was almost fully occupied against railway targets and V-1 launch sites, and there were more raids against other targets such as Kiel, Stettin and Danzig during the rest of the year. One highlight was the attack on Walcheren on 3 October. Two hundred and fifty heavy bombers attacked the sea walls around this low-lying island, flooding the inland defences. Visiting the squadron at Mepal, White was 'thrilled to find so many lads I had met before... It was wonderful to notice the high morale and great camaraderie and how it all worked together in one big team.'[60]

Another unit sent to battle the V-weapons was 488 Squadron, under R G Watts, by this time equipped with Typhoons. They were visited at Dymchurch in late October 1944 by White, who had come across to England from Canada on a lightning tour. He found the airmen were 'doing a great job shooting down buzz-bombs and beating up anything they could find along the enemy coast line... The pilots loved the aircraft and considered them better than Spits.' Moving on, White found 487 Squadron at Thorney Isle. 'Our arrival was heralded by a flock of 150 DC-3's, which had been diverted from elsewhere — we were lucky to get down first... Our personnel here are a wonderful lot, many of whom I knew... it seemed to me that the pride they had in their aircraft was reflected in the manner in which they looked after themselves.'[61]

White visited the New Zealand squadrons in France in early November. On landing, he was 'met by the airfield commander, Group Captain Des Scott, and the Wing Commander... Scott was in great form, he had been to Boulogne and was able to give us each a bottle of champagne which had been looted by the Germans.' White watched raids in support of Canadians at Calais. 'We saw them all away and back again inside of 75 minutes.'[62] White's observations were no mere official puffery; by this time the Germans had lost air superiority.

Victory in Europe

Although Germany had been effectively defeated by early 1945, Hitler refused to consider surrender and in February the Allies calculated the European war would not end before June.[63] The decision was taken to heavily bomb several German cities. Dresden was to have been hit by United States bombers during 13 February, but the attack was called off after bad weather and the RAF launched its own raid that night. Lancasters of 75 Squadron arrived after incendiaries had set the city centre alight; the New Zealanders could see the firestorm from 160 miles away and smelled the smoke over Dresden at 17,000 feet.

By this time the end of the war was in sight, and many New Zealand airmen finishing their tours were discharged. Others longed for the moment. Jim Martin, who spent the last half of 1944 as an instructor, spent some time in February 1945 'trying to get home but no luck.' The problem was his experience:

> *Our contract is for 3 years and the RAF will not release me as I am an experienced instructor — yet other chaps finishing tours today and who*

> *have only been away 2 years are going home simply because the RAF won't train them so I'll have to stay.*[64]

He confided to his parents that he was 'completely fed up with it all.'

During March, 75 Squadron joined raids against oil plants at Kamen and Bochum. There were also raids against Cologne and other attacks on targets adjacent to the Rhine, preparatory to the Allied crossing. On 9 April, squadron aircraft joined nearly 1000 others in a strike on Kiel which sank the *Admiral Scheer* and damaged other units of the German navy. On 24 April the squadron conducted its final raid of the war against railway yards at Bad Oldesloe. No. 486 Squadron were sent in early 1945 to Vokel airfield in Holland — pitting their Tempests against Me-262 jet fighters and winning. No. 488 squadron was based in France during the last months of the war and during one of its final patrols on 25 April destroyed a Focke-Wulf Fw-189. The last operational sorties by 75 Squadron were humanitarian. Western Holland was still in German hands and had been cut off. A truce was organised to air-drop food, and 75 Squadron was one of several units given the task of flying cargo into these dubiously friendly skies.

Victory came as a relief. 'Well it's come at last,' Jim Martin wrote to his parents soon after Victory in Europe (VE) day:

> *... and we can rest in this part of the world. There is still a big job to be done in the Pacific yet but I don't think that will take so very long. Maybe a year but I don't think any longer. I went to London last Saturday and of course ran into the peace celebration. The crowds were terrific... Monday night at about 9 the people suddenly decided to celebrate ...and confusion started everywhere. The streets were packed mainly with a lot of youngsters at 10 am Tuesday Trafalgar Square was packed out and ...I returned to camp. I couldn't see much occasion for such wild celebrations as there is still another war which a lot of people over here would like to forget.*[65]

After VE day, 75 Squadron Lancasters repatriated prisoners of war, bringing some 2219 people back from France by 24 May. In June, the squadron was slated to join 'Tiger Force', a unit Bomber Command was preparing to join the assault on Japan. Orders came to prepare thirty crews for tropical service and for conversion to the Avro Lincoln II. Training began at RAF base Spilsby on 24 July, and word went about that they would be operating from Okinawa. But the Japanese surrendered on 14 August, and the decision was taken to repatriate the New Zealanders as soon as shipping could be arranged. During September, squadron aircraft were involved in 'Exercise Exodus', returning British troops from Italy.

Before disbanding, the squadron flew past the *Andes*, loaded with 1500 New Zealand airmen on their way home. One of the passengers was Jim Martin, who had been waiting for passage. 'It is a fast trip,' he told his parents 'which is a blessing as our eating quarters are no better than a pig sty.'[66]

CHAPTER FOUR

Pacific Defensive 1941–42

'I feel really awful at having come out here and having left you, but I really think it is better to try and stop trouble ever reaching NZ's shores'

– Edwin Glanville to his wife from Malaya, 3 December 1941.

Although New Zealand airmen saw extensive action in Europe, the RNZAF itself was more directly involved with the Pacific war. The first overseas deployment was to Malaya in mid-1941, part of the 'Singapore strategy', where the RNZAF was among the Commonwealth air forces deployed there that bore the brunt of the initial assault. It was a tragic irony. The development of New Zealand military aviation had been strangled during the 1920s because of the naval focus on Singapore. Now, New Zealand airmen with obsolete equipment were trying to save the base.

Main fleet to Singapore

The Pacific conflict of 1941 was directly triggered by the second Sino-Japanese war which erupted in 1937. Britain and the United States positioned themselves behind the Chinese, as did New Zealand, where firm diplomatic efforts were undertaken during 1940 to help curb Japanese aggression. Western logistic support kept the Chinese going, and the Japanese turned their attentions to cutting the supply routes, even clashing with British troops over the Burma Road during 1940. Spurred by the fall of France, they also blocked the southern supply route by occupying northern French Indo China, and then in mid-1941 declared Japanese authority over the entire colony. Britain and the United States responded sharply, freezing Japanese assets and enforcing an oil embargo. Prime Minister Konoe attempted to negotiate, but was forced to resign in October by his war minister, General Hideki Tojo. Negotiations continued while the Japanese made preparations to invade Malaya and secure its oil resources.

Japanese forces committed to this assault were small; Colonel Manasobu Tsuji, preparing the plans to invade Malaya, calculated he would be outnumbered 2:1 on the ground. However, this perception was not shared by the two South Pacific Dominions, particularly as reverses in Europe made it likely that the expected despatch of a significant fleet to Singapore would not materialise. Fears that New Zealand might be directly invaded rose. Coates, then in the United States, discussed war material, but the United States government was more concerned about Europe. The British continued to reassure New Zealand — Churchill even offered to abandon the Mediterranean to release forces if the Japanese attacked. He made the same assurance to Roosevelt, but told the President he was worried by the 'disastrous military possibilities' that would probably follow.[1]

In practise the British Chiefs of Staff had little option but to trust Singapore's defences, but equipment was short, and new squadrons manned in part by pilots from New Zealand were set up with the obsolescent aircraft that Britain made available for what was at that stage a less critical theatre than Europe. Then in late June 1941, the British asked for a complete New Zealand fighter squadron and construction crew to be deployed to the island. This was achieved by deducting pilots from the quota that would have gone to Europe. The aerodrome construction crew were first to leave. This unit — the first of its kind in the world — formed in July as the No.1 Aerodrome Construction Squadron Unit 24. It comprised older men, often from the Public Works Department, many of them experienced engineers, surveyors, and mechanics.

One of the men who enlisted was thirty seven year old surveyor and artist Edwin (Ted) Glanville. Like many of his fellows, he was not a career military man, but was worried by the war and wanted to do what he could to protect his wife and daughter in Gisborne. He enlisted in the army in January, but transferred to the RNZAF to join Unit 24, forming part of the Advance Survey Party which left New Zealand on 22 July. Glanville found the voyage to Malaya somehow remote from the war. One day during the voyage, the men stayed on deck until midnight, watching the islands slip past in the moonlight.

> *It was all very peaceful and beautiful and it is harder than ever to realise that there is a war being fought in all its horrible stupidity... When the Germans are defeated you will find I never want to leave NZ again, although, of course, if you can come too it will be very different.*[2]

Glanville arrived in their base camp at Tebrau, not far north of Singapore, to discover work still under way on the buildings. He compared his sergeants quarters to the 'wreck of the Hesperus'. But they were soon 'making quite good progress' and he found the work relatively easy. 'We are not troubled by any snakes, insect pests or anything like that,' he wrote on 19 September. 'Actually we are working alongside a bitumen road with cars and traffic passing all day so don't imagine me away out in an impenetrable jungle. The conditions are better than most survey jobs in NZ so it is really a luxurious "war" time job.'[3] The rest of the squadron went to Sydney for training in August, left for Malaya on 10 October, and by the third week of the month some 15 officers and 140 ranks were working at the base.

The Malayan deployment was the first experience overseas for many of the Kiwis, and when opportunity permitted they explored Singapore. Glanville had always wanted to go to Malaya, but admitted his current sojourn had removed his curiosity. The climate was 'not too bad' but the scenery was 'not a patch on NZ in any shape or form. I certainly appreciate the scenery, people and living conditions in NZ which are just marvellous compared to those in the east.'[4] Others 'goggled ...through the city streets and native bazaars... marvelled at the fine buildings and the places we'd read so much about, Raffles Hotel for instance.'[5] Cabarets were a strong attraction and some New Zealanders were able to buy tickets to dance with 'taxi girls.' The city was a mass of different people — Chinese, Malayan, English and even Indian — many unfamiliar to the New Zealanders. Glanville had a chance encounter with a 'well spoken Singhalese' who:

> *took me to the Johore Gardens which I had previously missed and we went through a fernery filled with hundreds of ferns, then he showed me a huge circular pond with wonderful waterlilies — white, cream and flaming red... When we took leave of each other I was most grateful for his thoughtfulness and courtesy, but what stumped him was "why did you leave your family and come all this way? What made you do so and WHY?" I am darned if I could answer. All the usual blurb about patriotism and so on seemed too stupid, so I just told him it was sort of an obligation we felt towards our own people. But he, like others I have met out here, seemed mystified that we should think it necessary.*[6]

They began building an airfield at Tebrau amid plantations of dense rubber trees. 'Today they had a shot at pushing over some rubber trees with an RD8 which is a huge and ferocious looking caterpillar tractor and the local inhabitants must have wondered what was going on,' Glanville wrote.[7] The trees were cut up for firewood. Deep drains were dug alongside the planned runways, initially by 18-ton tractor but finished by contracted gangs of Tamil labourers. Heat and monsoon hampered progress. Stripped to the waist, the New Zealanders laboured in the tropical sun. Some even shaved their heads. Rain threatened their work and the tractors rapidly bogged down in the mud, forcing the men to wait until the downpours stopped. These down times were an opportunity to maintain the equipment; in the end, earth moving was done in the mornings or later at night.

The air forces being sent to Singapore took a little longer to organise. No. 488 fighter squadron assembled at Rongotai in September and initially comprised nine officers, eleven pilots, and 132 ranks. Ninety six officers and men were despatched on the Dutch liner *Tasman* and a second group followed six weeks later. The unit was led by Squadron Leader Wilfred Clouston, a New Zealander who had fought in the Battle of Britain. He arrived at RAF Kallang on 29 September with his two principal officers, Flight Lieutenant John MacKenzie and Flight Lieutenant John Hutcheson. Their men arrived eleven days later.

Clouston was under no doubt as to the amount of work that had to be done. His pilots were newly trained; the most capable aircraft any had flown was a Harvard, the advanced trainer. They were equipped with twenty one Brewster F-2A3 Buffaloes inherited from 68 Squadron. These were step up from the Harvards, but nonetheless obsolescent, and the New Zealanders soon discovered that all were also in 'various stages of repair and modification.' Worse, as Flight Lieutenant Cecil Franks later recorded, 'the unit equipment comprised six trestles, six chocks, one repairable ladder, and six oil draining drums.'[8] Plans to put the pilots through a refresher course at nearby Kluang air station had to be put on hold while the aircraft were made serviceable. Work was hampered by an acute stores shortage. Efforts to procure more were hampered by bureaucracy, but supplies were eventually procured direct from the depot at Seletar. Ground crews under W A 'Andy' Chandler performed near-miraculous repairs, mounting armour under the pilot's seat, fitting radios, and keeping the aircraft flying during the training period. 'After repeated efforts', all officers were even issued with .38 calibre Smith and Wesson revolvers and twelve rounds of ammunition.[9]

The new Japanese military government in October set alarm bells ringing, and in Malaya, RNZAF personnel wondered when they would have to fight. 'I will never regret that I am able to do what I can to prevent, even in the smallest and most indirect way, the war ever coming to NZ,' Glanville wrote to his wife on 12 November.[10] In Singapore a few days later he asked an:

> *extremely polite old Jap (where I bought the little china ornament) whether he would go back to Japan. He said how could he, as he has lived here for thirty years and has a Chinese wife and his children only speak Chinese and English. he said his business was all he had. He seemed genuinely upset and I felt so sorry for him. It will be a great day when it is possible for all the nations to live in harmony together again and all militant spirit is washed out.*[11]

Peacetime routines still prevailed — including evening sports, weekend leisure activities and a half-day holiday on Wednesdays, and flying was restricted to five hours a day. 'We are about three hours flying distance here from the Jap occupied areas in Indo China and a huge town the size of Singapore does not even have a blackout!' Glanville marvelled.[12]

Talk of a Japanese invasion of Malaya ran wild during November and contingency plans were laid to pre-empt it with a British assault on the Kra isthmus. Even so, there was no thought that war might be imminent until 28 November, when reports circulated of a planned Japanese attack on Siam. Two days later a Japanese invasion fleet was seen near British North Borneo. The modern battleship *Prince of Wales* and First World War vintage battlecruiser *Repulse* reached Singapore on 2 December amid official concern that they were being deployed too far forward; but the arrival of what was shortly dubbed 'Force Z' gave heart to the New Zealanders. 'It is great to think that they are sufficiently strong in Home waters to be able to spare ships for the Pacific,' Glanville wrote to his wife on 3 December. 'I feel really awful at having come out here and having left you, but I really think it is better to try and stop trouble ever reaching NZ's shores.'[13]

On 8 December reports came that the Japanese were landing at Singora and Khota Baru in Malaya. There was an air raid on Singapore that morning, and — although they had yet to be declared combat ready — Buffaloes of 488 Squadron were airborne on defensive patrols. At Tebrau, Frank McCarthy was 'sleeping lightly' when he heard distant air raid sirens. Soon everybody was awake. Half an hour later the men heard aircraft in the distance, and searchlights and anti-aircraft artillery erupted into action.[14] Next day the RNZAF unit discovered the Japanese had bombed a village north of Singapore, smashing houses and killing many civilians. Some corpses had already been laid out for burial. Other bombs fell into Singapore, some near the barracks occupied by the New Zealanders preparing the Short Singapores for flight to Fiji.

Admiral Sir Thomas Phillips consulted his staff, and they decided to attack the invasion force in a fast hit-and-run raid with the two heavy ships and supporting destroyers. It was a decision wholly in the spirit of Royal Navy tradition and, given the British assessment of Japanese capability, not as reckless as it might have seemed in hindsight. The *Prince of Wales* and *Repulse* sailed at 5.35 pm on the 8th, but at 10.35 pm Phillips was told there would be no air cover over Singora. The airfield was already in Japanese hands. The Japanese were alerted and Vice Admiral Nobutake Kondo hoped to engage the British in a surface action, but was unable to find them; air units despatched from Saigon in filthy weather also failed to locate the force. Phillips decided to abandon his mission on 9 December, but at midnight heard the

Japanese were landing at Kuantan and changed course to investigate without informing Singapore. Reconnaissance early on the 10th revealed the harbour was empty. Phillips then set course for Singapore. At 11.10 am his force came under heavy attack from eighty Mitsubishi G4M1 'Betty' and Nakjima G3M3 'Nell' torpedo bombers, 170 miles northeast of Singapore. These aircraft were part of the 22nd Air Force based at Saigon, and were on their way back there after an unsuccessful search when they encountered Force Z.

Buffaloes flown by the RAAF were available to provide air cover, but in order to avoid alerting the Japanese, Phillips kept radio silence and nobody in Singapore knew where Force Z was; the first hint of trouble did not come until the *Repulse* signalled that the squadron was under air attack. The RAAF immediately deployed fighters, but it was too late. Kiwi pilots joined the effort but were simply instructed to fly in pairs at half-hour intervals to a particular location and protect unidentified ships. When the first pair flown by MacKenzie and Sergeant W J N MacIntosh arrived, the two capital ships had already been sunk. MacKenzie and MacIntosh were not the only New Zealanders in the air at the time. One of the three Short Singapore IIIs intended for Fiji was patrolling sixty miles south of the battle and afterwards found a Supermarine Walrus amphibian floating in the open ocean. This turned out to be a spotting aircraft from the *Repulse*, which had been in the air during the attack and run out of fuel. It was subsequently towed to Singapore by destroyer.[15]

The fall of Singapore

The Japanese success over Force Z was, symbolically, the death-knell of the 'Singapore' strategy that had driven New Zealand's defence policy for twenty years. The British were stunned; Churchill himself had 'never received a more direct shock.'[16] However, RNZAF personnel on the spot were philosophical. 'Losing the two big ships was quite a blow,' Glanville admitted to his wife 'but the British have survived Dunkirk, which was a thousand times worse calamity.'[17] Within two days the Japanese had occupied airfields at Khota Baru, Kuantan and Alor Star, and 488 Squadron pilots found their obsolescent fighters outclassed. Even Japanese reconnaissance aircraft proved immune to the Buffalo, as MacKenzie discovered while pursuing one on 15 December.

Loss of the airfields in northern Malaya prompted renewed efforts by the RNZAF construction unit to finish work at Tebrau, and they adopted a modified plan to bring a 1200-foot runway into action. However, the speed of the Japanese advance caught everyone by surprise and a large detachment of Unit 24 was sent to build a new fighter strip at Bejok, while another group of 28 men went to Singapore Island to work on a strip at Sungei Buloh. Other men were withdrawn to help repair existing aerodromes, and a further group went north to snatch abandoned equipment from under the noses of the Japanese. Constant air raids hampered work; Glanville found them tiring and irritating. 'Why the Japanese bother tiddly winking about with these silly little raids absolutely beats me as the damage is absolutely nil from a military point of view.'[18]

No. 488 Squadron flew extensively on 3 January to bring a convoy safely in to Singapore, notching up more than 64 operational hours that day alone. New Zealanders with 233 Squadron shot down the first Japanese aircraft on the 10th. Glanville watched the fight begin. 'My cabin mate on the way over, Bert Wipiti from Taranaki, got a Jap plane today about 25 miles from here,' he wrote. 'They passed overhead as he was chasing it, just after breakfast.'[19] On 13 January, eight 488 Squadron Buffaloes under MacKenzie were ordered to intercept an incoming Japanese raid; but this included 27 Zeroes and Type 97 fighters. MacKenzie ordered immediate evasive action, but lost two aircraft within seconds, and five others were damaged. Next day eight Buffaloes under Flight Lieutenant Hutcheson attempted to intercept thirty Type 96 bombers, but ran into heavy defensive fire from the tightly packed Japanese formation. Four aircraft were written off and one was damaged. Hutcheson crash landed at Kallang. Only William Greenhalgh managed to engage the bombers, but was hampered by gun failure.

Glanville had been amazed that peacetime routines continued in Singapore in the weeks before the war — but incredibly, and to the irritation of the New Zealanders, the British continued these arrangements even after the Japanese began their advance down the peninsula. Captain N H North, seconded to the RNZAF construction unit, was later critical of this decision:

It was with considerable alarm that one found the usual peace time office hours being maintained in the Far East Command, even though the enemy had advanced a considerable distance into Malaya. The usual mid-week holiday was not dropped until an absurdly late stage in the campaign. As Unit 24 had left New Zealand imbued with the urgency of the situation, this state of affairs was to say the least most aggravating.[20]

Equipment was so short that even mess facilities were difficult to organise. When war broke out, 488 Squadron was given the task of also supporting a Dutch unit. Their mess at Kallang, equipped for 400, now fed 1500 men and 'was lamentably short of plates, cups, cutlery, cooking utensils, dish-washing facilities and towels; insufficient rations being drawn from the food depots; there was no planning in the preparation of meals, while the mess room and cook houses were in a drab and filthy condition.'[21] The New Zealanders came to the rescue; Flight Lieutenant Franks took over and managed to restore order.

Unit 24 had almost completed the strip at Bekok, but the speed of the Japanese advance was unprecedented and the area had to be abandoned. The New Zealand unit felled trees across the near completed strip and laid mines to deny it to the enemy. The runway was blown up on 15 January, and the men returned to Singapore to begin building another airstrip at Yio Chu Kang. Morale was still high; British ground forces still outnumbered the Japanese. 'Sooner or later we will make a stand and the Japs will be slowed down,' Glanville wrote hopefully '...the other day well over a hundred Jap planes were turned back by anti-aircraft fire and a few of our fighters, so when we get better tools they will just mow the Japs down.'[22]

The problem was that the Japanese had total air superiority; and the arrivcal of 51 Hurricanes on 13 January did little to dent the Japanese dominance Pitting their elderly Buffaloes against vastly superior Japanese aircraft, the New Zealanders fought on without respite, suffering steady losses as the days went on. On 19 January, MacKenzie and Flight Lieutenant H J Meharry conducted a daring flight more than 100 miles behind enemy lines to reconnoitre Kuala Lumpur, which turned out to be the main Japanese base. The Dutch withdrew from Singapore the same day. Losses continued, both in the air and on the ground as the Japanese raided the airfields. By 24 January, No. 488 Squadron had just two serviceable Buffaloes left. The squadron was allocated nine Hurricanes, but before they could begin conversion an air raid damaged or destroyed the fighters. Three aircraft were made serviceable by the 27th.

The RNZAF Aerodrome Construction Squadron continued to labour in heat and frequent rain. Glanville had 'never seen or heard such rain in my life — it was tremendous.' The advance of the Japanese brought a new sense of haste and desperation:

> *As we do our construction work huge piles of rubber trees are rolled to the sides by the big 14 ton caterpillars. Usually Chinese contractors buy and take away the timber but on this job the locals are just helping themselves... I have been at work again tonight on plans and so have little time before lights out. Tomorrow will be a busy day as on this particular job there are only three of us on [CENSORED] work and we have periodic spasms of activity when we have to hurry to keep ahead of the [CENSORED]. Our boys are doing a great job of work on this particular location and I only hope it will soon be used to good effect...*[23]

By 24 January the men could hear heavy gunfire when the tractors were turned off. The Japanese were just 88 miles north at Mersing. Tebrau airfield was abandoned and blown up to deny it to the enemy. The newly completed Rifle Range field at Johore also had to be blown up — the New Zealanders soon ran out of demolition charges and had to supplement them with 500lb British and 700 lb Dutch bombs. Glanville still hoped they might finish an aerodrome before the Japanese over-ran it. To him the airfields were like sand castles built in front of the incoming tide:

> *... and our boys have worked like Trojans too. They come out trumps and deliver the goods every time. Our present job should be of great value when finished, but it all boils down to a race against time, and all this should have been started and finished years ago... If the British talked less and did more one would have a little more confidence...* [24]

But time was running out, and as January ended it was clear the RNZAF aerodrome squadron would not complete its desperate task. A few days later they were pulled out.

> *Halfway through the day our job was knocked on the head and our machines immediately commenced undoing all our good work again. As*

this was our last and only attempt that may have been in a position to be of use it is a bit of a knock. I just hope we can still be of use somewhere or other. We have at least tried to do something to help.[25]

The RNZAF construction unit was the last New Zealand group to leave the Malayan peninsula. The British destroyed the causeways linking the island with the mainland and Singapore became a besieged fortress. 'We have done what we could in our own line here and although our work is now gone for nothing, we did at least try... One feels absolutely mortified by this whole show,' Glanville wrote to his wife. He was in no doubt that the catastrophe had come about as a result of British ineptitude. 'With a little foresight and proper planning ... much, if not all, of the reverses of the past month could have been avoided.'[26]

Japanese propaganda showered down from the skies. 'Do not dedicate your lives to fatten the British "High Hat"!' declared one pamphlet hopefully.[27] Other propaganda was intended to separate the British from their Commonwealth allies; a pamphlet portraying defeated Indian soldiers was dropped in late January, unfortunately with a caption in Malay. These people were only a tiny minority in Singapore. Glanville picked one up and 'showed it to about 40 Chinese today, but not one could read it, so that bit of Jap propaganda misfired... Several of them fluttered down and I was glad to get one as a souvenir.'[28]

The Japanese seemed able to rapidly find and attack dispersed and camouflaged equipment in Singapore. Some New Zealanders believed the Japanese had a very efficient espionage system.[29] The Japanese were certainly able to use the airfields built by the No.1 Aerodrome Construction Unit despite the demolition effort. 'Repairs were made by throwing into craters any large rocks, rubble etc which were to hand,' Flight Lieutenant P L Laing reported after he had returned to New Zealand.[30]

Congestion and the vulnerability of the airfields to shellfire from Malaya restricted air operations to a few fighters working from Kallang. The construction unit worked frantically to fill in bomb craters and establish new fighter strips on the island. Kallang was heavily bombed and the squadron offices, ammunition store, equipment and oil stores were virtually demolished. The squadron was given notice to evacuate within a few hours and loaded their gear into seven lorries, which were dispersed, but then word came that they were to assist 232 Squadron and the trucks were unloaded again.[31] Meanwhile the pilots pulled their aircraft out of range of Japanese artillery — at Sembawang, F S Johnstone actually took off amid a bombardment. Frank McCarthy discovered the construction unit's new home was between Japanese artillery and a British battery, and there was a rush to dig trenches.

There were a surprising number of New Zealanders in the city by this stage, including thirteen of the twenty six engineers who had been assigned to repair the Short Singapores. When the last of the Singapores departed on 13 December, the maintenance unit was reassigned to No. 205 Squadron to help maintain its Catalinas. On 31 January they left for Batavia on board HMS *Kedah*, which was also crowded with women and children. Next day the No. 1 Aerodrome Construction Squadron began their own withdrawal, initially on board the SS *Talthybius*. All loading was done by the squadron in the absence of dockside help; some 2400 tons of equipment was put aboard in just sixteen hours, despite air raids. However, a raid next day scored a direct hit. Ray Tyers and other crew emerged from shelter to see fire raging in the No.6 and 7 holds, and badly burned men crawling from them on to the deck.[32] There were seven casualties; two died later in hospital.

The decision was taken to unload what could be saved, including the heavy earth moving machinery, but the ship was sunk at the dockside next day by another raid, taking down 17 Caterpillar tractors, 12 scoops, a grader, 32 tip trucks, a dragline shovel and a good deal of other equipment.[33] On 6 February, the RNZAF squadron was ordered to leave on board the SS *City of Canterbury* and the 1900 ton coaster *Darvel*. The former was overloaded, but her captain declared that he had evacuated New Zealanders from Crete and would do so again from Singapore. The *City of Canterbury* sailed on the night of the 6th, but the *Darvel* was recalled because at seven knots she was too slow, and an attempt next day was aborted by bad weather.

The *Darvel* finally sailed on the 8th, leaving during an air raid with a scratch crew supplemented by the RNZAF construction unit. Japanese forces dominated the skies, and her captain hoped to brave the narrow Banka Strait at night. However, the ship was delayed two hours assisting the SS *Kiritak* that had run aground at the entrance of the strait, and was still in the danger area at dawn. They anchored near an abandoned steamer in the hope of hiding from Japanese patrols, but twenty seven bombers launched an attack late the next morning. Frank McCarthy described the event in the RNZAF's official magazine:

> *There was a minute or two of suspense as the drone of many aircraft engines grew louder... then came the rush and whistle of falling bombs, and hell seemed let loose in a pandemonium of noise. Terrific explosions shook the ship. She tossed and rolled like a cork as bombs exploded and churned the water all round. Columns of spray shot up and drenched those flattened out on the decks. There was a hiss of steam from burst pipes and clatter of falling debris. The bombs stopped falling. A burst or two of machine gun fire, then all was quiet.*[34]

Glanville 'had the satisfaction of cackling away with a light machine gun when the bombers came low but one could have done just as much good with a pea shooter for all the notice they took of it.'[35] Five minutes later another raid swept overhead, sinking the abandoned ship nearby, and leaving the *Darvel* riddled with shrapnel and flooding. Abandoning ship was not an option; the lifeboats were so badly damaged as to be useless and 'it was decided to weigh anchor and drive the ship all out for Java.'[36] The men were ordered to move to the starboard side in an effort to keep the damaged port side out of the water, and the RNZAF construction crew got to work with anything they could find to plug the holes.[37] The four orderlies under Harris helped the wounded; one man died from his injuries and was buried at sea.

After two hours the immediate danger to the ship had passed, and the RNZAF was later officially credited with saving the vessel. Still listing and with wooden plugs protruding from her hull, the *Darvel* limped into Batavia on 12 February to the cheers of men watching from the quays. Glanville was relieved to be safe, but disillusioned by the experience. He wrote to his wife that:

> *I think the Dutch will put up much stiffer resistance than the British in Malaya. The whole Malayan business will go down in history, when the story is really told, as one of the most disgraceful shows on record. Criminal incompetence, official stupidity, and all round bungling by those in authority. The whole wretched show was hopeless from the start... add to it all the fact that Malaya was starved of essential arms, planes, tanks,*

navy and of practically every essential and you will understand that it was just a gigantic bluff — which did not come off.[38]

The unit moved to Buitenzorg before being evacuated back to New Zealand. Meanwhile, No. 488 Squadron pulled out of Singapore. Many of the pilots had already withdrawn to Batavia, sailing on HMS *Danae* and the SS *City of Canterbury*, but the ground crews continued to work on the island. The Japanese landed on 8-9 February and ground crews under Flight Sergeant Chandler tried to make one Hurricane serviceable to evacuate Clouston, but the effort was not successful and he was captured after Singapore fell. On the 11th the ground crews were evacuated on board the *Empire Star*, which came under air attack as they left the docks. Next morning they were attacked at sea by more aircraft and put up stiff resistance with machine guns and rifles, shooting down one aircraft and damaging another.

No. 488 Squadron pilots withdrawn to Batavia landed at Tjililitan airfield, minus their equipment, and Franks recalled that:

A search was made for possible quantities of equipment, and a number of cases of diverted stacks of tools and accessories, originally addressed to Singapore, were discovered. From this the squadron was equipped with essentials in tools and C-class stores.[39]

Two New Zealanders — Meharry and Pilot Officer Sharp, then joined a unit taking nine Hurricanes to Palembang, but they arrived amid a Japanese paratroop assault. Only Meharry was able to land, and the other aircraft crashed in the jungle or were shot down. Sharp survived the crash of his Hurricane and avoided capture.

Singapore surrendered on 15 February. By this time the Japanese were advancing with unprecedented speed and threatening Java. The British handed over to the Dutch and withdrew. MacKenzie was ordered to leave six pilots and his aircraft behind to help bring No. 605 squadron up to strength; the rest of his unit was evacuated to Australia on board the *Deucalion*, the 450 men mostly sleeping on deck. The ship had only limited supplies for its passengers, but Franks took an inventory and organised menus, with the result that two hot meals and one cold were served every day. By the beginning of April they were back in New Zealand.

The air defence of New Zealand, 1942–43

The fall of Singapore sent shock waves through New Zealand; the Japanese 'blitzkrieg' seemed unstoppable and there were early fears that both Australia and New Zealand would be invaded. In fact, while the Japanese Naval General Staff believed holding Australia would improve their defensive perimeter, the army believed it would take the entire Combined Fleet, 12 divisions, and 1.5 million tons of supplies to do so — more than had been allocated for the whole South East Asian campaign — and they wanted to end the war in China first. A strategy also had to be found to face the Americans in the central and northern Pacific. In the end, a compromise was adopted which met neither aim and involved a strike on Midway while simultaneously securing Port Moresby as part of a defensive perimeter from New Guinea to Fiji and Samoa.

This was not known to Allied powers at the time, and in the face of a rapid Japanese advance through South East Asia, both Australia and New Zealand feared invasion was imminent. It was a critical situation; the bulk of the armed forces of both nations were overseas and New Zealand had no modern fighter aircraft, a position not helped by the fact that the country had 'slipped through the cracks' of the Allied command structure. Unified command in the South West Pacific was initially established under General Sir Archibald Wavell, extending from Burma to Dutch New Guinea and Northern Australia. After the fall of Singapore the situation was confused until the Americans offered to take over east of Singapore, but the resulting South Pacific Command split New Zealand from Australia in April 1942. Admiral Robert L Ghormley, appointed to command the South Pacific Area, had no authority to support New Zealand, even though he was based in Auckland.

The British proved completely unhelpful. A request for Hawker Hurricanes was turned down, and so was a further request in December 1941 for four complete fighter squadrons. The squadrons had to be complete because the RNZAF had no experience of modern fighters, nor the manpower to operate them — another legacy of the long inter-war funding drought. There was no alternative to procurement from Britain; New Zealand could only access the American Munitions Assignment Committee via the British chiefs of staff — a situation that left Kiwi orders subject to change if the British had higher priority elsewhere. The British finally offered to send 142 Kittyhawks from the Middle Eastern theatre to Australasia, of which New Zealand received eighteen. A further 36 Hudsons and 80 Kittyhawks were allocated in March, but the British diverted 36 of the Kittyhawks to Ceylon in April 1942. More Hudsons were allocated after personal intervention by Prime Minister Peter Fraser. It was not the first time he had been forced to plead for assistance — nor the last.

Part of the problem was that from the viewpoint of the United States and Britain, New Zealand was merely a small nation on the fringe of the Pacific theatre. Politically, there was also a heavy focus on the European war, which Roosevelt formally reaffirmed after the Pearl Harbour attack and underlined in a concrete fashion by not replacing the Pacific battleships with units from the Atlantic Fleet. Indeed, as late as January 1943, only fifteen percent of Allied military power was being employed in the Pacific. The colossal military expansion programme on which the US had embarked in mid-1940, after the fall of France, took time to begin producing armaments in quantity, particularly aircraft; new-generation fighters such as the P-51 Mustang and P-47 Thunderbolt were still essentially on the drawing board in 1941. Full production was not achieved until 1944, by which time the United States arms industry was supplying their own needs, while simultaneously supporting the entire Commonwealth, China, and the Soviets.

Consequently it was up to the RNZAF to organise New Zealand air defence during early 1942 with the limited resources it had available. Emergency preparations known as FAFAI included a scheme to utilise the training squadrons in combat. Every flyable aircraft and crew was given tasks ranging from maritime attack to strafing invasion forces. Operational training was squeezed between regular training courses. The fact that the service had to seriously consider putting Baffins and Vildebeestes up against Zeroes reveals the depth of the crisis faced during the critical early months of 1942. This was the real price New Zealand paid for minimising its own armed forces during the inter-war years.

The Malayan experience was not forgotten. Officers who had served with 488 Squadron and the No.1 Aerodrome Construction Unit provided lengthy reports giving detailed advice on everything from ways of minimising injuries in slit trenches to bomb storage. 'The storing of bombs as done at Hobsonville appears to be "asking for trouble",' P L 'Lofty' Laing reported on

1 April.[40] The bombs at Hobsonville were pulled out of range of water-borne attack and re-distributed to Te Rapa.

Command and control was another early priority, and the RNZAF formed three administrative groups — inevitably called Northern, Central and Southern — coinciding with the three military districts. These were centred on Combined Headquarters in Auckland, Wellington and Christchurch, complete with separate operations rooms in Auckland and Wellington for bomber and fighter squadrons. A co-ordinated chain of control ran from the Air Department through a Central War Room to groups, stations and squadrons. A comprehensive observer and spotting network was also established, but radar lagged behind. The Department of Scientific and Industrial Research (DSIR) had obtained plans from Britain, but imported electronic components were in short supply, and complete units were not delivered from Britain at anything like the required rate. One of the first went to Fiji to bolster defences there, and the national radar system was not in place until May 1943, well after the main threat of invasion had passed.

New squadrons were established as equipment trickled in. No. 14 Squadron formed in April 1942 around the survivors of No.488 Squadron at the Fighter Operational Training Unit at Ohakea.[41] The unit moved to Hood Aerodrome near Masterton, working with Harvards until its Kittyhawks arrived. No. 17 Squadron formed at Ohakea under Squadron Leader J V A Reid, again equipped with Kittyhawks. No.8 Squadron formed as a bomber-reconnaissance unit equipped with Vincents and was sent to Gisborne. No. 15 Squadron formed at Whenuapai in June for deployment to the Pacific, where some second-hand Kittyhawks were waiting for them at Tongatapu, and No. 16 Squadron formed at Blenheim in August, equipped with Kittyhawks. New airfields required a good deal of work. While British aircraft could generally operate from short grass strips, American aircraft were best flown from long concrete runways, and the United States Government requested runways at Ohakea and Whenuapai capable of taking their heavy bombers.

By this time Bradshaw was attached to air headquarters, where he organised emergency aerodromes for No.2 General Reconnaissance Squadron and took on responsibility for national airfield maintenance. 'There was no problem regarding those occupied by the Air Force,' he later wrote 'as these had a resident Public Works engineer but there were dozens of others and the powers that be wished them all to be kept completely serviceable just in case they may be required some time.[42] Later he was asked to find two sites in Canterbury, one for heavy bombers and a shorter strip for fighters. He flew to Harewood with two public works engineers and an officer from the Aerodromes branch of the Public Works Department. 'We landed in all sorts of weird places,' he later wrote. Some fields were too small to take off from with a loaded aircraft and he had to leave his passengers behind. The bomber strip was located at Hereat and completed in two months, but the fighter strip was never built.[43]

In June 1942, the RNZAF formed Aerodrome Defence Squadrons to supplement army forces, but personal weapons were in short supply and although the army provided 800 rifles, 90 light machine guns and 70 Thompson guns, only a third of the men could be armed. Britain responded to a request for anti-aircraft weapons at the end of 1941. Sixteen 3.7-inch guns and twelve 40-mm Bofors cannons arrived in New Zealand early in 1942. These and other light guns were mounted by September around five airfields. Plans were also laid to destroy airfield structures in case of attack, and nearly £250,000 was spent on camouflage and decoys that included 254 fake Kittyhawks, Hudsons and Hurricanes. These were completed by the middle of 1943. Stores also received attention; apart from shifting the bombs at Hobsonville to Te Rapa, equipment was further dispersed to sites in Auckland, Wellington and Christchurch. A second depot had already been established in the Centennial buildings near Wellington, and a third was set up at Te Awamutu. Fuel was another issue; New Zealand did not have enough storage to meet an American requirement and new tank farms had to be set up. Bradshaw got the task of locating one new fuel dump, which went into a copse of bluegums alongside the railway near Bankside. Work was slowed in all locations by lack of heavy machinery.

The real 'front line' during these desperate months was Fiji. It was generally accepted that Japanese conquest of Fiji would open the door to attacks on New Zealand. Japan also had a strong submarine fleet; air reconnaissance and anti-submarine patrol work from the islands was critical. When the war broke out, RNZAF forces in Fiji included six Vincents and two DH-86 Dragon Rapides. Major extensions to Nandi airfield were well under way and the flying boat base at Lauthala Bay was under construction. The Short Singapores began operations from Suva in late November 1941 as No.5 (General Reconnaissance) Squadron, but one was lost almost immediately when it rammed a coral outcrop during an over-long takeoff run caused by failure of the tail trimming equipment. Serious maintenance difficulties continued to plague the type during its early operations, limiting it to local flights. Forces on the island were further reinforced by four Hudsons, which arrived on 21 December.

Island life was a sharp contrast to what most of the Kiwis had been accustomed to at home. Corporal R Neal was stationed in Suva during 1942 and his description of Fiji provides something of the flavour:

> *Their music is all yah yah yi yum sort of style... it would be pretty hot in swing time, oh yeah!... As regards my coming home with a Fijian wife as I said no Mum, I have changed my mind entirely, not for me. The Fijians are very nice, obliging & clean, they have as many as three showers per day & that's dinkum... The average person lives on 15/- per week that's the whites as well... The weather varies a terrible lot, you may think a person would get quite brown well it is just the opposite, sun bathing here is rather dangerous. The best time is after 4 pm then one gets into trouble from insects, they are nippers, they don't just have a snack a proper feed & invite all relations to make a dinner of it. One can tell it is a wet climate by the vegetation of the island, very green. Also the nice fields give that indication; it is quite an education to one to even come to Suva, there's no amount of old methods of native life & primitive stage, even the oxen in the cart & plough.*[44]

The United States took responsibility for all forces in Fiji in July 1942, but the islands remained a centre for RNZAF operations throughout the war. A Short Singapore commanded by Ronald MacGregor attacked a suspected submarine in July 1942. The following month the Singapores moved to Lauthala Bay. The Vincents were withdrawn in late 1942, and Catalinas replaced the Singapores in early 1943. No.4 Squadron was re-equipped with Hudsons and continued its anti-submarine patrols. Japanese submarines continued to operate occasionally in the area, and 4 Squadron aircraft were involved during May 1943 when three US freighters were attacked south of Fiji. Six submarines were sighted the following month, and one was attacked by a Hudson 180 miles southwest of Suva, while the RNZAF were escorting a convoy. The boat was listed as a 'probable'.

The problems the RNZAF faced during 1942 stemmed largely from the years of fiscal starvation in the decades before the war. Funding issues became less relevant in the war emergency, but the new bottleneck became procurement, which initially relied on a beleaguered Britain. Wartime funding came in part from increased exports — particularly under 'lend lease' where food was essentially exchanged for military equipment — and loans, some raised overseas but others drawn from the population of New Zealand. 'You must help them strike,' blazed one poster offering five year 'Bomber bonds' at three percent in 1942. 'Give the RNZAF a break and they'll be there when the whips are cracking... Every penny subscribed will be used to increase the striking power of the Royal New Zealand Air Force.'[45]

Manpower was another bottleneck. The RNZAF's domestic commitments had to be met without reducing output to Europe. More than 16,000 new recruits nonetheless enlisted during 1942 — a significant number given that the Air Force had to compete with Army and Navy as well as essential services. Recruiting drives told little about the realities of warfare. 'It's a great life, Chaps,' declared one poster with Bigglesian optimism.[46] Schools established to meet specific trades included a Preliminary Technical Training School at Rongotai and Radio Selection Pool at Wigram.

Women began joining the air services in April 1941, when the first draft of 200 assembled at Rongotai under Frances 'Kitty' Kain, a graduate of Otago University and a specialist dietician.[47] At first, the Women's Auxiliary Air Force (WAAF) was not regarded as part of the RNZAF, and in line with the thinking of the day the women were cast as cooks, mess hands and clerks. In 1942 the WAAF was integrated into the RNZAF and adopted military ranking. By the end of that year women were employed in tasks ranging from radio technicians to general aircraft maintenance. Women also joined the RNZAF's first motor boat training course in mid-1943. Much early development was achieved through Kain's work. She left the service in December 1943 and was awarded an OBE in 1949. Some 4750 women served with the WAAF during the Second World War.

CHAPTER FIVE

Pacific Offensive 1942–45

On one occasion a Jap ship was thought to be in the vicinity which caused a good flap, especially for the armourers ... as they had to bomb up six Kittys with 500 lb AP and no-one knew anything about fusing American bombs.

— Basil Berry with 15 Squadron at Fumota airfield, Tongatapu, 1942.

The RNZAF's largest campaign of the Second World War was fought into the Pacific. Between 1942 and 1945, the service deployed some thirteen squadrons into that theatre, peaking at more than 7000 personnel in early 1945. Casualties were remarkably low — just 348 men were killed during the entire campaign, despite periodically intense fighting. Aircraft taken on inventory included 297 Curtiss P-40 Kittyhawks, 202 North American PT-6 Harvards, 139 Lockheed PV-1 Venturas and 48 Grumman TBF-1 Avengers among other types. Towards the end of the war the fighter squadrons converted to several models of Chance Vought F4U Corsair, of which 424 were ultimately fielded — numerically, the most important aircraft of all time to enter New Zealand service. It was also one of the most capable fighters of its day.

All this was accomplished without slackening the effort to send pilots to Europe — not an easy task. A 1943 report noted that 'the expansion plan for the Pacific threw a considerable burden on the whole training organisation.'[1] New Zealand's contribution to the Pacific air war was disproportionately high in context of the national population and general Kiwi military effort worldwide. However, the RNZAF never did enter the war to the degree envisaged in 1942. Lack of credibility — another legacy of the inter-war funding drought — was the main hindrance. Until the RNZAF could prove itself, many higher US commanders were dubious about the infant service. The RNZAF consequently paid a good deal of attention to squadron composition, swapping experienced personnel — usually at the main base on Espiritu Santo — to ensure that front line squadrons received the most battle-hardened individuals. In practise, New Zealanders achieved startling results. Kiwi fighter pilots were preferred escorts among US bomber squadrons, and the entire RNZAF was well respected at operational level.

Conflicting plans

Arguments raged in Washington during early 1942 over the best strategy for defeating Japan with minimal resources. There were two possible approaches; direct assault across the central Pacific, or an 'island hopping' thrust to roll back Japanese forces in the southern Pacific. The former was favoured by Admiral Ernest King, the Commander in Chief of the US fleet and Chief of Naval Operations. but left Australia and New Zealand under threat. General Douglas MacArthur preferred the latter, in part because it would enable him to return to the Phillipines. In the end the Americans took both approaches — a compromise that initially left both campaigns short of men and equipment. The island-hopping strategy itself devolved to a two-pronged campaign; a joint US/Australian drive through New Guinea under MacArthur; and a US/New Zealand/Australian assault on the Solomons, under Vice-Admiral William F 'Bull' Halsey.

There was no doubt in New Zealand that the war would have to be carried into the Pacific. By April 1942 the RNZAF had developed a scheme for expansion to twenty squadrons in twelve months, of which a proportion were to be earmarked for offensive operations. Unfortunately, equipment relied on supply from the United States, via Lend-Lease arrangements with Britain. The US Joint Chiefs of Staff did not believe the RNZAF could expand effectively to more than ten squadrons, and consequently recommended four bomber squadrons equipped with Hudsons, five fighter squadrons flying P-40s, and one army co-operation unit. The British had yet another opinion, suggesting sixteen squadrons equipped with Hudsons, Kittyhawks and sixty four B-25 Mitchells. This was closer to the RNZAF's thinking, but British supply policy left New Zealand little choice but to follow the American plan. Even so, supplies were far from guaranteed. Theoretically, the Arnold-Towers-Portal Agreement between Britain and the United States, signed later in 1942, confirmed American procurement and logistic support for the Dominion air forces, but supply was not automatic and the arrangement also did not give the RNZAF a guaranteed role in theatre.

In August, RAF Air Vice-Marshal Sir Victor Goddard visited Washington to argue New Zealand's case for inclusion in the American command structure. He had an uphill battle. King was opposed to integration and preferred New Zealand to remain inside British supply structures. The British, heavily pressed in Europe, the Mediterranean and the Burma front, were not prepared to do this. In the end King grudgingly agreed to put the New Zealand Chiefs of Staff under Ghormley. Supply was confirmed in September 1942 with a Mutual Aid Agreement by which New Zealand essentially traded food for American arms. A central RNZAF Equipment Liaison Office was set up in Washington which also handled requests for British equipment. Even so, logistic support was not properly sorted out until June 1943 when the United States decided to treat allied squadrons as if they were American for supply purposes. This formalised an arrangement that had been in existence at local command level for some time. The RNZAF was never properly integrated into US command. Units came directly under the commander of US South Pacific air forces (COMAIRSOPAC), but in practise were employed as required by local commanders, often in the 'forward area', one step back from the combat zone.[2]

This treatment contrasted sharply with that meted out to Australia, which was strategically in a similar position to New Zealand during the period. The Australians were able to procure some aircraft from their own resources, adapting the T-6 Texan/Harvard — constructed in Australia under license since 1939 — into the CA-12 Boomerang interceptor. The United States also viewed Australia as a forward base for operations against the Japanese and in these circumstances there was no question of Australia being left off command and procurement structures. The Australian government ordered more than 2000 aircraft from US and Australian sources during 1942, and the RAAF ended the war as the fourth largest air force in the world after the United States, Britain and Russia, with 6000 aircraft and 182,000 personnel.[3]

The Guadalcanal Campaign 1942–43

Japanese war strategy was based around developing an in-depth defensive perimeter that would be too expensive for the Americans to break, forcing the United States to the bargaining table. However, the campaign in New Guinea stalled in May 1942 after the battle of the Coral Sea, and the surprise American victories in the battle of the Coral Sea and at Midway in early June tipped the balance. The Japanese then planned a modified perimeter running through the Solomons to Fiji, which would cut off Australasia from American support. They had occupied Tulagi in April, and began developing further forces to attack the remainder of the Solomons, threatening the main Allied base in Espiritu Santo at the northwestern end of the New Hebrides. The Japanese invaded Guadalcanal in July 1942, forcing the United States into an early counter attack. This campaign, dubbed Operation Watchtower by US commanders and Operation Shoestring by the men, devolved into a lengthy struggle to control Henderson airfield. Matters stood in the balance until the 7th Marine Regiment arrived at the end of September. The Japanese then renewed their efforts to reinforce their units on Guadalcanal by sea, and heavy fighting broke out on 24-25 October, followed by several disastrous naval night actions during which both sides suffered heavy losses.

The RNZAF was not directly employed during these phases of the campaign; the service had yet to recieve aircraft via lend-lease, and at that stage also lacked credibility with the Americans. However, Rear Admiral John McCain, commanding US air forces in the South Pacific (COMAIRSOPAC), believed the service could assist in the 'forward area', and in mid-1942 requested six RNZAF Vincents to supplement anti-submarine patrols around New Caledonia. Ground crews were despatched from New Zealand on 1 July on board the *Makinac* under Squadron Leader C J Kidson. They arrived off

Noumea on 5 July and were about to land when a strong Japanese naval force was reported just two hours away. There was virtually nothing in Noumea to stop them, but next day the Japanese were located heading for the Coral Sea. The New Zealand contingent disembarked without further incident and were trucked 180 miles to the Plains de Gaiacs.

Equipment was short; lend-lease still had to get under way, and prefabricated huts, vehicles and emergency rations had to be made up from stocks in New Zealand. Aircraft, too, came from New Zealand's existing domestic resources. There was a feeling that New Zealand should be seen to contribute as effectively as possible, and the decision was taken to substitute Hudsons for Vincents in the forward areas. Six were found by reducing the number operating from Fiji and depleting 1 and 2 Squadrons back in New Zealand. The first pair were flown in on 19 July by Edward St John Spicer and G S A Stevenson. Active work began two days later with a dawn anti-submarine patrol along the coast. Three more aircraft arrived on 23 July, bringing Squadron Leader D E Grigg of Ashburton to command what was established as No. 9 Squadron. By November 1942 the squadron included 36 officers and 245 ranks, with twelve Hudsons; and it remained in New Caledonia until March 1943. No submarines were actually spotted during the nine months of operations, apart from a possible sighting in early February 1943. The deployment nevertheless gave the RNZAF valuable service experience.

As the Guadalcanal campaign gained momentum during September, US Colonel F G Schneider of COMGENSOPAC told RNZAF air staff that the unit 'now at Plains des Gaiacs was doing excellent work and ...General Harmon was anxious to have an additional squadron ...located at the Plains des Gaiacs to enable the squadron already there to be sent to a forward base.[4]

The RNZAF agreed in principle, but deployment was dogged by problems that stemmed ultimately from lack of staff liaison between the RNZAF and COMGENSOPAC. At first, the move to the Plains des Gaiacs was expected in two months — ample time for No.3 Squadron to prepare. However, the formal American confirmation on 10 September required an immediate move to Vila instead. The RNZAF believed the squadron was ready, but a further change of destination on 18 September to Espiritu Santo strained the Air Department's administrative resources. The War Cabinet approved the move four days later.

Espiritu Santo, in the northwestern corner of the New Hebrides, had become the main Allied advance base in the South Pacific, but nothing was known in New Zealand about conditions there. Nevill, now Deputy Chief of Air Staff, recommended postponing the deployment if United States arrangements did not appear satisfactory. He flew to the island to consult with McCain and was told that the squadron was required for reconnaissance work. There was no time to send an advance party, but Nevill made a personal survey and reported that a wide range of gear was needed, including mosquito netting, water tanks, beds and timber. Unfortunately his message arrived only five days before the squadron was due to depart.

To make matters worse, the ship which the Americans had promised to carry the men and equipment to the island did not materialise; deployment had to be conducted at short notice with New Zealand resources. Fortunately the *Wahine* and *Taybank* were available. There was criticism of the Air Department for this confusion, which Nevill blamed on US staff planning. 'The move took place under very difficult circumstances,' he reported 'chiefly owing to the ignorance and vacillation of our friends; I consider that branches did remarkably well under such conditions.'[5] A draft history of the event took a slightly different view. 'A fair criticism would be that a lack of anticipation had been shown in planning at a high level.'[6] Nothing went smoothly. There were problems kitting the men for the tropics. Even departure was made difficult by a last-minute decision to arm the airmen, after the small-arms had been brought on board in packing crates and stowed away. The situation was further complicated by the fact that many men with 3 Squadron had been classified as medically unfit for overseas service. This resulted in a good deal of shuffling and, as the RNZAF's draft history laconically noted: 'The nominal roll of the unit was subject to change up to few hours before embarkation.'[7]

The *Wahine* finally left Auckland on 22 September with the bulk of the personnel, including John Morgan, one of the ground engineers. He found shipboard life a contrast to service on land. 'Walked around till tea time and afterwards had a nog at canteen,' he recorded in his diary on the day they left. 'Nominated for submarine watch tomorrow...Cabin like pigsty, gear all over the show.'[8] He did not get seasick, unlike some of his fellows, and was able to take close interest when they were over-flown by a Hudson. By 26 September they had reached Vela and saw their first real signs of war.

Cpl Jack Meggett came in to say we were in a harbour, generally supposed to be Vela in southern end of Hebrides. Alongside tanker early. Not many houses in sight. Very mountainous looking show, with plenty of bush and palms, also several locals rowing around in outrigger canoes. Pulled in alongside tanker & spent most of day refuelling. Pulled away and anchored until 1745. Several boys started fishing overside, but though many fish were about, caught none. Lot of mixing with Yanks on tanker going on and a few swaps. A lot of Yank planes around. A dozen in formation in morning, a couple of Fortresses & 3 or 4 floatplanes...[9]

The *Taybank* left New Zealand on 25 September with 317 tons of equipment and arrived on 8 October. The squadron set up in jungle at the north end of Pallukula airfield, where they were immediately bogged down in mud, an experience that gave the place a 'bad reputation which lasted until the end of the war.'[10] Curiously, although the New Zealand contingent had to bring most of what it needed, they found stacks of petrol cans stamped with RAF markings and British ammunition dated 1936, which seemed to have come from Singapore. Logistic problems plagued the men even after they arrived. Warrant Officer M Harris, a medical sergeant, landed with a small supply of first aid equipment. This was fortunate as the medical stores on the ship did not come ashore for some days. 'When they did,' he recalled on interview after the war 'it was found that none of the stuff ordered had been sent.'[11]

Thirteen Hudsons flew from Whenuapai under Wing Commander George Fisher, reaching Pallikulo via Norfolk Island and New Caledonia. The squadron were ordered to make anti-submarine patrols in Segond Channel, where the majority of US naval units in theatre were anchored. To do this the aircraft — built to meet British weapons specifications — had to be fitted with racks to take American depth charges. Morgan spent most of 13 October 'fitting carriers & putting on special ones for VS 325 lb depth bombs (had to cut nicks out of main spar!!) Heat pretty terrific. Dirty as all hell too.'[12] Next day, Nevill addressed the men and explained that their progress would draw a good deal of attention back home. Morgan recalled that Nevill:

Caused amusement & unseemly mirth from ranks by swiping at flies all the time he was talking. In afternoon went onto bombs & had a bit of bother with fuses (Mk 3 anti-sub) but got things straightened out.

> *Probably put them on tomorrow. Fred working on them now. Rocked to find one sent over with smashed tail. Had hell of a job getting ballistic caps to stay on noses.*[13]

Life settled into a routine marked with intermittent action from the Japanese — including an apparent shelling on 15 October:

> *Most of chaps said they heard heavy firing and whistle of shells over camp. Supposed to be sub shelling island. No panic at all. On fusing anti-sub bombs part of morning & got gota from Yanks on fusing their 325 lb depth bombs...Two air raid alarms, one about 8 pm and one at 10. Both fizzled out. Fortress coming in to land nearly cleaned up searchlight at end of runway. Missed by about 10 ft. Searchlight crew & self bolted. Got extra 30 rds of ammo and went up to camp for rifle & tin hat. Plane loads of wounded arriving from Guadalcanal all night. Put bombs on 3 planes. Story about Jap naval force on the way down. Our planes left for Vila about 3.30 am with some ground crew... Guadalcanal trip washed out now that Japs are attacking it again. Went to bed about 2 am. Hudson crashed and blew up in sea taking off. All killed, though plane and names of crew unknown yet.*[14]

Morgan spent most of his time fusing bombs. It rained heavily on 27 October. 'Place like a bog,' Morgan penned. Mud prevented work the next day. 'Sat around most of day, but filled in part of time making up belts. Strict blackout at night. Clearly heard what was probably sea battle going on. Heard rumbling & detonations. F O'Neill on guard said he saw many gun flashes in sky.'[15]

Tropical heat caused problems and after a while the ground crews routinely took incendiary ammunition out of the containers on the aircraft because they tended to smoke. Heat affected the men too. Many spent their days clad only in shorts. Nudity was officially frowned on but the practise — particularly when swimming — became widespread. Morgan was told to restrict his swimming to the sea 'as we're supposed to wear trunks at least, on account of Yank nurses coming into big new hospital at Surrenda Bay.' There was only one problem. 'Have no trunks,' he wrote in his diary, adding wryly 'haven't seen any nurses yet.'[16]

A request for further RNZAF assistance came hard on the heels of No. 3 Squadron's move to Espiritu Santo. The service was still waiting on adequate supplies of modern aircraft consequent on the lend-lease arrangement; General Harmon suggested in October that New Zealand crews could meanwhile conduct anti-submarine patrols with two dozen P-40's abandoned in Tongatapu by a departing US Army Air Force squadron. Wing Commander B M Lewis flew from Suva to Fumota airfield to investigate, discovering that the New Zealanders would have to supply their own transport, accommodation, clothes, and tool kits. But it was an opportunity not to be missed, and No. 15 Squadron hurriedly formed for the purpose under Squadron Leader A Crichton. Once again the RNZAF was forced to despatch men classified for home service. Men were even seconded into the squadron on the day it was due to leave. Basil Berry found the squadron was short of drivers. 'They pumped me (and some others) full of injections and gave me leave from 4.30 pm on that same day until 7.00 pm that night to say my good byes.'[17]

The squadron departed Wellington on the USS *President Jackson*, arriving after dark on 27 October. Despite the blackout the men immediately unloaded to lighters and drove to Fumota, where they found twenty three dilapidated P-40s that had been left behind by the Americans. 'The first thing our men noticed was that not one machine gun on the planes was serviceable owing to rust and coral dust etc,' Berry recorded.[18] This was only the tip of the iceberg. Everything needed repairing. J J Mackie condemned the aircraft as no more than 'worn out crates.'[19] Maintenance crews under Flight Lieutenant Smith discovered there were only fifteen spare engines on the island and no parts apart from spark plugs, but through a tremendous round-the-clock effort the aircraft were made flyable. Operations began a few days later — but the squadron almost immediately had its first tragedy. 'One of the young pilots was flying too low and the plane crashed into bush upside down and caught fire.'[20]

The unit operated from Tongatapu for three months. Lack of bomb racks meant that at first the New Zealanders would have been limited to strafing, despite an administrative suggestion that pilots could carry anti-submarine weapons in their laps. Racks were eventually provided for the 325-lb depth bombs. For the most part the dawn-and-dusk square searches proved fruitless, but there was occasional excitement:

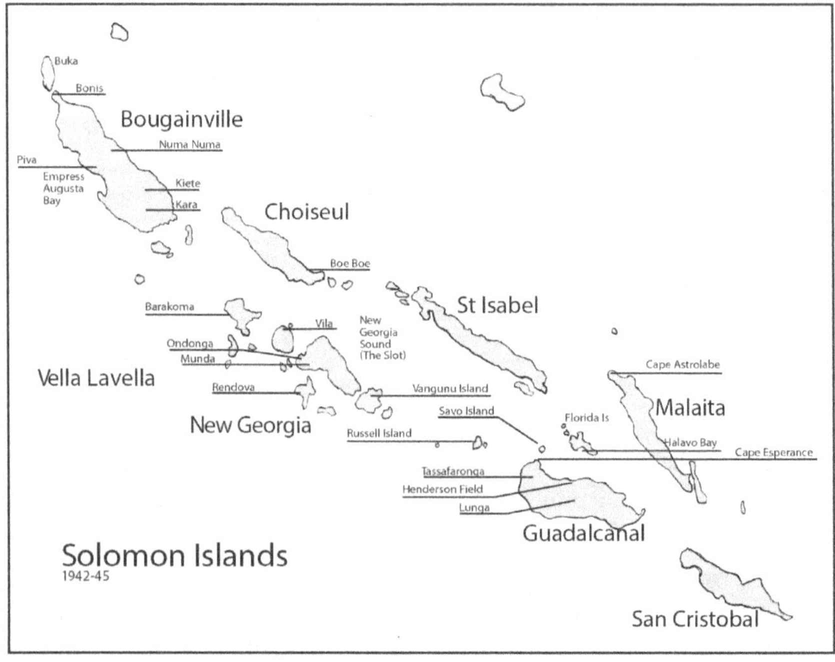

on one occasion a Jap ship was thought to be in the vicinity which caused a good flap, especially for the armourers and Flight Sergeant Hawkins, as they had to bomb up six Kittys with 500 lb AP and no-one knew anything about fusing Americans bombs.[21]

The Kittyhawks — though mediocre by 1942 standards — were the highest performing aircraft the New Zealanders had flown. Some pilots succumbed to the temptation to 'stretch the envelope'. On one occasion, John Scott dived a Kittyhawk from 22,000 feet, running the airspeed indicator off the clock to what squadron personnel thought was about 600 mph — and tearing most of the fabric from the horizontal tail surfaces and rudder.

The airfield had been built by the New Zealand Public Works Department — and 'being beautifully grassed, it was not easy to detect until extension runways of coral had been laid.'[22] Life for the most part was idyllic and a sharp contrast to Whenuapai. Fruit plantations were a great novelty; to be able to simply pick and eat fresh fruit was a new experience for many airmen and something, Berry recalled, they could have done with later on Guadalcanal.

The Tongans were 'very friendly to New Zealanders and would give us native mats of Tapa cloth and shell beads... but after the Americans would pay them any price they asked they soon found out the value of the almighty dollar and there were no more free gifts.'[23] Mail was a problem. 'Letter mail was fairly frequent,' Berry wrote 'but parcels and newspapers failed to arrive.' It turned out that the mail was going to Espiritu Santo, and in a fit of administrative idiocy the accumulated pile was burnt after eight months — long after the squadron had actually arrived there.

The squadron moved to Espiritu Santo in February 1943 to back up US fighter units at Guadalcanal. Such a long over-ocean journey was unprecedented for single-engined aircraft, but the New Zealanders did not hesitate to make the journey. The Kittyhawks were fitted with 110 gallon belly tanks and escorted by Fortresses and a Catalina. The first long over-ocean hop of 3 hours 15 minutes took them to Nandi; then they flew four hours to Efate Island before a final hour-long flight to Espiritu Santo. The Nandi-Efate flight was the longest over-sea ferry mission by single engined fighter aircraft to that time.

The Tongan deployment had a curious post-script after the war. The second-hand P-40s were not included in Lend Lease, and in such a poor state when the RNZAF got to them that they were almost worthless. The New Zealand government evidently believed it had been able to collect the run-down aircraft for nothing until June 1945, when a bill arrived for $1,586,173 — including delivery charges of $335,107.[24]

The RNZAF became directly involved in front-line work in November 1942 when the Japanese began a major effort to recapture Guadalcanal. Six No.3 Squadron aircraft and eight aircrew were sent to the island for operations from Henderson Field. This was the principal airfield in Guadalcanal at the time, and was crammed with men and machines; the New Zealanders found room to camp in a nearby gully. By this time the Japanese had been reduced to ferrying supplies at night down Georgia Sound from Bougainville. The RNZAF unit was attached to the Search and Patrol Group of TF-63's Air Search and Attack Command to find the so-called 'Tokyo Express', and also made low-level day searches for staging posts in nearby islands. Until the New Zealanders arrived, the Americans had been using dive-bombers in this role. They were not well suited to the task, and US commanders began employing the six Hudsons very extensively. Up to five flights a day ranged as far afield as New Georgia and Santa Isabel. Serviceability fell behind as a result, and more aircraft were brought over from Espiritu Santo in early December to assist.

Guadalcanal was very much in the front line — this reconnaissance work contrasted sharply with the unrewarding searches of earlier months. On the very first day, George Gudsell and crew found a tanker, two transports and a destroyer near Vella Lavella, and were then engaged by three floatplanes. There was no damage to either side, but three days later Gudsell's Hudson was ambushed by three Japanese fighters while he tried to investigate a Japanese task force. Gudsell rallied his crew and the adrenalin-pumping seventeen minute engagement that followed resulted in little damage to the Hudson and no casualties. There was more action on 2 December west of New Georgia, when Flight Sergeant I M Page dropped his Hudson low to investigate what he thought was a canoe. It was actually a small Japanese submarine, and Page pressed an attack with the limited armament he carried on his reconnaissance mission, dropping two 250-pound bombs and two depth charges. One bomb fell on the diving submarine, and a patch of oil was observed on the surface, but the 'kill' could not be confirmed.

These activities had their effect back in New Zealand, where the training schemes were modified to cope with higher demand for airmen. Hudson crews going into the Pacific had to undertake specific conversion training for a wide range of operations including aerial gunning, high-level and anti-submarine bombing, formation flying, aerial photography, advanced navigation and fighter co-operation. Captains also had to attend a course in the New Plymouth School of General Reconnaissance. Bradshaw went there in November 1942 and found it 'excellent'.[25] He narrowly avoided one accident when the pilot of his Anson clipped a hedge on landing. This was not the only incident at Bell Block. Nolan Wynn recalled seeing a difficult landing in which an Anson tore out nearly 150 yards of fencing as it came down.

RNZAF aircrews played an important role in convoy battles in the Solomons during December 1942. An RNZAF Hudson also launched the first attack on a new Japanese airfield at Munda, on New Georgia island just 150 miles from Guadalcanal. Christmas came, and the New Zealanders each received 500 cigarettes from the Americans. John Morgan 'thought it decent of them to include us.' He spent the afternoon of Christmas Eve moving an ammunition dump and removing the turret from Hudson NZ 2039, which he did not finish until the next day, even though Christmas was a 'day off for everyone.' A stripped-down Hudson flew in from New Caledonia with a free beer issue. 'Really sweated our return to Santos and landing,' Morgan recorded 'as it had 5 bottles per man aboard.'[26] Christmas cheer brought Americans and New Zealanders together:

> *Got squadron photo taken at 2 pm before going to work. Told after photo parade that we would be getting 2 quart bottles of hooch issued free at 4 pm. Cut 2 out before tea, one of my own & one got by impersonating non-drinker, Vic Connell. Fred O'Neill, Laurie Easton did same by poising as two more non-drinkers. Got pretty boisterous affair at night. Good feed dished up by Sgts. Bit of singing going on in mess. CO made a speech, but is as unpopular as hell & got cold shoulder. Got back and found Yank met today back in tent with books... Went to his tent for a visit & spent a couple of hours. Took his tentmates down at "Blackjack", which Yank name for Pontoon. Good bloke, name of Bob More, from Kentucky. Pumped couple of beers into him. Got back & made own supper. Then Newton went to Yank camp with me. Supper in our tent pretty boisterous with lot of ballet dancing & other foolery.*[27]

During the festive season on Espiritu Santo two drunk American pilots took off in a B-17 for Vila to get more beer. One had reportedly made a bet with the other that he could not take off 'hands off'. Although a sergeant drove a jeep on to the runway in an effort to stop them, they bounced the aircraft over him and took to the air. They did not get very far. 'About 1/4 mile from end of runway one wing dipped & hit trees,' Morgan later recorded. 'Sent plane out of control. Ploughed gap in jungle about 200 yards long & burned. Nasty mess.'[28]

The Japanese made a further effort to bring supplies to Guadalcanal during early New Year 1943, and RNZAF Hudsons made up to seven reconnaissance sorties a day. There was also low-key bombing work, including an attack on Munda, and in early January the RNZAF helped provide air cover for a task force sent to shell the island.

Morgan was sent to Guadalcanal on 11 January with only one day's notice. He had time to draw new trousers and an emergency chocolate ration, and to change his boots. He landed in Guadalcanal — code named Cactus — about 1 pm the following day and:

> *noticed right away difference in atmosphere from Santos. Hot & breathless, like an oven, and peculiar smell around which is hard to place. Everyone looks pale & yellow from malaria... Very dusty... Yank pointed out Lib (B24) which took off just after we got out of plane, and said that the last white women on the island was aboard it. She is a nun who had been hiding in the hills... Went to camp about 15 miles on far side of runway from sea, near it on place called 'Bloody Ridge (or knoll) where 2200 dead Japs buried... Front line only 600 yards away, but several high ridges in between. Camp is down in valley to right of ridge, steep sides 1/4 mile long, 200 yards wide; choked full of Bongan trees & dirty big creepers. Green swamp on bottom as there doesn't seem to be any outlet. Stinks like hell. Tents themselves on side of hill, all cock-eyed because of roughness of ground. Dirty great tree at other end of valley fell just as I was going down track for first time... Found bed in US Marines tent (NZ bods attached to US Marine Air Group 14) for night & hope to find one in NZ tent tomorrow. Yanks OK, and one in particular named Kelly from Alabama... Expecting visit from Jap plane called Washing Machine Charlie, named this because of sound he makes rather resembles machine. Charlie almost a legend here. Didn't show up however... Yank 105 mm battery just over ridge opposite tents shelling off & on all night. Have a curious double report, probably echo. Can hear shells hissing all way over us till they burst further up valley. Flashes annoying, also blast, which puffs out mossie net like a sail. Could also hear gunfire all afternoon down on airstrip; from up coast a bit. Battery on airstrip also shelling lines over camp.*[29]

Morgan's work began as soon as he arrived, preparing Hudson NZ 2050 for a raid on Bougainville. A few nights later 'Washing Machine Charlie' turned up with an escort:

> *AA opened up & put up barrage some of which seemed to go close. Planes seemed to fly right overhead & I thought bombs were going to land fairly close. Come down with peculiar whistling noise, a ground shock with*

concussion. Landed on opposite side of camp from where we were. Came back twice more, but lights scared him off. Fighters went up but didn't catch up.... Had first experience of AA shrapnel. Didn't realise what noise was, until Yank in telephone exchange said to come under cover. Loud, peculiar humming sound that seemed to come from everywhere... Heard some pieces hit but ground & trees break off branches also ricochet around. Noise caused by thousands of fragments from AA shell.[30]

Japanese forces counter-attacked on 1 February. A major convoy was spotted by an RNZAF Hudson, and Henderson Field came under very heavy air attack. But this was preparatory to evacuation, which the Japanese completed on the night of 7-8 February.

Central Solomons Operations

Low-key action continued in the Solomons into 1943, while the United States prepared a major offensive to push back the Japanese who were firmly lodged in the western islands. No.3 Squadron went to Guadalcanal, where they were largely employed on shipping patrols, a monotonous task 'lightened by a variety of odd jobs.'[31] Maxwell W McCormick shot down the RNZAF's first Japanese aircraft in April; during an eventful patrol he had depth-charged a Japanese submarine before he came upon a floatplane which was evidently unaware of his approaching Hudson. Next day a Hudson shot down a Japanese aircraft off Vella Lavella. Later in the month, other Hudsons engaged in sporadic air combat with Japanese float-planes.

Fifty works personnel under W E Puddy arrived at Guadalcanal on 7 February in response to urgent requests to improve RNZAF base accommodation on the island. They brought their own sawmill which was powered on site with the engine of a captured Japanese light tank, and built a new camp for the New Zealand contingent, complete even down to wooden floors for the tents. Morgan left Guadalcanal at the beginning of April and returned to Espiritu Santo.

Up early & packing. Got ready pretty soon & over to plane by 9 a.m. Put stuff aboard & got photo taken with rest of armourers on wing of

> *Hudson. Had to leave one bloke behind as there were too many besides myself. Smeaton the armourer, Bob Campbell & Henry Bruce, riggers, a prisoner from construction outfit on board. It was his escort we had to leave. Plane took a hell of a takeoff run, full length of runway almost (strip 1 1/3 miles long) and still just lifted over Palm trees on overshoot area. Could smell rubber from tyres burning, inside aircraft. Sorry to be leaving boys behind in one way, and wished I could have seen out double tour. Missed by 11 days by doing 3 month tour instead of 65 weeks. ...Kissed Guadalcanal goodbye, also Tulagi & rest of Solomons. Landed at Buttons about 1 pm. Put gear on truck & went up to new camp in coconut grove to let officers off. Hardly knew the place, as it has changed so much. Met up with Len Newton first then Fred O'Neill later. Pleased to see me (I think).*[32]

By this time the RNZAF had set up a headquarters unit at Espiritu Santo in the camp vacated by 3 Squadron. No.1 (Islands) Group Headquarters came under Sidney Wallingford, now an Air Commodore, who had authority over all RNZAF operations in the Pacific. Wallingford — a veteran of the NZPAF's first operations in 1930 — reported to US Rear Admiral McCain, Commander Aircraft South Pacific. The unit included the No.4 Repair Depot, set up to provide stop-gap maintenance facilities until the United States could establish their own unit. No.9 Squadron and No. 14 Fighter Squadron arrived in March and April, the former as a reserve for No.3 Squadron. Isitt noted later in the year that the 'camp is very well laid out, good coral road, the only disadvantage being its situation between two aircraft strips and it is fearfully noisy.'[33] A Base Depot was also completed on Guadalcanal by November 1943, including the No.2 RNZAF Hospital. This brought the number of New Zealanders serving on the island to 1196.

Survival after being shot down in the tropics was a major issue as ever larger numbers of New Zealanders entered the Pacific theatre. Each bomber was equipped with an emergency pack that contained — among other things — a first aid kit, a two-cell torch with spare batteries and bulb, a whistle, ten packets of razor blades, fishing lines, hooks, revolver oil and 48 rounds of ammunition, six flares, six tins of fresh water, seven packets of emergency ratios, a compass, and a packet of shark repellent. Airmen were told what to do if they crashed in a booklet entitled *Survival Hints for Aircrew.* This comprehensive survival guide included instructions on dinghy drill — including ways of avoiding puncturing it — and rigging sails and sea anchors. The section 'meeting bodily needs' revealed that only a quarter of a pint of water daily could maintain life in extreme emergency. There were pictures of dangerous fish — grimly labelled 'Never eat these' — and instructions about what to eat on tropical islands. Of course, the Solomons were hardly deserted and aircrew were assured that the locals were 'almost all friendly to a white man.' An addendum contained useful phrases in pidgin. Probably the most crucial advice was buried in the middle. 'However bleak the outlook,' the authors in RNZAF Intelligence intoned 'do not give up.'[34]

Air-sea rescue was an important part of the RNZAF's effort to preserve the lives of its airmen — and those of allied nations. So-called 'Dumbo' units — taking their name from the Disney character — were intended to rescue downed airmen from rafts in the Pacific. The RNZAF had ordered 24 Catalinas for its units in Fiji to equip two squadrons, though in the end insufficient aircraft were actually delivered to do so. Shortage of equipment proved an early problem for No. 6 Squadron which formed unofficially in January 1943 at Fiji, eventually coming under Wing Commander George Stead. The Americans thought the squadron was fully operational and wanted it for work at Efate in the New Hebrides, but the unit was seriously under-manned and under-equipped and could not be sent. In early May the squadron rescued nine survivors from the torpedoed freighter *Vanderbilt*, 120 miles south of Suva. The seas were rough; Ronald MacGregor flying Catalina NZ 4001 was unable to land and circled the rafts for three hours waiting for rescue boats. When none came, he risked the landing, damaging the Catalina — and saved the seamen. He was awarded the Air Force Cross. More Catalinas were delivered that month and the squadron was officially formed on 25 May, still short of crew but with enough men to become fully operational. Tragically, MacGregor was killed in early June while flying back to New Zealand to collect more men.

In late April 1943, No. 3 Squadron rotated from Espiritu Santo back to New Zealand with little warning. Morgan had been in hospital for several weeks with a tropical bug, and returned to duty late in the month to find that 9 Squadron had virtually taken over from his own. The same day they received word they were heading home. 'Wish I had known of the shift sooner,' Morgan wrote. He hastily packed:

Got everything into bags & got them down to orderly room. Said goodbye to Fred... Newton & Bowden. On trucks and on our way by 1 am. ...Shipped out in barges to boat USS Rixey. Got stuff aboard & down to quarters after lot of trouble. Felt sorry for Johnny Fulton as we left in barge, as he got left behind. All hands sang out to him anyway. All of us put down below in large room, with bunks 4-5 high & only one door. Not too keen on that, as my bunk is right against outside hull.[35]

The return journey was uneventful, and Morgan arrived in Auckland with the rest of the squadron on 26 April, overflown as they came south by a Vincent from Waipapakauri. An American band was playing on the Auckland wharves when they arrived. Morgan was pleased to be back:

Pretty wild looking crew, as no haircuts for weeks or months, and clothes in tatters in some cases. Up to YM [YMCA] for feed served to us by waitresses! They probably wondered what they had struck. Up to Banks Bros buildings to draw great-coat and change money & from there to 'Albion' for big do, where most of us had first booze up for months.[36]

No RNZAF fighter units had yet been deployed into the combat zone, but No.15 Squadron had been preparing for the move to Guadalcanal since arriving at Espiritu Santo in February; and No. 14 Squadron was working up in New Zealand for eventual deployment into the Pacific. In late March No. 14 Squadron was ordered to fly their Kittyhawks to Espiritu Santo to swap them with No. 15 Squadron's worn out examples. The first group to deploy north, under Flight Lieutenant Stanley Quill, ran into trouble as they approached New Caledonia on the long hop from Norfolk Island. Low on fuel, they found their destination shrouded in low cloud:

Through insufficient briefing and inadequate intelligence, pilots had not been advised of alternative landing grounds, one of which was later reported to have been in clear weather. With darkness descending rapidly, and little fuel left, Flight Lieutenant Quill located a small beach near Noumea and ordered his pilots down. All four landed successfully, three with little damage to the aircraft, but Flying Officer MacDonald's aircraft over-ran the available space and finished in deep water, the pilot being rescued by Americans. Flight Lieutenant Quill himself, having no room to land, baled out and was picked up, some 6 miles from the shore, 4 hours later.[37]

Shipping had been promised to deploy 15 Squadron to Guadalcanal, but in the event it never turned up. The pilots took their new aircraft north on 26 April but the ground crews and radar unit remained on Espiritu Santo for several weeks. Even when the ship eventually arrived, wartime secrecy kept many in the dark about their destination. Basil Berry embarked on 25 May, realising that the large destroyer escort probably meant a forward area but not knowing where. They arrived off Guadalcanal shortly afterwards.

Meanwhile the squadron aircraft were employed on short-range patrols near Henderson field, and the first encounter with the enemy did not come until May. Squadron Leader Michael Herrick and Flight Lieutenant S R Duncan were escorting a Hudson when the bomber crew spotted a Japanese float plane and went in hot pursuit. The Japanese aircraft disappeared into a rainstorm. The fighters followed and eventually attacked the floatplane, which crashed into the sea. There was another engagement in the middle of the month when Flight Lieutenant I R McKenzie brought his Kittyhawk back riddled after an inconclusive tussle.

Air raids over Henderson Field were a daily occurrence — made worse because the Japanese seemed able to exploit a blind spot in the radar. The biggest attack came on 16 June. Berry watched 'hundreds of planes in the sky'. Ominously, 'some of the Jap planes that got through our fighter screen spent some time flying low and strafing anything and anyone they could find. Again at night over they came and we were very glad when that day was over.'[38]

The shortage of air transport facilities — which had even seen RNZAF personnel hitch rides on Liberators passing through Auckland — was partly rectified when No.40 Squadron formed in June 1943, equipped with six C-47 Douglas Dakotas and nine C-60 Lockheed Lodestars. By August there were scheduled services between Whenuapai and the islands. In September, the squadron absorbed the Pacific Ferry Flight, which had been shuttling Catalinas and Dakotas to New Zealand from the continental United States.

By the middle of 1943, the Allies had built up sufficient forces for a sustained assault into the Solomons. The first target was New Georgia, directly northwest of Guadalcanal and protected by Munda airfield. Halsey planned to seize Segi point, Wickham anchorage, Viru harbour and Rendova island before securing New Georgia itself. The Japanese observed the invasion build-up and tried to foil the assault with a pre-emptive strike on Henderson field. Kittyhawks of 15 Squadron shot down six Japanese aircraft for no loss during these intense battles. They were relieved in the middle of the month by 14 Squadron, but the Americans again employed the New Zealanders on combat air patrols over the air base where there was little action, though one Kittyhawk was shot down on 12 June when the Japanese tried to establish air superiority over the island. A third Japanese air attack on 16 June was also foiled; the RNZAF No. 52 Radar Unit played a significant part in detecting this force and providing air control. However, for the most part the work was boring and fruitless. 'Another of these wretched patrols, ending with the usual results,' the unit historian noted in the operations book on 18 June. Later the same day eight aircraft were scrambled to Cape Esperance where radar plots indicated 70 enemy aircraft were approaching. 'This raid, however, never materialised and our aircraft landed at 1625 without incident.'[39]

The New Zealanders were hampered during these battles by the fact that the Kittyhawk — derived from a mid-1930s design — was inferior to the Japanese Zeroes and obsolescent by comparison with more modern USAAF aircraft in theatre such as the Lockheed P-38 Lightning. Success under these circumstances derived entirely from pilot skill. The Kiwis had a further chance to demonstrate their abilities at the end of the month when the Allies attacked Munda. Bad weather on 30 June forestalled a blitz over Kahili, but squadron pilots nevertheless flew almost continuously — with tragic results when C T Guild's P-40 collided with another on the runway. The pilots had been in the air for most of the past eight hours without food and the accident was formally put down to fatigue.[40] The squadron also began daylight patrols began over Rendova island, operating between Guadalcanal and spartan forward bases in the Russell islands, northwest of Guadalcanal.

On 1 July a unit of eight 14 Squadron aircraft under Flight Lieutenant E H Brown saw enemy aircraft 5000 feet below them:

> *All carried out attacks forthwith. Brown leading, a series of dogfights ensued, but owing to adverse cloud conditions everyone was split up. However confirmations for seven aircraft were obtained... To these must*

be added three probables... Brown's aircraft had a sharp burst into the engine and he was forced to retire towards base. His motor seized and he baled out. Owing to his parachute pulling him under even though he had dropped out at 5 feet he lost his dinghy and was picked up in poor condition some four and a half hours later. In his own estimate he owes his life to FO MacDonald.[41]

Flying Officer MacDonald took off in his own Kittyhawk at 2.45 to look for Brown and Flying Officer Burton, who had also baled out. He found Brown, who was picked up 'in poor condition' after four and a half hours in the water and later said that he owed his life to MacDonald.[42] However, Burton was not seen again. Two days later eight 14 Squadron aircraft on patrol were 'jumped by many enemy aircraft and ... badly mauled.' There were actually about forty Zeroes — 'Zekes' in official terminology — against the eight New Zealanders. In the melee that followed, Quill — pushing the fight hard — shot down a Zero but was wounded in the shoulder, crash landing in Russell Island. Two other Kittyhawks were hit by cannon shells. Geoffrey Fisken downed three Zeroes. Nairn 'did battle for almost an hour by himself against some 40 enemy aircraft'[43] — an astounding feat in which he shot down one Zero without damage to his own aircraft.

One Hudson, under William Allison, was attacked by eight Zeroes near Vela Lavella on 24 July. A running fight followed, during which one Zero was probably shot down, but the Hudson was set on fire and Allison had to crash land in the sea. The crew escaped, but one of the Zeroes spent ten minutes strafing the swimmers, killing all except the tail gunner, Trevor Ganley. Wounded, he swam four miles to a deserted island where he found an abandoned American raft still containing some chocolate. He supplemented this with coconuts and survived on the island for nine days while he repaired the raft, which he then paddled to Vella Lavella. This was still in Japanese hands and Ganley was found by armed locals as he reached the beach. Bradshaw later recorded that they 'demanded "American" or "Japanese", to which Ganley foolishly replied "New Zealand."' Luckily, one of the islanders had been educated in New Zealand, and 'this literally saved his life.'[44] Ganley was not turned over to the Japanese occupying forces — despite the risk of major reprisals if his rescuers were found out — and returned to his squadron a few weeks later.

No.14 Squadron rotated back to New Zealand in July. Meanwhile, the US government requested a second RNZAF fighter squadron for front line operations in support of the offensive, and No. 16 Squadron formed at Ohakea in June 1943 for the purpose. They deployed in late July to begin operations in the bomber escort role over Munda. First combat occurred on 31 July, when their P-40's engaged thirty Zeroes for the loss of two.

This was only the beginning of a major effort over the next two months. When the squadron rotated back to New Zealand in mid-September, it had notched up 2100 operational hours.

Other New Zealand forces committed to the campaign included the light cruiser HMNZS *Leander*, torpedoed at the Battle of Kolombangara on 13 July, and the two-brigade strong Third New Zealand Division. Munda fell on 5 August. Halsey then decided to bypass the Japanese garrison on Kolombangara, thought to be 10,000 strong. The more lightly held island of Vella Lavella came under attack in mid-August; the Third New Zealand Division landed to mop up survivors, and the Japanese evacuated New Georgia by early October. New Zealand's fighter contribution continued at the two-squadron level, with a third in reserve at Espiritu Santo. No. 17 Squadron deployed in September to replace No. 16, while No. 15 came out for a second tour, and No. 18 deployed to Espiritu Santo.

Reconnaissance and bomber activity rose to fever-pitch during these intense months. At one stage, No.3 squadron pilots flying reconnaissance missions from Guadalcanal found themselves playing regular hide-and-seek with a lone 'Betty', also on regular reconnaissance work. This aircraft was faster than the Hudson and better armed.[45] The squadron had a radar equipped Hudson, which the New Zealanders sent out with two Kittyhawks by way of a trap. Bad weather foiled the attempt. The Americans then put two P-38's up with the Hudson to ambush the 'Betty', but found nothing. Later the men heard that a 'Betty' had been shot down by a B-25 and deduced that this was their persistent companion.

By this time the construction crews had finished their work on Guadalcanal and Bradshaw found accommodation fairly comfortable, but the men were very complacent and often remained in their beds when air raid sirens went off. Manpower shortages were a particular problem. His regular navigator was sent back to New Zealand for medical reasons, and no replacement was available. Bradshaw discussed the situation with his crew and decided that he would make the takeoff and climb, then hand the aircraft over to the co-pilot while he did the navigation until it was time to land.[46]

The decision to bypass Rabaul

Still hoping to achieve a combat strength of twenty squadrons, the RNZAF requested additional Catalinas, Dauntlesses, Venturas, Avengers, Kittyhawks and transports in late 1943 along with F-4U Corsairs. Audaciously, the service also requested 100 B-24 Liberator heavy bombers to form two squadrons with attrition reserves. These were turned down. On re-think, the service then decided not to commit to such a large number of different aircraft types, and cancelled the Dauntlesses and Avengers in exchange for more Corsairs — though Dauntlesses were taken on strength when the service had the opportunity to take over second-hand American aircraft, and some of the Avengers were delivered.

The Japanese had established their main base in theatre at Rabaul, on the northern tip of New Britain. It was heavily fortified, and taking it was clearly not going to be easy. MacArthur hoped to land in western New Britain after the defences had been reduced from the air, but at the Quadrant Conference of August 1943, Roosevelt and Churchill decided to bypass the island altogether on the advice of the Combined Chiefs of Staff. MacArthur was instead ordered to take Manus in the Admiralty Islands and Kavieng in New Ireland, preparatory to advancing along New Guinea to the Vogelkop peninsula. MacArthur saw this as prelude to being sidelined in favour of the central Pacific campaign, but after rapid lobbying was permitted to begin planning an assault on the Phillipines.

These decisions dictated the Allied strategy for New Ireland, including the work of the RNZAF. Halsey had originally intended to bypass Bougainville, which was heavily garrisoned, but now needed airfields there to keep Rabaul suppressed. The southern part of the island was thought to hold 60,000 Japanese soldiers, and Halsey came up with a compromise scheme for occupying only the northern end. Forces moved up to make the assault included RNZAF 16 and 18 Squadrons. These two units were at Guadalcanal and ordered to Munda on 4 September. The Americans proposed a further move to Segi, but the RNZAF objected; the runways at Segi were short, and with poor brakes the squadron's P-40N's were at a disadvantage. Instead they went to Ondonga — mid-way up the eastern coast of New Georgia — on 19 October, where RNZAF Station New Georgia was formally established under Trevor Freeman.[47]

Poor weather hampered the move. The administrative units had been there some days before the aircraft began arriving on 23 October. Mackie, by this time with No.18 Squadron, tried to fly to Ondonga next day but had to abandon the attempt when the weather refused to co-operate. 'Waited all morning and didn't get away,' he noted in his diary.[48]

Accommodation was set up in a coconut plantation that fast became a sea of mud. Little was ready when the aircraft arrived. 'The mess hall had not been completed,' the war history remarked 'and the first meal which was a credit to the cooks, was eaten by all ranks wherever they could find a dry spot to sit down.'[49] Until early October, Ondonga had been under artillery attack from emplacements on Kolombangara. The Japanese had evacuated that island by the time the New Zealanders arrived, but the base was also within 120 miles of Japanese airfields on Bougainville, and the first air raid took place on 27 October. Foxholes had yet to be dug. 'The experience proved ...unnerving,' a draft official history dryly noted.[50] There were eight raids while the New Zealanders were at Ondonga.

Operations began at the end of October, and the RNZAF Wing flew up to ten sorties a day in support of diversionary land attacks on the Treasury islands by the 8th Brigade Group of the New Zealand Third Division. 'A very busy day,' Mackie noted on the 27th 'our troops landed on the Treasury islands and all the fighter squadrons were on patrol from dawn till dusk... 3:40 flying... had a dam [sic] sore seat.'[51]

Halsey ordered an assault on Choiseul and deliberate reconnaissance of the Shortland Island area to convince the Japanese that Bougainville would be attacked from the south. In fact, landings were made at the beginning of November in the west by the 3rd Marine Division. The Japanese were caught unawares, and in what Mackie called a 'pretty exciting time', eight P-40s of RNZAF No. 18 Squadron under Waimate-born Flight Lieutenant 'Jimmy' Balfour intercepted nearly sixty Zeroes flying in V-formation down the centre of the island, apparently unaware of the Allied attack. In the battle that followed the New Zealanders scored seven kills and one probable. Two were shot down by Balfour. Flying Officer K D Lumsden was forced to ditch his P-40 after battle damage, and was picked up by a barge. Mackie went up at noon to support the air assault. 'A big bogie was reported coming in,' he later wrote 'so we dumped our belly tanks and climbed up to 25,000 feet. Circled around and heard a lot about bogies but [I] had [to] return with Souter as he was short of petrol.'[52] Next day the RNZAF Wing was involved in further air fighting over the beach-head. No. 14 Squadron arrived at Ondonga — referred to in Squadron histories as 'Ondongo' — on 8 November, finding their quarters in the Navy Pilots camp a 'most satisfying experience.'[53]

That month the Japanese reinforced the base with the air groups of the carriers *Zuikakau*, *Zuiho* and *Shokaku*, a total of some 173 aircraft. At this stage Rabaul was only within effective reach of US carrier aircraft, and Halsey ordered a massive naval air assault during November. Lt-General Koga, in command of the Rabaul defences, was forced to withdraw his own carrier air groups to prevent their annihilation. Rabaul ceased to be an offensive threat, and by December the Allied focus had switched to merely keeping the Japanese subdued.

During this period the RNZAF wing was heavily engaged over Bougainville, escorting raids or strafing enemy positions. Typically the first operations began at dawn, with other raids forming during the afternoon. To achieve these sortie rates, maintenance crews usually worked during the night to prepare aircraft, and were often hampered by air raids. By this time the squadrons operated in colour-coded divisions, and on 13 November 'White' flight of 14 Squadron:

> *discovered a small barge being rowed from Asie to Fauro Island. Weber was first in and appeared to kill half of the 20 occupants. The balance went overboard, but by the time the strafing ended there was no activity and only bodies floating in the water. At one stage Weber must have received a small bullet in his oil system as it packed up on the way home and he baled out, with great difficulty from the low height of 4-500 ft between Wana Wana and Arundel Islands.*[54]

Weber was picked up two hours later by the US Army and brought back to base by crash boat. Two days later, 'Green' and 'White' flights were engaged in so-called 'Cherry blossom' and 'Charlie search' missions, during which they met some anti-aircraft opposition, but nevertheless:

> *put bursts into buildings at Numa Numa and Tenekau plantation house. Kieta was given a thorough doing, Stanley and Meharry leaving 2 probable oil barges burning and Bullen sinking a small boat by a jetty... A natty looking 30' boat moored to a jetty in Taimonapu Bay was strafed and left burning.*[55]

Fighter-bomber missions in early December destroyed a bridge and damaged Japanese positions at Kieta, an airfield in south Bougainville. Balfour shot down another Zero on 22 November and was awarded half-share on a second 'kill'. Mackie recorded two days later that 'about ten we were vected [sic] on to point Day coming down at 450 mph we found two SBD's there and some new barges which we strafed and set on fire.'[56]

There was excitement behind the front line. Mackie was rotated out of Ondonga with 18 Squadron on 24 November, returning to Guadalcanal in the afternoon:

> *to be met with one of the greatest sights one could see an ammunition dump about four miles square going up. There was smoke and cloud in gigantic waves. This carried on most of the night while every now and then the tent would shudder as a huge explosion went. Camps all round and a hospital had to be evacuated.*[57]

Direct action over Rabaul became possible for the RNZAF when an advanced refuelling strip was established on Bougainville at Empress Augusta Bay. This enabled fighters with long-range tanks to escort bombers over the Japanese base, and the first main attack went ahead on 17 December. Eighty fighters were involved, including 24 from the RNZAF Wing. They left Ondonga at dawn and refuelled at Torokina, reaching Rabaul mid-morning where the entire group was engaged by Japanese aircraft. The New Zealanders shot down five and the Americans four, but two New Zealand aircraft were shot down. Another attack a week later resulted in twelve 'kills' and four 'probables' for the loss of six RNZAF aircraft and five pilots.

While this went on, the RNZAF shifted their Ondonga camp into an area vacated by US Marine Corps squadron VMFG 215, as the original site had proven almost uninhabitable. Squadron padre Flight Lieutenant W Answorth reported that morale was high, 'not only because the men knew they were serving in the front line of the campaign but because of the outstanding personality of Wing Commander Freeman.'[58]

The bomber squadrons continued their work slightly further away from the action. No. 1 (BR) Squadron deployed to Guadalcanal in October 1943, equipped with new Lockheed-Vega PV-1 Venturas, but arrived without spares, and then discovered that there were none for the type in the operational area. Maintenance crews were reduced to cannibalising several PV-1's that had crashed near the airfield. New spare parts did not arrive from US sources until February 1944, by which time the tour was almost over. Although operating from Henderson field, a detachment eventually moved to Munda to more easily reach the patrol area. Offensive work included bombing warehouses and barges over Bougainville.

On 24 December two PV-1s under Donald Ayson and R J Alford were ordered to follow a Liberator raid, and were flying independently when both were 'bounced' by several Zeroes. G E Hannah, on Ayson's aircraft, managed to shoot down two, but despite the arrival of a Corsair, the bomber was having a difficult time. Ayson slammed on full throttle, reaching an airspeed of 300 knots with 57 inches of boost on the turbo-superchargers, but the rudder controls were shot away, aircraft commander S P Aldridge was wounded and navigator W N Williams took over control of the battle. Hannah damaged three more Zeroes before the attack was broken off, and Ayson managed to land without rudder control at Guadalcanal. Three Zeroes damaged the other PV-1, but were driven off and Alford managed to land his aircraft. Afterwards, Ayson and Williams were awarded the DFC, and Hannah — who was credited with three 'kills' — the DFM.

No.6 Squadron moved to Havalo Bay on Florida Island near Guadalcanal in December 1943, to provide Dumbo support in theatre and supplement the maritime patrols of the land based squadrons. This remained their home until September 1945 when the squadron was disbanded.

Encirclement: Rabaul and Green Island

By the beginning of 1944, the United States had enough forces in the Pacific theatre to advance in three directions; directly across the central Pacific, northwest from the Solomons, and through New Guinea. Meanwhile, positions were established around New Britain to encircle Rabaul. New Zealanders were prominently involved in this work. The RNZAF Fighter Wing moved to Torokina airfield on Bougainville in January 1944, occupying an American camp along with Nos 2 and 4 Servicing Units. Three raids on Rabaul followed, but during these battles No. 17 Squadron suffered high casualties, compounded by tropical disease, and was withdrawn. The following month, RNZAF fighters escorted US bombers over Rabaul on 20 days out of 29, totalling 404 sorties.

As a result of the Allied air activity over Rabaul, the Japanese decided in February to withdraw their 70 remaining fighters there to Truk, well north of theatre in the Carolines. There was a final clash on 13 February when RNZAF P-40's, escorting a raid of American TBF's against Vunakaku airfield, near Rabaul, were engaged by 25 Mitsubishi Zeroes. The New Zealanders shot down two for the loss of one P-40. This brought the RNZAF to 99 confirmed 'kills' for the Pacific campaign, and a few weeks later Air Vice Marshal Leonard Isitt reported great eagerness among the squadrons to shoot down the 100th enemy aircraft, but that 'since the middle of February the Jap air strength in the Solomons and Bismarck area has received such a thrashing on the ground and in the air that our fellows can get no reaction and have not made a contact for over a fortnight.'[59] Indeed, the score remained at 99 until the end of the war, and No. 14 Squadron operations book recorded that this period was notable for a 'complete absence of contacts.'[60]

On 15 February, New Zealand ground forces landed on Green Island, a coral atoll mid-way between Bougainville and New Britain, 125 miles from Rabaul. The RNZAF provided fighter cover — eight aircraft of Nos 14 and 18 Squadrons were above the island at any given moment — and by 19 February resistance had been quelled. Isitt visited two days later, remarking on the success just twenty miles from occupied Bougainville — a victory he put down to 'co-ordinated sea and air effort' which had captured the island 'for practically no casualties.'[61] United States 'Seabees' built an airfield on nearby Nissan Island, which opened on 7 March, enabling fighter-bomber operations against Rabaul. That day, twelve aircraft from 14 Squadron and eight from 18 Squadron armed with 500-pound GP bombs on modified drop-tank racks flew from Torokina, staged on Green Island, and attacked Rabaul. Incendiaries were also carried, and later 1000 lb bombs were toted into battle by RNZAF P-40s. Isitt was pleasantly surprised by 'what I saw of

No.1 (Islands) groups. The morale is very high, and the work of the squadrons and units is most efficient. This particularly goes for our maintenance.'[62]

In March, MacArthur was ordered to take Emirau, part of the St Matthias group due north of New Ireland. By this time some 30,000 Japanese troops had been cut off in Bougainville, and a further 50,000 in New Britain and New Ireland, where they were being pushed back to the Gazelle Peninsula. The final strike of No. 14 Squadron's tour in the area came on 26 March against Japanese units on the western tip of Talili Bay, west of Rabaul on the Gazelle Penninsula.

> *For the second time we carried 500 lb incendiary clusters and as the target was comparatively narrow, we released from 4000'. Apart from a few incendiaries which fell short in the sea the target was completely covered and left in a thick pall of greyish black smoke which prevented immediate observation of fires apart from two large ones from which columns of black smoke were rising. However the pilots consider it was one of the most satisfactory bombings they have done.*[63]

The Japanese attempted to push the Allies out of Bougainville the same month. By this time the Americans had established a four-mile deep lodgement around Torokina. The Japanese planned to breach the perimeter and drive the Americans and New Zealanders into the sea, where they would be annihilated by naval bombardment. The airfield was protected by a variety of units including the Torokina Airfield Defence Force, partially manned by three RNZAF companies. Intercepted messages gave a little warning, and the attack began a day late on 8 March, opening with an artillery bombardment. Bombardments continued daily until 20 March; for safety, the aircraft were flown to Green Island each night. Meanwhile, Japanese infantry attacked with only desultory effect, and the Japanese came under heavy air bombardment, including strikes by 14 Squadron P-40s armed with 1000 pound bombs, just six miles from the Torokina airstrip.

Nos 25 and 30 squadrons arrived in the middle of the assault, equipped with Douglas SBD-3 Dauntless dive-bombers and Grumman TBF Avengers respectively. The equipment was fortuitous; the RNZAF had been able to take over the aircraft of US Marine Aircraft Group 14, originally stationed at Seagrove near Auckland. Their arrival at Torokina was postponed until it was clear the Japanese attack on the airfield would fail, but even so, personnel were camped only 1000 yards from the front line. Some of the tents were hit by rifle fire on the night of 17 March, only two days after squadron advance parties arrived. Both squadrons joined American aircraft for an attack on Kavieng airfield at the end of March, but the aircraft of 25 Squadron were unable to make a rendezvous and had to return.

Attacks on Rabaul continued, principally against Vunakakau and Tobera airfields. The RNZAF Fighter Wing also operated against targets in Bougainville. Squadrons rotated at approximate six-week intervals, and in May 20 Squadron deployed to Torokina with the first F-4U Corsairs, under Squadron Leader S R Duncan. When 25 and 30 Squadron were withdrawn in May, 31 Squadron deployed forward under Squadron Leader M Wilkes, again equipped with Avengers. They continued operations against targets in Rabaul and Bougainville, spraying diesel on crops grown by the besieged Japanese. This involved precision flying at low level, exposed to rifle and light-calibre AA fire. No. 14 Squadron returned to Torokina, and a mission on 14 July resulted in bombing which was described as 'quite good', though 'the only observed results were three native huts which were demolished by the blast from two bombs.'[64]

Meanwhile, RNZAF bomber squadrons operating from Munda achieved a variety of successes. A PV-1 of No.2 Squadron attacked a submarine off New Ireland on 20 February, but was unable to determine whether it was a 'kill'. Operations around Rabaul began in February with coastal sweeps for barges and an attack on a radar station. There was more action against submarines in April, and at the end of the month the squadron moved to Piva, near Torokina, where there were better maintenance facilities. It was replaced by No. 9 Squadron in late May after completing 3758 operational flying hours. No. 9 squadron, under A C Allen, then began offensive operations against Rabaul, a task which RNZAF Venturas continued for the rest of the war.

RNZAF sidelined, 1944–45

By mid-1944 it was clear in Japan that the war was lost. The Tojo cabinet fell on 18 July, but the new government of General Kuniaki Koiso and Admiral Mitsumasa Yonai were not yet prepared to admit failure. Certainly the unconditional surrender demanded by the Allies was unacceptable. So the war continued, though its outcome was inevitable.

The RNZAF enjoyed an excellent reputation by this time. American bomber pilots preferred being escorted by RNZAF fighters because of their combat discipline. However, all New Zealand forces in theatre were sidelined during the year partly as a result of a political spat that erupted over the Canberra Pact. This arrangement, technically the Australian-New Zealand Agreement, was a principally Australian response to ongoing exclusion from post-war planning by Britain, the Soviet Union and the United States. Bilateral discussions between Australia and New Zealand on defence issues began as early as 1938, when Savage called for closer consultation, but did not gain momentum until late in the war when Australian concerns developed at ongoing exclusion from Allied planning. In late 1943, Churchill, Roosevelt and Chiang Kai Shek agreed to strip Japan of all its Pacific island territories, without consulting Australia or New Zealand. This move set the tone for bilateral talks in Canberra. Neither Australia or New Zealand informed the other Allies, a perhaps unfortunate oversight. The pact was negotiated over three days of 'friendly but nevertheless candid'[65] talks in Canberra which culminated in agreement on 21 January 1944.

What irritated the United States particularly were Clauses 13, 14 and 16. The first called for a regional defence zone extending to Western Samoa and the Cook Islands. Clause 14 requested Dominion involvement in the United Nations, and Clause 16 stated that wartime use of territories was not a basis for claiming those territories afterwards. This was interpreted by the Americans as an effort to reduce their post-war influence in the Pacific, and the Joint Chiefs of Staff decided in April to restrict the RNZAF to garrison and low-key reconnaissance duties in the South Pacific, scrapping all fighter squadrons. It was a significant blow to which both the RNZAF and the New Zealand government reacted quickly. Isitt revealed the fundamental problem to Fraser on 5 April:

> *lack of forward planning by the higher United States staffs in Washington seems to relegate the bulk of the RNZAF in the South Pacific zone to garrison duty in the immediate future. Our object is to press for employment in the combat zone and it is still more important that plans should be developed for the ultimate employment of the RNZAF in active*

operations against Japan in order that adequate representation is secured at the termination of hostilities.[66]

This was the key issue; sidelining the RNZAF reduced New Zealand's voice in any post-war settlement. Isitt later noted that the decision by the US was 'largely due to repercussions here from Australian-New Zealand Agreement', but thought the decision was primarikly a 'service one not political.'[67] In a sense he was right: the RNZAF was not a large service and there were difficulties finding roles. However, the over-riding problem actually was political, and Fraser visited Washington personally to lobby for New Zealand. He issued an oil-on-water press statement on 18 April, which the media misunderstood. The same day he talked to the Senate Foreign Relations Committee, and with Walter Nash, Minister for New Zealand in the United States, argued the cause with Admiral Ernest King, Chief of Naval Operations. Talks were fruitless. King agreed to refer the employment of the RNZAF to the Chiefs of Staff — opening up the possibility that they might reconsider their decision. Later the same day, Fraser and Nash received a sharp and somewhat demeaning dressing-down from US Secretary of State Cordell Hull.

Fraser and Nash believed they had made some headway with King, but the Americans had not changed their minds and at the beginning of May the New Zealand Air Mission in Washington were informed that there was 'no prospect of active employment for RNZAF squadrons in Pacific west of longitude 159 east or north of equator.'[68] The only role was garrison duties in the Solomons and New Hebrides, requiring major reductions. The New Zealand War Cabinet decided to accept this as 'necessary in [the] interests of British prestige in Pacific', but sent Isitt to Washington to argue for further employment of the now surplus squadrons in the combat zone, ideally under Halsey. The American decision also alarmed Fraser, then in London. 'The decision from Washington is... completely at variance with our understanding with King,' he telegraphed to Nash, ordering the minister to see King immediately 'and advise me of his views.'[69] Before meeting the Admiral, Nash responded that:

whilst King may be living up to his statements ...he is certainly not acting in the spirit for long range use of our forces. I know unofficially

> *that Halsey would like the New Zealand Squadrons to work with him but I also know from a reported personal conversation that King has stated that the operations in the Marshall Carolines area where Halsey is to control are to be exclusively undertaken by USA forces. King is also reported to have said "the Australians and New Zealand... apparently want a say in what is to be done with the Marshalls and Carolines and neither Australia nor New Zealand are going to have a right to claim a say in what is to be done with these islands on account of their having taken part in the operations for the capture of them." ...King's views I am told are personal to him and are due to his strong resentment to the clause 26 in the Canberra Agreement.*[70]

Nash went to see King and on 23 May reported that the Admiral had not refused to consider employing the RNZAF in the central Pacific, but the issue was tangled with an over-supply of US forces in the same theatre, US command changes, and plans to clear up Japanese pockets in the South West Pacific. In a second note to Fraser, Nash added despondently that 'King, it appears to me, has a complete case on the disposition of our forces.'[71]

The Americans certainly did not seem willing to compromise at government level, although New Zealand's contribution to the Pacific war — which included supplying food for the campaign — had been accomplished without diminishing output to Europe and reflected a very high level of national effort. The development of the RNZAF in particular was a very major achievement, expanding the service from a thousand men and a handful of obsolete aircraft to a modern combat force able to make a real contribution to the war. All this had been done through extreme personal and national sacrifice — manpower levels back in New Zealand were critical by 1944. In return, New Zealand had been excluded from post-war planning and now was being cut out of the Pacific war.

Yet there were still glimmers of hope. The RNZAF had made a favourable impression at the 'sharp end', and Isitt visited COMSOPAC at the end of May to discover strong local support for continued RNZAF operations. Armed with this news he went to Washington to 'obtain final agreement for the continued employment of our squadrons with the South Pacific task force during the next few months, and also to our proposals for the deployment of the RNZAF combat force after the Bismarck operations have been concluded.'[72]

A compromise solution was eventually reached in August, when Isitt attended a conference in Brisbane with South Pacific commanders. The decision was taken to permit the RNZAF to operate seven squadrons on garrison duties in the southwest Pacific. This included two fighter squadrons at Espiritu Santo, two at Guadalcanal, a bomber and a flying boat squadron at or near Guadalcanal, and a fighter squadron at Los Negros. Another fighter squadron was permitted to stay on Bougainville, and two more at Green Island and Emirau respectively, along with RNZAF bomber-reconnaissance squadrons. Isitt estimated 8500 officers and men including 1000 officers would be required for the Pacific theatre, needing an intake of only 1900 men per annum from New Zealand.[73]

The RNZAF group came under a new South West Pacific command, and the units in the Solomons became the New Zealand Air Task Force (Zeairtaf), headquartered at Bougainville. Isitt did not anticipate much combat. 'The chances of air fighting in the Bismarck area are most unlikely at the moment.'[74] Most of the construction work was also done by the RNZAF, although the Americans were meant to have done it. The unit was intended to take over air authority in the northern Solomons from the 1st Marine Air Wing on 1 November 1944, but in the event the change did not take place until July 1945. Operations were hampered by lack of sea transport, because the majority of available US shipping was in the central Pacific.

There was further political tension later in 1944 when the RNZAF purchased four Short Sunderland Mk III flying boats for £60,000 each. These were initially intended for military purposes, but the United States government interpreted the delivery as an early effort by New Zealand and the Commonwealth to set up post-war commercial air routes, and as a result of American pressure the Combined Munitions Assignment Board in London refused to ratify the deal. After further negotiations consent was given in August and the four aircraft left Britain for the delivery flight in October, under Donald Baird. They arrived in early December and were met by a Lodestar sent to photograph them, but the 'shoot' was marred by near catastrophe when the Lodestar and one of the Sunderlands collided. Although badly damaged, the Lodestar recovered to Whenuapai. The Sunderland landed in the sea and was eventually towed to Auckland by a fishing boat.[75]

The restriction of the RNZAF's operations to the north-western Solomons meant that only No.40 Transport Squadron continued to range far out into the Pacific. By early 1944, squadron aircraft flew a regular route that embraced Norfolk Island, New Caledonia, Fiji, Tonga, Espiritu Santo, Guadalcanal and Honolulu. Later in the year, Samoa was added to the list, along with other bases in the Solomons. Bradshaw was posted to the squadron at the end of 1943, and after a few initial VIP flights with Lodestars, changed to the Douglas C-47 Dakota, which he flew for the rest of the war. With two 100-gallon auxiliary tanks, the Dakota could reach Espiritu Santo direct from Auckland. The RNZAF typically flew the type at an all-up weight of 31,000 lb, markedly higher than the US civil limit of 25,500 lb.[76]

Bradshaw's experience paid off when he flew the RNZAF band around the Pacific camps on a concert tour. Six C-47's were needed for the job. The trip went smoothly until they left Tontouta in New Caledonia. Bradshaw arrived at his loaded C-47 to be told by a worried engineer that the tyres and main oleos seemed flat. The loading sheet assured them the aircraft weighed only 29,500 lbs. Bradshaw insisted on having the cargo re-weighed, despite the fact that no facilities could be found closer than an American depot two miles distant. The load was some 3000 lb heavier than Duncan's figures indicated, but it turned out that the band had spent up large at the local Post Exchange, and 'packed their loot around their band instruments' — a ton and a half of it.[77]

Mopping up in Bougainville

Although hampered by late deliveries of the Lockheed PV-2 Harpoons that were intended to supplement the Venturas, the RNZAF worked closely with the Australians to crush Japanese resistance in Bougainville, and continued operations against Rabaul — although by this time the Japanese seldom put their heads up. No. 14 Squadron spent Christmas Day on Green Island, 'hard at work putting up 85 hours on a 4 plane patrol over Rabaul for negative results.'[78] On the last day of the year the three squadrons on Green Island put up three Rabaul patrols each 'with one doing a scramble alert dawn & dusk patrols one day then Dumbo the next.'[79]

Australia took over from the United States in Bougainville in late 1944, and by November, Australian troops had been deployed to wipe out the last Japanese resistance. Eight aircraft of the RNZAF's No. 15 Squadron under

Squadron Leader D P Winston gave close support to Australian infantry on 7 December, discovering that depth charges had enormous destructive effect in thick jungle. The service gave extensive assistance to the Australians on Bougainville for the rest of the war, particularly after April 1945 when fighter garrison duties on Espiritu Santo ended and the Corsair-equipped squadrons could be sent directly to Bougainville. Isitt visited the island in March and reported that 'the co-operation is excellent and the mutual admiration and trust between the RNZAF and the Australian military forces would be hard to improve.'[80] Morale was high.

No. 14 Squadron was deployed to Bougainville on 2 April and began operations two days later with six searches of two aircraft each, 'the result being two beached canoes and a rowboat damaged by strafing.' Next day they struck a road east of the Puriata River. Four aircraft joined the first strike and eight the second. 'These strikes were successful,' the squadron operations book dryly noted 'as the Australian Brigadier sent along a message of thanks.'[81] Strikes continued daily and depth charges became the weapon of choice, favoured for their blast effects in jungle. On 4 April, four aircraft under Flying Officer David Corbett dropped eight 325 lb depth charges on the east-west road just east of the Puriata River. Later the same day the strike was repeated with 14 500 lb 'daisy cutters' and two 325 lb depth charges. A few days later 18 325 lb depth charges and six 500-lb bombs were dropped over Japanese troops on the east bank of the Puriata. All available aircraft were put up on 26 April in preparation for an advance down the Buin Road, south east of Hiruhiru. The target area was only 1000 yards long, and the Australians requested that bombing should begin 300 yards ahead of their own positions. The RNZAF put the ordinance directly on target, which:

> *was devastated; some dead Japs were found and those alive in the vicinity were "punch drunk". Some Australian troops were forward of the indicated positions and an Australian Colonel, who had taken up a forward position, was knocked over by bomb blast... some time later he said he thought close air support was very effective.*[82]

By the end of the month the squadron had flown 892.15 hours operationally. A total of 10,592 sorties were eventually flown by the RNZAF against the Japanese on Bougainville, until the surrender in August.

Activity elsewhere was limited during 1945. Logistic support west of Meridian 159 was taken over by the US Seventh Fleet based on Manus in December 1944, but their expected move out of theatre in March 1945 created a requirement for logistic support which Isitt admitted the RNZAF was 'quite incapable of meeting... as we had no shipping.' Nor could they provide full base support for deployed units in the field 'on account of the man-power situation in New Zealand and also lack of personnel trained in these duties.' Isitt estimated the service needed 2500-3000 men for these tasks, and negotiated with the Australians, the Commander Allied Forces GHQ, 'and various US naval commanders' among other authorities to get them. In the end he was able to get continued gasoline and ordinance from the US Navy, and the RAAF agreed to provide airfield maintenance facilities.[83] During April there was talk of completely reorganising the RNZAF in the Pacific, giving administrative control and logistic support of all operations in the Northern Solomons-Bismarck area to COMZEAIRTAF and abolishing the No.1 Islands Group.

Until May, RNZAF squadrons operated from Green Island against residual Japanese forces on the Gazelle peninsula, but they moved to Jacquinot Bay that month. Other units at Emirau were ordered in June to advance to Borneo, via Los Negros. This base had suffered an air raid in April when remaining Japanese air units at Rabaul launched a torpedo attack against shipping in Seeadler Harbour. However, by this time the Allies were knocking on the gates of Japan and the war was clearly approaching its end. There were rumours that RNZAF units on Los Negros might find a role in Japan. But in the end no RNZAF units moved beyond the operational areas to which they had been restricted by the United States.

No. 14 Squadron finished the war at Emirau, patrolling Kavieng and New Ireland against negligible Japanese resistance. Pilot Officers Richard Soar and Jennings had a rare burst of activity on 1 August when the dusk Kavieng patrol 'gave [them]... the chance to do some accurate bombing when they landed 4 x 650 lb depth charges within 20 yards of each other on a suspected hutted area at Fangelawa Bay, but the jungle obscured observation of results.'[84] One of the final missions of the war was a sweep on 3 August by John Killian and Flight Sergeant Bell who 'concentrated their bombing on huts between Uluono and Kapsu Plus, destroying one hut. The Dawn Patrol overshot their target at Kimidan but two of their depth charges cratered the coast road.'[85]

The New Zealanders were at the end of a long and at times desperate road. For 14 Squadron the journey ended on 7 August when — in the last entry of their first wartime operations book — the squadron was 'secured as from 1200 hours'[86] and began packing for a move to Borneo via Los Negros. The war ended before they became operational there.

Initially, the war was not expected to end as early as August. There was no indication of a Japanese surrender and plans were laid to invade Kyushu in November — Operation Olympic — and Honshu in March 1946 — Operation Coronet. Conservative estimates suggested 1,000,000 Allied casualties, and this was one of several factors prompting US President Harry S Truman to authorise deployment of a new weapon: the atomic bomb. Hiroshima and Nagasaki were devastated, and the US threatened to target more cities. After some confusion Emperor Hirohito took direct action, and a cease-fire was declared on 15 August. The Australians made arrangements with local Japanese commanders in Bougainville to accept their surrender; RNZAF aircraft continued to patrol enemy positions and were fired on. Isitt signed for New Zealand at the formal surrender ceremonies on board USS *Missouri* in Tokyo Bay on 2 September.

The RNZAF was involved in a variety of repatriation programmes in the immediate aftermath of the war. New Zealand prisoners at Singapore were an early priority, and Squadron Leader M L Pirie had Dakotas fitted out as air ambulances soon after the Japanese surrender. However, he could not despatch them until Singapore was formally relieved by the British on 2 September. The first RNZAF Dakotas landed at Kallang on 13 September and eventually brought back 156 New Zealanders.

Demobilisation was already well under way — strident public voices were calling for reductions even before the fighting in the Pacific ended, and the RNZAF actually began shedding men in July 1945. A very large number of aircraft were on order — part of a re-equipment programme intended to replace the F-4U Corsairs with P-51 Mustangs and the PV-1 Venturas with PV-2 Harpoons. All but four Harpoons were cancelled, along with the last 89 Corsairs which had been delayed first by snowstorms at the factory, and then by lack of transport into the South Pacific. However, 60 Corsairs which had been in transit arrived at Los Negros between June and August — the United States would not take back aircraft that had been despatched. The New Zealand government also cancelled orders for 167 Mustangs and 41

Douglas C-47 Dakota transports, but thirty of the P-51's were also in transit and had to be accepted at a cost of $US61,000 each, plus shipping.

Bases in the Pacific were rapidly closed down. Some squadrons were disbanded almost immediately; No.6 Squadron ceased operations on 9 September. Other units flew their aircraft back to New Zealand, supported by 5 Squadron Catalinas in 'Dumbo' role. Other Catalinas filled a transport role. Many men were brought home by Nos 40 and 41 Squadrons, and about 2000 came back on the *Wahine*. By the end of the year, only 700 servicemen remained in the Pacific, about a tenth of those who had been stationed there in February. However, the demobilisation pools at Auckland, Wellington and Christchurch discharged only a hundred men a day each — they were hampered by lack of medical examiners — and there was substantial ill-feeling, even a mutinous mood among men desperate to return to civilian life. Many of those remaining in the service were formally discharged in July 1946.

CHAPTER SIX

Post-war deployments 1946–60

'The transfer of 14 Fighter Bomber Squadron is essentially the transfer of part of our defence obligations from the Middle East to South East Asia'

– Keith Holyoake, 1955

After the Second World War, New Zealand initially looked to traditional ties with Britain for security. Although the government had decided to accept the Statute of Westminster — which made New Zealand a sovereign nation within the Commonwealth — there was no question of moving away from close security orientation with Britain. At the 1946 Commonwealth leaders meeting, Nash expressed a hope that a Commonwealth acting in unity might become a third world power to balance the predominant United States and Soviet Union. From New Zealand's perspective, the Commonwealth certainly offered the only means of collective security at the time. New Zealand was still on the outer as far as the United States was concerned and there were ongoing arguments over the use of island bases in the Pacific. It was through the British connection that the RNZAF was involved in the occupation of Japan and the Berlin airlift. Airmen were also sent to serve with the RAF, and a strong RNZAF presence was maintained in the Middle East for some years.

The immediate post-war years nonetheless brought uncertainty for the RNZAF. The main focus was on demobilisation. Squadrons were disbanded and wartime bases closed down. Hundreds of surplus aircraft were put out to pasture at Rukuhia and eventually scrapped. Until the post-war size and role could be determined, the 'interim' function of the RNZAF was mainly limited to operating a variety of civil airline routes until the National Airways Corporation could take them over. The only operational role was the contribution to the Japanese occupation forces. Weary of war and eager to demobilise, New Zealand had yet to consider the shape of its post-war armed forces. Certainly there was no question of continuing wartime levels of expenditure; and it was also clear that any peacetime levels would be minimal. The only real certainty was that the post-war RNZAF would take its place alongside army and navy — there was little chance of repeating the lean decades for the air services that had followed the First World War. In 1919, air force had yet to take its place alongside sea force as a key element of maritime power projection; New Zealand defence thinking of the day had reflected the priority of the navy. The change had occurred in the mid-1930s, and by 1945 the lesson had been driven well home.

Japanese Occupation, 1946–48

The Japanese surrender in August 1945 opened the way for the Allies to enter Japan itself, and arrangements were quickly made for representative forces from all allied powers to do so. At policy level, New Zealand's involvement reflected the deep national need to be involved in any post-war-settlement; but the Kiwis were still *persona-non-grata* with the United States government and became involved through British auspices. No. 14 Squadron was selected to join the British Occupation Forces in Japan, under twenty eight year old Squadron Leader Jesse Julius de Willimoff. Amid the general mood of demobilisation a call went out for volunteers. Nolan Wynn was one of nearly two thousand men who offered to go — and one of the few selected. 'Once again I was up before a selection board,' he recalled 'followed by two weeks of ceremonial drill.'[1] Squadron Leader J E Dunnan, 'The Bull', organised training. By early 1946 the men were ready to depart. They were paraded before Isitt at Ardmore on 15 February and on 8 March marched in farewell down Queen Street. Then the men, their twenty four Goodyear-built FG-1D Corsairs, and three months worth of supplies and equipment were loaded on board the light fleet carrier HMS *Glory.*

For some, the sea was an unfamiliar world, made worse because the carrier rolled badly. Hammocks were a blessing. Even so, some men were seasick and spent their time prone on the flight deck. Nolan Wynn photographed some of them and later recalled:

> *We mustered each day at the rum locker for a rum ration which was charged on your pay sheet. I not being used to and not being very fond of booze used to give it away to sailors for I did not wish to be seen turning it down. ...Each morning the bosun's whistle would blow early with the injunction 'rise and shine you've had your time and I've had mine. Up guard and stowage hammocks.' Upon this command you rolled out of your hammock, took it down, folded it up, and stowed it away to make room for your flight members to have breakfast. It was uncomfortably hot under steel decks in the tropics, so we were issued with salt tablets to swallow to replace salt lost in heavy perspiration. I believe horses sweat, men perspire. I know I sweated a lot. It was much better to sit in the gun sponsons where there was a bit of breeze and watch the flying fish leap out of a wave and dart away. It was a non-stop trip to Japan and the closer we got the colder it became. ...It took sixteen days to sail to Kobe in Japan and wind up in a partly bombed barracks on Iwakuni airfield.*[2]

Winter still held a grip on Japan. Flying from Iwakuni airfield, seventeen miles from Hiroshima, the squadron was charged with keeping a wary eye on the Japanese who, after four years of desperate warfare, were not trusted. Certainly their remaining military strength had come as a surprise; American estimates of 700 aircraft left intact in Japan were hopelessly optimistic. In fact the Japanese had 12,775 aircraft including 1,131 built in the last month of the war alone. There were also 3,350,000 trained troops, 4,000,000 reservists and a 'home guard' of 28,000,000 men, women and children. Fears of renewed Japanese militarism remained high and the Allies were vigilant. Among other tasks, the Kiwi pilots had to overfly airfields to make sure the Japanese were not filling in bomb craters. The RNZAF also located several 40 mm anti-aircraft cannon and radar sites which the Japanese had not announced. Regular patrols over the Sea of Japan also bore fruit during September as the squadron was able to locate the boat refugees escaping the post-war settlement that divided Korea into northern and southern zones.

The New Zealanders found Japan a 'whole new world, the people, the houses, the countryside with its fishing villages surrounded by paddy fields, for rice was the staple diet, although the population was basically starving and would eat anything. There was an illegal though thriving black market.'[3] They were stationed only fifteen miles from Hiroshima. Nolan Wynn thought the 'devastation there was unbelievable, with piles of concrete rubble and an air of desolation pervading the whole area.'[4] The Inland Sea was 'littered with half sunken ships, the result of American bombing.'[5] Later, some of the men were sent to Tokyo 'to show the flag and see the sights.' Here too the scars of war remained:

> *Large areas of the city were devastated by fire, following American bombing, but it was still home to many millions of people. There was a loop line running around the city with trains running in opposite directions day and night. Streets were numbered from north to south and east to west. There was also the underground and a rail system as well as on road level, and plenty of rickshaws. We marched through the city singing 'you can't piss us off any more etc'. ...The Japs would stop and bow to us for they had no understanding of English. Social contact with people outside of the services was lacking. This was starting to have a detrimental effect on morale, which was probably the reason for the spontaneous singing outburst.*[6]

Despite the proximity of Australian, British and American forces, many New Zealanders felt alone and isolated from the familiar fields of home. Mail was eagerly awaited:

> *A Dakota mail plane would arrive on station about once a month and the grapevine would send the word round the station that it was an hour or so away, so the station personnel would eagerly cluster at the airstrip*

awaiting their mail with each letter being flung out of the plane and a person calling out Smith, Brown, Jones etc. Not much finesse in that but very effective.[7]

The Dakota mail run by 41 Squadron was one of the longest scheduled mail routes in the world, and some 104 flights were made during the deployment, carrying 1477 passengers, 114,420 lbs of freight and 248,711 lbs of mail.

There was a strict non-fraternisation policy. Women were forbidden; posters were even put up in the barracks warning that particular women were 'dangerous'. Food was another subject close to the men's hearts. Meals were very poor at first, and the men quickly discovered that some of the rations meant for the squadron were being diverted to the British officers' mess in Kure. The food the British rejected was sent to Iwakuni — including green meat and weevilly flour. It was an impossible situation that the 'erks' remedied with home-grown ingenuity. Blockade and bombing had wrecked the Japanese economy and there was little to be had locally; indeed, the men were warned not to eat Japanese food and Nolan Wynn recalled seeing starving Japanese rummaging through the squadron rubbish bins looking for scraps. Nevertheless, cactus stoves soon appeared in the barracks. Nolan Wynn recalled these were built of:

a Yank petrol can lying flat with part of the top section removed, a piece of metal suspended in the aperture with a can of old oil with a pipe leading down to the suspended plate. A chimney at the far end of the can to make a 'draught', a piece of rag flung on to the plate which soon became saturated with oil, and when this was lit the cactus stove was soon roaring regulated by the flow of oil. Eggs which we bought from the Japs were cooked as well as some tinned food brought from the canteen, so we then had no need to go to the mess for meals. Not the Ritz but we managed.... I lost a lot of weight for I did not thrive on this diet and when I ultimately returned to NZ I weighed only 9 stone 5 lbs, but felt reasonably well.[8]

He recalled that the American Post Exchange canteens were a 'magnet'; the RNZAF had nothing to compare with them, though their own canteen was 'wet' as opposed to the 'dry' of temperance-minded Americans.

'Unfortunately the nearest PX to Iwakuni was several miles north.'[9] The food situation eventually prompted a general strike and demands for immediate improvement.

There was only one casualty despite constant air operations. Flight Lieutenant C W N Wright was killed when his F-4U Corsair crashed during take-off. But there were a number of other incidents, including one frightening moment when a petrol dump erupted into flames during a replenishment operation. Nobody was hurt, but the men hurried to roll drums of volatile fuel out of the way as other drums began exploding. Half a million gallons were lost.

The first men deployed to Japan were rotated home in December 1946, after a brief ceremony attended by Air Vice Marshall Cecil Bouchier, commanding the British Commonwealth Air Force in Japan. Some of the men flew back to New Zealand by Dakota, island-hopping through South East Asia to Australia and across the Tasman. Their replacements remained at Iwakuni under Squadron Leader Douglas St George. In early 1948 the squadron moved to Bofu. After a further change of personnel, the entire squadron returned home in November 1948, making the voyage on board the *Westralia*. Their aircraft were left behind in Japan and burnt.

Berlin Airlift, 1948–49

Iwakuni was the only overseas squadron deployment by the RNZAF in the first few post-war years, but RNZAF pilots saw action over Berlin during 1948 as a direct outcome of the effort to pursue closer ties with the Commonwealth. At the end of the war, the Soviets gave the Allies access to the western half of Berlin through a narrow 'corridor'. However, relations deteriorated steadily, and in 1947 the United States, prompted by Secretary of State George C Marshall, launched what was formally known as the European Recovery Plan to bolster the West against Soviet aggression.

This scheme raised Stalin's hackles, and the crisis was not long in coming. In February 1948, British, French and American officials discussed re-industrialising Germany. A German parliamentary assembly was authorised in June, and on the 23rd, the Western powers announced that the new Deutschmark would apply in their sectors of Berlin. Stalin took this as provocation and closed the 'corridor' the next day, isolating West Berlin with its two million souls.

The city required thousands of tons of supplies daily, mostly coal and food. US Army General Lucius Clay recommended an armoured assault to reopen the corridor, but Air Force Generals Curtis Le May and Henry 'Hap' Arnold favoured an air bridge. They received prompt political commitment, and within two days the first American aircraft were moving supplies into the city. Operation Plainfare remains the world's largest airborne supply operation; between July 1948 and May 1949, when Stalin finally admitted defeat, 184,000 flights moved 1,500,000 tons of cargo, enough to keep the Western sectors of the city alive.

Three RNZAF crews from 41 Squadron operated British owned C-47 Dakotas during this massive operation. The three crews were led by Flight Lieutenants C J Fraser, J D Philips, and G Haslop. Originally despatched for six months, they served for thirteen, working twelve-hour days, typically completing two or three round trips from their base at Lubeck. The biggest problem was exhaustion and traffic congestion. There were three official air routes into Berlin; a northern route from Hamburg; another running centrally from Hanover; and a third from the American sector near Frankfurt. All converged on just two airfields, the Tempelhof and Gatow. At the height of the airlift, aircraft were landing and taking off at Gatow every three minutes. The tricky operation left no room for error, and there was barely enough space for the C-47's, C-54's and other large transport aircraft involved to clear each other's slipstream. Fog often interrupted operations, but the RAF air controllers who had responsibility for the entire operation seldom seemed to get ruffled.

A typical flight for the New Zealand crews began at Lubeck; they flew towards Berlin down the 'Hamburg' corridor for about seventy minutes before homing on the radio beacon at Frohnau, sixteen miles from Gatow. Here they would descend to 1500 feet and receive landing instructions. They went straight in; there was no room to circle the airfield. On the ground, the Dakotas could typically be unloaded in half an hour, then immediately take off on the return flight.

Legend has it that the New Zealanders moved only coal, but in fact they toted a whole range of cargoes. Phillips arrived on 4 November and on his second flight took 6830 lbs tea and flour to Gatow, a similar quantity of coal on his third flight, then more flour, then coal again. However, by 20 November his loads had become highly variable. He took 6880 lbs of sultanas that day, and on the 22nd toted 6908 lbs of noodles, followed by 6893 lbs of baby food. Next day he carried 6858 lbs of dehydrated eggs and flour; the 6820 lbs coal that followed during his second flight of the day was the first coal he had carried for some time. Two days later he and his crew made two journeys toting 6885 lbs of dried peaches, and on 26 November he carried 6860 lbs of newspapers. Coal was a rarity during these days. Flights back were seldom as heavily laden; Phillips and his crew evacuated refugees, took what the manifest called 'misc. freight', and even moved goods produced by Berlin industries such as refrigerators.[10]

The RAF requested further assistance after the blockade was lifted, and a relief crew was sent from New Zealand, joined periodically by other New Zealanders on their way to serve with the RAF's No. 24 Commonwealth Squadron. The last RNZAF-piloted Dakota left Berlin on 11 August 1949. Some 1577 tons of coal, among other cargoes, were shifted by the RNZAF pilots during the blockade, in 473 sorties.

Restructuring the RNZAF, 1947–51

The RNZAF entered a waiting phase during the first years after the war. Government had agreed only to an 'interim' air service until policy could be sorted out. Leadership during these difficult years fell Nevill. Made Air Vice Marshal, he had an uphill battle with a demoralised service and indifferent government eager to slash defence spending from wartime levels. Recruiting depots were opened in early 1946, but efforts principally revolved around shedding men. Apart from deployment to J-force and the low level ongoing exchange with the RAF, there was little activity. Some civil air routes were established and operated by Short Sunderland Mk III flying boats. The RNZAF began a regular Fiji-Auckland service in June 1946, flying the route until October 1947 when the National Airways Corporation took over both task and aircraft.

American aircraft dried up with the end of Lend Lease; eighty De Havilland DH98 Mosquitoes, including thirty new-build aircraft, were ordered in July 1946 at bargain prices as interim equipment for three squadrons until post-war policy could be sorted out. This decision was not entirely well advised and many of the aircraft remained in storage for years. In October, the British Air Ministry gifted the 75 Squadron number to the RNZAF in recognition of services the New Zealanders of the squadron had contributed during the war. The name was given to the former No.2 (Bomber Reconnaissance squadron) of the RNZAF, based at Ohakea and re-equipping with Mosquitoes. Early plans for a slimmed-down service reflected a return to pre-war thinking by which regional security was secondary to the wider ties of Empire. Although New Zealand recognised that British power in the Pacific had declined sharply, relations with the United States remained mediocre.

For the RNZAF the practical result was a plan fielded in 1947 to establish five regular and five territorial squadrons, with strong long-range bomber capability, able to contribute to Commonwealth defence in the South Pacific and the associated 'vital strategic zone.'[11] This was essentially an updated version of the scheme Cochrane had devised ten years earlier, notably with the focus on Singapore and long-range bombers. But demobilisation had left the RNZAF in a relatively unbalanced state. There were not enough men left to fill the ground trades, and skilled personnel had to be recruited from as far afield as the United Kingdom, where former RAF officers and experienced tradesmen were offered work. Compulsory military training provided some manpower after 1949, by which time the RNZAF stood at around 4000 personnel. An Officers School opened at Whenuapai, flying training got under way again at Wigram, and the No.1 Repair Depot was transferred to RNZAF Woodbourne. Operations continued at Lauthala Bay with the flying boats of No.5 Squadron. One hundred women were recruited from England in 1951. One fell sick while on the way out, and the group became known as the 'Ninety Nine' in WAAF service. The WAAF was officially dubbed the Women's Royal New Zealand Air Force in 1954 by Queen Elizabeth.

Jet aircraft were slow to arrive. A Gloster Meteor FIII was supplied to New Zealand as a demonstrator in December 1945, flown by Squadron Leader Bob McKay, and a Jet Propulsion Unit formed around it at Ohakea. Fifty six pilots were trained to fly the Meteor, but structural fatigue led to speed restrictions and the aircraft was retired in mid-1947. In the end, Meteors were never ordered, but the aircraft was a useful introduction to jet operations.

Although more than 400 aircraft remained on inventory by the end of the 1940s, the RNZAF's equipment was essentially worn out. Nevill pointed out that New Zealand was the only British Dominion without modern aircraft. Given the need for inter-operability with the British there was no question regarding the source. The outbreak of the Korean war prompted action, and a modest procurement programme got under way to bring the RNZAF into the jet age. Aircraft delivered up to the mid-1950s included twelve Bristol Freighter 170 Mk 31 transports, four Handley Page Hastings transports, eighteen de Havilland Vampires, and six two-seat Vampire trainers. Only one squadron was usually equipped with Vampires at a time — No. 14 Squadron received the first batch of eighteen, later handing them over to No. 75 Squadron and picking up leased examples for overseas service. More were procured during the decade, however, both to make good attrition losses and also because the Vampire had only a short airframe life — generally about 700 hours — as a result of its balsa-plywood fuselage construction.

Total deliveries eventually came to forty six single-seat and eleven two-seat examples. Other aircraft of the day were more durable. Twenty eight de Havilland Devons were purchased in the early 1950s, and the last did not leave service until 1980. Sixteen Short Sunderland MR5 Flying Boats were reconditioned and entered service as maritime patrol aircraft. They were supplemented by the wartime fleet of North American T-6 Harvard trainers. The thirty P-51 Mustangs that had been in storage since the end of the war went to the territorial squadrons.

War Plans and the Middle East

New Zealand defence thinking reverted to its traditional pro-British form during the late 1940s. The defeat of Japan had ended the forty-year tension between British and Australasian defence perception, and New Zealand perceived no threat in the Pacific. The main fear was that Stalin might launch an assault through the Caucasus, threatening trade lines to Britain through the Suez Canal. Prime Minister Peter Fraser discussed specific war plans during visits to London in 1948 and 1949. From these meetings came the general conclusion that New Zealand forces were best employed in the Middle East — a traditional destination in two world wars.

Two Royal New Zealand Navy vessels went to the Mediterranean for six months in 1950, and in June 1951, at the Commonwealth Ministers of Defence meeting in London, Defence Minister T L MacDonald opened preliminary discussions to deploy an RNZAF squadron to the same area. The new Prime Minister, Sydney Holland, took the matter up with Sir John Slessor, RAF Chief of Air Staff, and the decision to deploy air forces was finally taken in early 1952. No. 14 Squadron was selected because of its experience with Vampires; the squadron was to surrender its aircraft to 75 Squadron and fly borrowed RAF aircraft in the Middle East. Holland believed the move would be 'very valuable to the RNZAF which should profit greatly in efficiency.'[12] The move was mirrored across the Tasman; the Australian government despatched a Vampire wing to Malta the same year.

An advance party under Flight Lieutenant H A Farrar flew to Cyprus in late September 1952. The rest of the squadron followed in October. The unit came under Squadron Leader S M Hope, who had flown in the Pacific and served with the squadron in Japan. His deputies, Flight Lieutenants T R Rabone and J D Waugh, had also served in the Pacific. The unit were equipped with Mk IX Vampires from RAF stocks and came under the operational command of No. 205 Group RAF, part of the Middle East Air Force headquartered at Abu Sueir near the Suez Canal. No. 14 Squadron itself was based at RAF Nicosia, in Cyprus. This base consisted of three airfields, Nicosia, Timbou and Lakatamia, and was also home to the No. 26 Armament Practise School.

Operations ranged across the entire Middle Eastern theatre. The squadron deployed on occasion to the Suez Canal — under an hour away by air — for exercises with RAF squadrons. In 1953 the squadron flew alongside the RAAF to defend Malta against naval attacks by US Sixth Fleet aircraft. Some 125 sorties were flown in 96 hours with twelve aircraft, a very high serviceability rate. The squadron also developed two aerobatic teams, and fifteen aircraft conducted display flying in East Africa during mid-1953 as part of the celebrations to mark the coronation of Queen Elizabeth II. Code-named Long Trek Two, the squadron deployed in three flights of five. One aerobatic team went to Kenya, and Uganda, and a separate display flight went as far south as Tanganyika. The aircraft deployed down the Nile along the old flying boat route. One hop included landing at a rough airstrip to refuel from jerry cans.

By early 1955 the New Zealanders had become a familiar sight in Cyprus and nearby airspace. Work began that year with 29 sorties on 3 January 'with the pilots doing pairs tailchasing, continuation and battle fours.' However the year did not get away to a very good start:

> *Flying Officer Currin had an engine failure in Vampire WE 111, and after the first flight in WR 125 it was found that the port wing by the air intake and No.1 rib was badly wrinkled... Flying Officer Currin who was flying in the Maiphou area when his engine failed glided the twenty two miles back to the airfield and made a successful wheels-down landing, without any further damage to the aircraft.*[13]

The deployment gave the airmen opportunity to fly with aircraft never seen in New Zealand. At the end of the month, Flying Officer M R Hawkins and Sergeant Pilot Morgan were about to take off when a Convair B-36D made its way past. Nicknamed the 'aluminium cloud', the enormous bomber was the largest aircraft of the day, able to carry nuclear weapons direct from the United States to targets in the Soviet Union. The two New Zealanders promptly chased it and 'formated on the monster which was cruising at 20,000 feet on six of its 10 engines. It is a most impressive looking machine and a Vampire looks ridiculously small alongside it.'[14]

One of the benefits of being posted overseas was the opportunity to turn tourist at government expense. The RNZAF aircrews at Cyprus lost no opportunity. Even three years after the squadron deployed there, turnover meant that a steady stream of new airmen were arriving, all eager to experience the sights and sounds of foreign lands. Egypt, just a few hours flying away, was a particular attraction, as it had been for Kiwis posted into the Mediterranean theatre since the First World War; and in late February 1955 a large number of Kiwis from the squadron went on leave to Cairo, a place familiar to many New Zealand service personnel since the First World War. The Squadron historian M R Hawkins recorded that:

> *The highlight of the trip was of course the visit to the pyramids but the shine was taken off this a bit, by the locals who plagued us like flies, offering us camel rides, together with pictures of the pyramids etc... Unfortunately a large crowd of American tourists were also visiting the city at the same time as we were, and everything was priced "for the Yankees", which automatically put the prices of things above our means.*[15]

New defence priorities, 1955–60

The RNZAF's work during the late 1950s was dictated by a major shift in defence thinking. For New Zealand, a return to the British 'fold' after the war was a comfortable step, but the developing bi-polarisation of the international system forced dramatic changes. The Cold War seemed confined to Europe until Mao Zedong's 1949 victory in China drew attention to Asia. Although this did not immediately change Kiwi defence thinking, a No. 41 Squadron detachment was sent to Singapore as a response to the general situation.

The real change for New Zealand was driven by events surrounding the Korean civil war. The outbreak of this conflict in 1950 prompted fears in the United States that Japan might also be vulnerable to communism. The result was a very favourable peace treaty with the Japanese, even permitting rearmament. There was considerable alarm in both Australia and New Zealand as a result; memory of the desperate days of 1942 was too close for comfort. Relations had begun to thaw after the Canberra Pact debacle, and the prospect of alliance with the US against a re-armed Japan was raised by the Australians in February 1951, when Secretary of State John Foster Dulles visited Canberra. The Americans were initially reluctant, but a pact had been prepared by July, was formally signed in September, and came into force in April 1952. The name ANZUS was adopted in August. There was no expiry date; the only possible cancellation was outlined in Article X, which stated that any party could cease to become a member by giving twelve months' notice to the government of Australia. As an alliance ANZUS was not automatic protection — it simply promised consultation in event of war in the Pacific, and did not signal an immediate shift away from Britain or reduction of traditional defence interests in Europe. Indeed, the pact noted that New Zealand and Australia both had military obligations outside the Pacific area, and as late as 1955, Holland was describing the United Kingdom as having 'a great deal to offer as an ally.'[16] Nevertheless the arrangement became fundamental to New Zealand defence thinking and policy.

Focus on Asia continued to develop through the 1950s. Uncertainty surrounding the Korean War prompted a modest procurement programme for the RNZAF, and the fact that communism had evidently spread from China to Korea also prompted concerns that other nations would fall. These fears were genuinely held at the time. While the flaws of communism were made obvious after the end of the Cold War, the 1950s were years of psychological *hubris* for a West that had been utterly victorious in the Second World War. In the United States, Senator Joseph McCarthy saw 'red', and while not everybody shared his view of rot from within, there was genuine and widespread belief that a communist threat existed to Europe and Asia. These sentiments were reflected in New Zealand where Prime Minister Sidney Holland utilised the 'communist threat' as a political tool to bolster support against the Labour party, and where the 1951 waterfront strike suggested to some that the radical left might have already taken hold. External policy was guided by the same thinking; New Zealand supported the Colombo Plan as a means of defeating Asian communism through economic means and gave arms to support the French in Indo China during 1952.

This war created a new focus for fear of Asian communism, and the siege of Dien Bien Phu in early 1954 by the Viet Minh prompted international response. New Zealand Minister of External Affairs, Thomas Webb, agreed with US and British proposals for new collective security arrangements in South East Asia. If the strategically important and resource-rich nations in South East Asia fell to communism, he argued, 'Australia and New Zealand would be gravely threatened.'[17] At the international conference held in Manila that September, New Zealand signed the South East Asia Collective Defence Treaty and Pacific Charter, which created the South East Asian Treaty Organisation (SEATO). This arrangement was subsequently responsible for several RNZAF deployments into South East Asia. New Zealand's motivation was only partly due to fear of the 'red threat'. Communism was being spread through rebel activity, itself destabilising regardless of ideology. A state of emergency was declared in Malaysia in 1948 in response to activity by 'communist terrorists'.

Against this background the Middle East was less important. To Holland, it had become 'increasingly clear' that the 'security of South East Asia, and... Malaya, are of special significance to New Zealand.'[18] A special Cabinet meeting in early 1955 discussed withdrawing 14 Squadron from Cyprus, and during a meeting in London, Holland couched the move in terms of relieving the British defence burden in Malaya. The British agreed. Keith Holyoake described the shift succinctly. 'The transfer of 14 Fighter Bomber Squadron is essentially the transfer of part of our defence obligations from the Middle East to South East Asia.'[19]

Operation Firedog — the Malayan Emergency

The return of the RNZAF to Malaya brought an operational role; RNZAF units at Singapore were intended to join the Far East Air Force (FEAF) to work closely with RAAF and RAF squadrons against the 'communist terrorists'. Plans approved at Cabinet level called for rapid crew rotation to ensure the men were 'at the same high state of operational efficiency as other Commonwealth airmen' — a self-deprecating idea that was probably unjustified.[20] Plans were laid to re-equip No. 14 Squadron with leased De Havilland Venoms, a Rolls Royce Ghost-engined derivative of the Vampire. The unit was joined in theatre by a transport detachment of No. 41 Squadron, re-equipped with Bristol Freighters. Long-range de Havilland Hastings freighters operating from Whenuapai supported the deployment, and there was talk of sending flying boats occasionally from Fiji for joint exercises. Total costs were estimated to amount to £1,000,000 per annum — a very significant sum for the time.

For the personnel of 14 Squadron the move from Cyprus produced mixed emotions. 'All things being equal the Squadron will be sorry to leave the area,' Hawkins wrote in the squadron operations book, 'as it has afforded them an endless variety on the Middle Eastern way of life, their visits to archaic castles and monasteries has been really worthwhile and they have had opportunities to visit places of interest that would otherwise have been denied to them.'[21]

The importance of the deployment to Malaya can be gauged by the fact that both Holland and Defence Minister Thomas MacDonald personally inspected the base at Tengah, near Singapore. Holland was enthusiastic, reporting that 'no better accommodation or amenities could be wished for.'[22] The airmen agreed — the advance contingent of 14 Squadron personnel that arrived in Tengah on 1 April under Flight Lieutenant McIntyre were particularly impressed by the 'fine swimming pool complete with 1, 3 and 5 metre diving boards.'[23] The first Vampire arrived from Cyprus on 9 April, the second five days later. Meanwhile, remaining Squadron personnel in Cyprus continued packing, and the last to leave were the married families who left on 29 April on the troop ship *Empire Clyde*.

The British delivered the first Venom on 24 April, but the New Zealanders soon discovered it had an old-model engine with unmodified flame-cans. These short-life items were due for renewal in just thirteen flying hours.

'This unhappy state of affairs was put right by exchanging our Venom for one of 60 Squadron's... we are pleased to note that 60 Squadron attempted to look quite happy.'[24] Flying had to wait for helmets that could be plugged into the Venom's systems. Meanwhile the squadron took to the air in its Vampires, practising against targets in the jungle laid by Army Austers. Flight Lieutenant S McIntyre tried taking the Venom up on 30 April. 'The noise of a [starter] cartridge bring fired is becoming a little less frightening,' the unit historian noted 'and fewer people are now flinging themselves to the floor to avoid the "rocket".'[25] However, the starter went unserviceable so there was no flying that day.

Offensive operations were code-named Firedog, and the first strike by 14 Squadron took place on 1 May 1955, when McIntyre led five Vampires against terrorist positions. 'A lot of valuable information was gained, particularly in timing.'[26] Five days later, four Vampires and the Venom took part in another raid. 'The Venom was flown by Flight Lieutenant McIntyre and we believe this is the first time a Venom has been used on active service operations anywhere in the world.'[27] Sixteen aircraft were leased, but the full complement did not arrive for nine months. The British also delivered late model Vampires, initially to supplement the Venoms until the squadron was up to strength, later to act as trainers.

Firedog missions were well under way by June. The squadron often flew with other RAF and RAAF aircraft types, including Avro Lincolns and Canberras. The Venoms were able to carry loads including two 1000 lb bombs or eight rockets, but the type was ill suited to the tropics, and on one occasion in June 1956, air-to-air firings had to be cancelled because there were only three Venoms with serviceable guns. Airframe life was eventually restricted to 750 hours for the same reason, and the squadron went through a large number of aircraft during their deployment — though the percentage written off due to accident was low. In one rare incident, Flight Lieutenant M F Palmer suffered engine failure while at low level over Johore Bahru. He attempted to trade speed for height, but the Ghost refused to restart and he ejected, landing in the water near a police launch which picked him up almost immediately. Vampires were also lost; Colin Rudd had a T.11 over the sea in April 1957 when he experienced engine vibrations. He crash landed in five feet of water near the beach and was quickly rescued. Next day the aircraft was dragged up, but found to have been ruined by its overnight immersion.

Nevertheless 'somebody got into the cockpit and was surprised when the flaps pumped up normally.'[28]

Air activity peaked in June 1956 with 'Operation Canterbury', heavy mixed strikes against targets in the Kluang area. On 18 June, the New Zealanders were behind eight RAF 60 Squadron Venoms over the target, 'and a most impressive sight it was to see the bombs exploding, with a visible shock wave going through the jungle.'[29] In October there were riots in Singapore, and 'the defence system of the station immediately went into action.' Next day RNZAF personnel took up guard positions — eight armed men and one officer stood at the gate — but there were no incidents.

In May 1957 the squadron was sent to Butterworth but they were back at Tengah by November. That month there was a brief flap when an unidentified 'bogie' was detected near the base. This 'turned out to be a met balloon and not a Sputnik after all.'[30] In early 1958 the squadron briefly deployed to Don Muang air base, Thailand, but their return to New Zealand was imminent. By April there were only ten serviceable Venoms, two of which could not carry bombs. There was an aerobatic farewell display in mid-May, and Squadron Leader Tucker received the Malay Kris in recognition of their work from the Malayan Federal Minister of Defence. Half the personnel completed a conversion to Canberras. In May the remaining Venoms were returned to the RAF; the RNZAF had notched up 12,365.4 hours on the type since 1955.

The return of 14 Squadron to New Zealand did not end RNZAF operations from Singapore. In the middle of that year, a detachment of No. 75 Squadron went to England under Geoffrey Highet to convert to the English Electric Canberra, Britain's medium jet bomber — an aircraft heavier than some heavy bombers of the Second World War. After training they flew their leased Canberra B.2's to Singapore to join other RAF Canberra squadrons, where they continued anti-communist work and conducted exchange visits with US squadrons equipped with B-57's — American-built versions of the same aircraft.

Antarctic operations

Scientific interest in the Antarctic flourished during the 1950s. Transport to and around the frozen sub-continent was transformed by aircraft. The Cold

War also gave political motivation, and by mid-1955 the United States had eight aircraft based at Wigram to support Deep Freeze scientific operations on the sub-continent. The British planned their own thrust in the form of the massive Commonwealth Trans-Antarctic Expedition. New Zealand was expected to play a key role, and air capability was essential. To prepare for work on the ice the RNZAF seconded Squadron Leader John Claydon to join US flights south during the 1955-56 season. The following year the RNZAF began flights of its own to support the huge multi-year programme, which had a variety of objectives intended to culminate in the first motorised crossing of the ice, and was one focus of the 1957-58 'international geophysical year' — an eighteen month period of unprecedented global study.

In May 1956 the RNZAF Antarctic Flight formed under Claydon, equipped with a de Havilland Beaver and a Mk 7 Auster. The Beaver had been purchased for £32,000 of which half was raised by public donation in Auckland, and was formally named 'City of Auckland' by Sir Edmund and Lady Hillary. Both aircraft were especially prepared for the ice, with additional instruments such as gyro-compasses, astro-compasses, radio transmitters, and radio homing beacons. Bomb racks were fitted to drop sledges and supplies. Training was intensive and included flights to support a training camp Hillary established on Tasman glacier. The Auster was damaged there in August when it overturned while testing ski landing gear. It was repaired in time to be loaded as deck cargo on HMNZS *Endeavour* for the journey south in December, but the port wing was accidentally rammed into a nearby freighter as the ship manoeuvered. RNZAF engineers the damaged wing in Port Chalmers, and after repairs it was taken to Antarctica by the United States, where it arrived in late January. The Auster took to the air on floats at the end of the month, but was re-equipped with skis for subsequent work.

Air capability had become critical to Antarctic operations by this time. One early mission was a mercy dash to rescue a member of a sledge party who had fallen ill, thirty miles across the Ross Sea ice shelf. Other tasks included finding sledge routes over the Victoria Land glacial fields and air supplying depots. Darkness and poor weather did not deter experimental winter flying — though snow drifts sometimes entirely buried the Auster. Two days before Christmas 1957, Claydon and Flying Officer W I Cranfield flew to the South Pole on a US aircraft. The RNZAF flag they left there was the first Commonwealth flag of any kind to fly at the pole since 1912.

Both the Beaver and Auster returned to New Zealand at the end of the 1957-58 season, after notching up more than 300 hours in Antarctic skies, and Claydon was awarded the Air Force Cross. The aircraft were on the ice again for the 1959-60 season, but the Beaver crashed in January 1960 in whiteout conditions near Beardmore glacier. Squadron Leader L C Jeffs and Flight Lieutenant P S Rule were not badly hurt, but efforts to get them out were hampered by poor weather and hazardous terrain. A US Navy attempt to extract them with a Dakota failed. Cranfield — now a Flight Lieutenant — took off on a two-day mission in the Auster to rescue them, landing several times on the ice in poor weather to refuel en route.

This ended RNZAF flights over Antarctica for some years. Scientific work continued, but the RNZAF did not have the capability to fly to the sub-continent, and although RNZAF pilots were attached to US Navy squadrons flying south in the early 1960s, the New Zealand Antarctic Research Programme had to rely on American support. Direct flights became possible when the RNZAF took delivery of three C-130 Hercules in 1965. No. 40 Squadron made the first flight to the ice that year. Carey Adamson, then a flying officer, recalled the event in the Air Force history *Charles C-130* :

> *We had to deliberately fly past a point of no return to a destination with no alternate. We had heard horror stories of the destination weather closing in with no warning and shutting down the airfield in a matter of minutes. Although we knew all the theory, we were not sure what landing on the ice would actually be like... When the coast of Antarctica came into sight, the intercom became silent as everyone took in the grandeur of the scenery and the alien nature of the continent. After seven hours and 10 minutes the first RNZAF flight to the Antarctic ended with an uneventful landing at Williams Field.*[31]

Hercules NZ 7003 carried 75,000 lb of cargo to the ice that season, beginning annual forays by RNZAF Hercules in support of New Zealand scientific work. The RNZAF was closely involved with recovery and investigation work after the 1979 crash of an Air New Zealand DC-10 on Mount Erebus. The C-130 Hercules NZ 7004 took a police and air accident team down to the site immediately, and subsequent flights by RNZAF Hercules brought back the bodies of the victims.

Operations over Antarctica re-commenced in 1985 when a No.3 Squadron UH-1D Iroquois was brought south for work on the ice. This became an annual pilgrimage. Painted orange for identification, the helicopter was soon dubbed 'Orange Roughy'. Helicopter operations on the ice itself went under the title Operation Snowbird. By the 1990s the RNZAF had a regular annual schedule of a dozen flights to the ice, named Operation Icecube, at a typical cost of around $18 million. Confidence in the ability to work with the aircraft grew to the point where even engine changes became possible. There were occasional incidents. In late 1996, Hercules NZ 7004 landed at Scott Base on three engines after a low oil warning light came on in No.4 engine. This complicated the landing rollout because directional control over the ice relied on differential thrust, but the aircraft landed safely. The problem was traced to a faulty oil level float switch.

CHAPTER SEVEN
Cold War Air Force 1957–85

The detachment ...made the men realise that their own service compared more than favourably with the US Air Force and that the living standards and way of life in New Zealand left little to be desired...'

— Squadron Leader C R Carter reporting on training in the United States, 1965

The late 1950s brought significant changes in defence thinking worldwide, notably a general shift from skeletal regular forces supported by part-time territorials to smaller 'forces in being'. For some nations these permanent forces were not so small; the United States conducted an unprecedented build-up through the decade, spurred by the 'red threat'. Protected by ANZUS, New Zealand did not see the need to follow suit, but changes were triggered in 1957 by a British Defence White Paper. This had profound effects on both British and Commonwealth defence policy. In a controversial move that had far reaching consequences for the aircraft industry, British Minister of Defence Duncan Sandys abolished new manned fighters for the RAF in favour of ground-based missiles. Both Australia and New Zealand followed this general lead. Fighters were the first casualty of a New Zealand Defence White Paper of June 1957, and for the second time in its career the RNZAF shifted from fighter/ground attack to bomber/interdiction. This defence review also imposed a variety of other reforms. Compulsory military training for Air Force and Navy was abolished, as was the Territorial Air Force.

New thinking: new aircraft

New Zealand security thinking focused on regional and Pacific affairs into the 1960s, through participation in regional alliances such as SEATO. Asia was one theatre where both super-powers were able to fight by proxy, and it was no coincidence that Soviet and Chinese support for communist groups in Vietnam, Thailand, Malaysia and Indonesia grew dramatically during this time. For New Zealand, the shift away from traditional Commonwealth thinking was accelerated by a further British White Paper of 1966 which heralded a sharp reduction in British defence interests in the Far East. The same year, both New Zealand and Australia joined the Asian and Pacific Council (ASPAC), a loose association that included Japan, Malaysia, Thailand and South Vietnam. New Zealand gained observer status with the Association of Southeast Asian Nations (ASEAN), formed in 1967. The transition away from British interests seemed complete at the end of the decade when the British government announced its intention to sever all military links with Malaysia by 1971, though the process actually took longer.

However, although New Zealand's attention was on South East Asia during the decade, a defence review in 1961 withdrew No.75 Squadron from Singapore as a cost-saving measure. In May 1962, Operation Scorpion took No. 41 Squadron, equipped with Bristol Freighters, to Korat as part of a SEATO response to communist forces on the border of Thailand. The unit was led by Squadron Leader B A Wood and came under the general command of US Lieutenant General James Richardson. It was withdrawn briefly to Singapore in December to support British operations in Borneo. Two freighters returned to Korat in January as part of what was known as the Special Logistics Aid to Thailand (SLAT) programme. They remained in theatre for two years, during which time the two aircraft flew 647 flights and carried 3,500,000 lb of freight, 15,877 passengers and 92,000 lb of mail.

The policy shift to bomber/interdiction was reflected by new procurement. Eleven English Electric Canberra B(I) Mk 12 medium bombers were ordered in August 1957. They were followed by an order for two T.13 training models two years later. The Canberra was a first-generation jet bomber that dated back to a 1944 Air Ministry requirement, designed by William 'Teddy' Petter around two Rolls Royce Avon axial flow turbojets developing 6500 lb thrust each. The type first flew in 1949 and the first production variant entered service with the RAF in 1950.

The RNZAF's decision to buy Canberras brought inter-operability with the RAAF. The Australians had been an early Canberra customer, ordering 48 modified B.2's for delivery from 1952. A detachment of 14 Squadron personnel went to England to convert to the type during 1959, and the first four Canberra B.12's arrived in New Zealand in October that year. The complex avionics caused many problems during 1960. The 'Blue Silk' bombing system was particularly troublesome, and there were difficulties with the bombsight computer and Mk 10 autopilot. Attrition was low, though NZ 6101 was lost as early as November 1960 when it suffered a flame-out during asymmetric landing practise at Christchurch.[1] Pilots preferred the bomber to the trainer, often referring to the latter as the T.4 although, it was technically the nearly identical T.13: 'The T.4 compares unfavourably in comfort and visibility with the B.12 and for a pilot who hasn't flown a T.4 for some months there is a rude awakening.'[2] Personnel became very blasé about the bomber's sparkling performance. When tailwinds blew a No.14 Squadron Canberra back from Amberley at a ground speed of 600 knots the event was 'just routine stuff for the Fighting Fourteenth.'[3] The last Canberra was delivered in January 1961.

The Indonesian Confrontation

The RNZAF's second major South East Asian deployment in the 1960s had little to do directly with battling the communist threat. In 1963, Indonesian President Sukarno, who had led Indonesia into independence by juggling a range of supporters, took exception to the official formation of the Federation of Malaysia. The new union was backed by the British and included parts of northern Borneo, which bordered on to Indonesian Kalimantan. Blaming the British for supporting separatist rebels in Indonesia, Sukarno launched his ***konfrontasi*** partly as a means of focusing support within his fragmented nation. Low-level air raids and incursions began across the Kalimantan border, followed in September 1963 by heavier raids and paratroop assaults. More paratroops were dropped into Johore.

New Zealand deployed 14 Squadron into the trouble zone under cover of Exercise Vanguard VI. Cabinet took the decision on 14 September, the RNZAF was formally alerted next day, and four of six Canberra B12s were on their way in just 37 hours. During that time they were repainted in RAF camouflage and equipped with UHF radio. They deployed via RAAF Edinburgh in New South Wales, Perth and then to Singapore via the Cocos island — a tortuous route designed to avoid Indonesian airspace. In Singapore they joined 96 other aircraft, including three Canberra squadrons, a detachment of Avro Vulcan heavy bombers, and Gloster Javelin interceptors. Tensions were initially very high, but the Indonesians did not make a concerted effort despite being equipped with MiG-15 interceptors, P-51 Mustangs and Ilyushin Il-28 Beagles.

Both the No.14 Squadron bombers and the 41 Squadron detachment that supported them were led in Malaysia by Wing Commander D E Jamieson, who reported to FEAF command. The two month stay was extended by the New Zealand government until March 1965, and then to October 1966 in response to continued high tension. No. 41 Squadron Bristol Freighters provided logistic support to the combat zone, usually by air-drop. There was a serious incident in October 1965. A freighter flown by Flight Lieutenant N J S Rodger was on a routine cargo mission near the Indonesian border. Flying at 500 feet near the drop zone they passed over Indonesian territory and were fired on. The mission was abandoned.

Vietnam operations

The RNZAF's involvement in the Vietnam War was relatively limited by comparison with their work in Malaya. The New Zealand government decided to attach 550 troops to Australian units; the Kiwis were deployed into theatre and supported by No. 40 Squadron. In July 1965 the squadron airlifted No. 161 Artillery Battery to Bien Hoa AFB. Departure from New Zealand was kept secret to avoid protests by the Progressive Youth Movement. Even the aircrew believed they were only going to Singapore until shortly before the first flight. During the seven day operation the aircraft carried 96 soldiers and 70 tons of cargo that included five 105mm howitzers and fourteen Land Rovers. One of the problems at Bien Hoa was that the Viet Cong held positions around the perimeter of the airfield and were able to fire at approaching aircraft. The only way around this was to make a spiral descent within the airfield confines from 20,000 feet. Bristol Freighters subsequently operated on a weekly basis into South Vietnam between 1968 and 1971.

Direct involvement came by secondment. Sixteen RNZAF helicopter pilots served with the RAAF No. 9 Squadron between July 1967 and December 1971, operating primarily from Vung Tau to support the 1st Australian Task Force at Nui Dat, a group that included the New Zealand soldiers. Their numbers included Douglas 'Punchy' Paterson of Woodville, who nursed a damaged Iroquois back to Ving Tau after being attacked during a resupply mission. Fourteen pilots, including Murray Abel of Whanganui, also flew Cessna O-2's as forward air controllers. A full roll of all the New Zealanders involved in South Vietnam was never kept — a nominal list was subsequently assembled from pay records.[4]

The RNZAF evacuated New Zealand embassy staff, nationals, and some Vietnamese from Saigon during the collapse of South Vietnam in April 1975. Two Bristol Freighters of 41 Squadron were sent from Singapore to Saigon under Squadron Leader R Davidson early in the month, making six flights in total. One of the freighters airlifted food to Phu Quoc, where 60,000 refugees had assembled. A C-130 of 40 Squadron operated between 6 and 19 April, to pull out New Zealand embassy staff. One of the Bristol Freighters was withdrawn, but the other remained in Saigon for the final evacuation. On 18 April, the RNZAF crew were ordered not to leave without the remaining New Zealanders, and three days later the decision was made to evacuate. Some Vietnamese were also taken off. Clearance formalities were not fulfilled — but there were no incidents and the aircraft reached Singapore safely.

The Morrison years: 1963–65

The 1960s did not start well for the RNZAF at home; the service was certainly the loser in a defence review which resulted in the 1961 decision to bolster the army and recall 75 Squadron from Singapore. The review confirmed that new maritime and transport aircraft would be needed, but did not say when, and there was talk of slashing the air budget in half. Shortfalls in long-range transport capacity were meanwhile addressed by transferring three obsolescent Douglas DC-6 aircraft from Tasman Empire Airways Ltd. Morale was not high; manpower was down to critical levels and there was a sense that direction had been lost.

All this was turned around the following year by the influence, drive and vision of one man. Air-Vice Marshal Ian Morrison became Chief of Air Staff in June 1962 and did much to redress the balance of defence spending in favour of the Air Force. He inspired officers and men alike with his vision of a revitalised service, re-equipped with modern aircraft, firmly bringing New Zealand's air defence into the jet age. He lobbied ceaselessly in the corridors of power to bring that vision to reality, focussing initially on a maritime and transport replacement programme, later on renewal of the strike aircraft. His frankness did not endear him to politicians, but he was effective, and indeed remains one of the RNZAF's most accomplished administrators, a man whose work had far-reaching effects both within the service and outside it, one of the half dozen movers-and-shakers whose personal influence and character can be said to have fundamentally shaped the service.

Born at Hamner Springs in 1914, Morrison was educated at Christchurch Boys High and in the early 1930s studied at the Joint Service Staff College and Imperial Defence College in Britain. He joined the RAF in 1935, but in 1939 transferred to the RNZAF where he served as a bomber pilot and staff officer in the South West Pacific. In 1944-45 he commanded a Ventura bomber squadron operating out of Guadalcanal and later Bougainville. He remained in the service during the lean post-war years and cut such a swathe that there was little surprise when, aged 48, he became Chief of Air Staff.[5]

Morrison envisaged a renewal of the transport, maritime and strike squadrons — a trident to make the RNZAF an effective and modern service, able to fulfil New Zealand government requirements anywhere in the world. He was particularly in favour of the Lockheed C-130 Hercules, a four-engined turboprop transport with excellent short-field capability that had recently entered United States service. Nothing else was in the same league, and initially Morrison envisaged that these aircraft would also fulfil the maritime patrol role. The aircraft was investigated by an air staff team that included Wing Commander Richard Bolt, son of the pioneering aviator, who recalled that he took the C-130 specifications from Lockheed brochures as the basis of the Air Staff requirement.[6] Plans for a maritime version were abandoned after a fact-finding visit by Air Commodore William Stratton to the United States, but they were accepted for the logistic role.

Three new C-130E Hercules were approved by Cabinet in June 1963 for £13.5 million, with spares and associated equipment that included a British-built procedural trainer. Production at the Lockheed Marietta plant in Georgia shifted to the C-130H-LM with the more powerful T56-A-15 turboprops the following year, and the RNZAF aircraft were built to this standard. A detachment of three officers and 32 airmen under Squadron Leader C R Carter went to Travis Air Force Base in June 1964 to begin an intensive sixteen week course on the type. They were met at their destination by Squadron Leader J E Hetrick of the New Zealand Joint Services Mission in Washington. The Americans welcomed the New Zealanders; Carter recalled it was 'obvious from the start that United States Air Force personnel were going out of their way to be helpful.'[7]

Lectures began at 7.45 daily, Monday to Friday, but were over by 2.30 — an arrangement that worked well as the men had trouble concentrating in the heat of the afternoon. The RNZAF personnel soon discovered their New Zealand training had given them far greater expertise than the Americans anticipated. 'If this had been fully realised by Air Training Command,' Carter noted 'the duration of the training in most cases would have been reduced.'[8] Twenty three men went home a month early. These were not the only differences. US Air Force maintenance standards were below RNZAF levels, and domestic arrangements differed. Meal allowances had to be increased; the standard of the food was lower than what was served in New Zealand. Carter believed this had a bright side, reporting that:

> *the tour was of great value, and the training received most beneficial... The detachment was also a very educational one apart from training and made the men realise that their own service compared more than favourably with the US Air Force and that the living standards and way of life in New Zealand left little to be desired in comparison to that which they came in contact with during the tour.*[9]

Three aircrews followed at the end of the year for conversion courses, arriving to find that part of their course included language training — and a written test to discover how well they could speak English. Carey Adamson, a Flying Officer with the unit, recalled that:

> *... it was quickly apparent that there had been a major misunderstanding. ... It was not possible to bring forward the rest of our training, so we spent the time at Lackland learning about the Constitution, the history of the United States, the federal system of Government, the philosophy and rules of American football, and the finer technical points of baseball. This information was not wasted and proved valuable in following years... We went to the Lockheed plant in Georgia to pick up our new aircraft and on 1 April 1965 our crew flew NZ 7002 for the first time. That was the beginning of a 13 year personal relationship with a magnificent and elegant lady. We went on a navigational exercise on 5 April to check out cruise procedures and left for New Zealand on 8 April 1965.*[10]

All three aircraft reached Rongotai on 14 April, to a formal reception by Prime Minister Keith Holyoake, and they were taken on charge next day. There were, however, delays in delivery of the procedural trainer from Redifon Ltd of England. Delivery slipped to September 1966, which the company explained was due to their own difficulties obtaining data from Lockheed, in part a result of security issues. Two further Hercules were ordered in 1967, entering service with No. 40 Squadron in early January 1969.

Morrison also required new maritime patrol aircraft for his new-look air force. These eventually focussed on five purpose-built Lockheed P-3B Orions, which were ordered in March 1964 for £8 million and delivered between September and December 1966. They replaced the Short Sunderlands, and the flying boat base at Lauthala Bay was closed. Commonality with the Hercules — which shared the same power plants — was played up at the time, but investigations during 1965 revealed key differences. There was only a five percent parts commonality between the S4H60-77 propellers of the P-3 and the S4H60-91 propellers of the C-130. Worse, the T-56A-14 engines fitted to the P-3 differed in 24 significant ways from the T-56A-15 engines of the C-130, which meant spares stocks had to exceed original allocations.[11] This did not undermine the value of the aircraft. The Orions were the most capable anti-submarine aircraft in the world, and brought the RNZAF's reconnaissance and maritime capabilities firmly into the post-war era.

All of this played out to a background of significant administrative change. All the New Zealand armed services were amalgamated into a single Ministry of Defence during 1963 and 1964. In September 1965 an RNZAF Operations Group gained authority over the Strike Wing at Ohakea, the Maritime and Transport Wings, overseas units, stores depots and the training schools. A Training Group was formed in February 1966 at Wigram, though the title was short-lived and the unit became the Support Group Headquarters under its first Air Officer Commanding, Air Commodore D F St George. There was a significant re-arrangement of Wigram accommodation and offices as a result of this restructuring. The same month, the term 'station' was formally abandoned, and Whenuapai and Hobsonville became RNZAF Base Auckland. Morrison retired that year, but he had accomplished his mission, stripping the last vestiges of wartime equipment and bringing the RNZAF into the modern era.

By the late 1990s both the Orions and Hercules were approaching a third of a century in service, but there were no plans to replace them. This unprecedented longevity was in part an outcome of the fact that aircraft performance technology plateaued during the 1960s. Subsequent improvements did not match the vaulting leaps of the previous thirty years, and by 1990 the usual replacement for an old P-3 Orion or Hercules was a new one — albeit with refined airframe and engines — but this was difference of detail rather than concept. Avionics were a different matter, but even so there was less pressure to replace the aircraft to keep up with foreign capabilities. Expediency also played a part. Funds were not available to buy new aircraft, so the RNZAF had to make do with the ones it had. To this extent, policy had to follow form and in retrospect, Morrison's re-equipment programme of the 1960s was fundamental to the development, use and function of the RNZAF for the rest of the century.

Rotary wing aircraft

The RNZAF received its first helicopters as a result of Morrison's reformation. The first to enter RNZAF service was the Bell 47G-3B1 Sioux, which had been flying with the US Army since 1948 and was still in production in the 1960s. With a 280hp Lycoming VO-435 piston engine the type was adequately powered for its intended training and army air scout role. Six were delivered new to No.3 Squadron in December 1965, and seven more were ordered in June 1968 for delivery in 1970. The Sioux were based for many years at Wigram, but were flown north to Hobsonville in May 1993 following the decision to close the Christchurch base.

In 1965, five UH-1D Iroquois were ordered from the Bell Helicopter plant at Fort Worth, Texas. The first was delivered in June the following year and all five were operational by the end of 1966. Powered by a single 1,100 shaft horsepower Avro Lycoming T53-L-11 turboshaft, the D-models were supplemented in 1970 by nine UH-1H models, with the more powerful 1400 horsepower L-13 engine. In 1981-82 the five D-models received L-13 engines, but minor differences with 'genuine' H-models remained.

To the public, the UH-1H became synonymous with search and rescue. Two helicopters and crews were kept on permanent two hour standby for the purpose, one at Hobsonville and the other at Wigram. However, the primary *raison d'etre* was always to support the army, including air mobile assault, tactical reconnaissance, air logistic support, and supporting SAS operations. Other roles included conversion training, operational and continuation training, aeromedical evacuation, support of police operations, search and rescue, and civil defence work.

The 1970s were lean years for the type. Four Iroquois were put into storage at Woodbourne in 1971 after defence cuts. Three more were allocated to No.41 Squadron at Singapore, supporting New Zealand Army infantry battalion; they were later joined by a fourth. One Iroquois, NZ 3810, crashed into a sand hill near Kaipara harbour in 1972 with the loss of three crew. This left only six serving in New Zealand, and a replacement aircraft, NZ 3815, was purchased in 1976. The mothballed units were gradually returned to service and the Singapore flight returned to New Zealand in July 1989.

Operations with the Iroquois were generally trouble-free, certainly in relation to the number of hours flown. However, two accidents marred the service record in the early 1980s. One crashed in Australia in October 1981, and another was damaged on Mount Cook during a rescue operation in January 1983. Both were recovered and repaired by Blenheim's Safe Air. There was another crash at the end of March 1995 when NZ 3813 aircraft was on a routine training flight with the Army at Waiouru. The aircraft was returning to the helipad when it suffered engine failure. Tony Fesche made a forced landing in the Ngamatea swamp, but the aircraft turned over as it touched down, briefly trapping Darran Goodwin. The four army passengers, Fesche, and co-pilot Chris Underwood, escaped from the wreckage. The Iroquois was too badly damaged to return to service and became a crash training hulk at Hobsonville.

By 1991, when the Iroquois completed twenty five years in service, the fourteen aircraft had collectively flown 79,000 hours. Tailboom cracks — a known fatigue problem — were discovered in seven during 1990. One aircraft was easily repairable, but the other six were less straight forward and a 'short term' fix was applied to four airframes by Pacific Aerospace in Hamilton, who had the only tail boom jig in New Zealand. The remaining two were repaired in Australia, but the fix was interim until a major upgrade of the fleet could be carried out. Then in November 1992, six of the fourteen were found to have fatigue cracks in the main rotor structure. Bell advised that this, again, was a known problem; the cracks did not affect structural integrity. A fix, applied by Blenheim's Safe Air, involved patching the spar caps.

There were no plans to replace the Hueys in the 1990s. Instead, a scheme was fielded to buy six second-hand units so the RNZAF could meet an Army requirement to lift a complete company. Longer term, there was a proposal to rebuild the fleet with new tailbooms, rotors, structural components, wiring, avionics and engines. The estimated cost of this scheme was estimated in 1995 to be approximately $58 million. The additional aircraft never eventuated, but two second-hand airframes were purchased from the United States in 1996, one for eventual rebuild and service entry, and the other as a spare. A defence review completed at the end of 1997 confirmed the need to keep fourteen Iroquois in service and confirmed the life extension programme.

One other helicopter type was also operated by the RNZAF from the mid-1960s. Two Westland Wasps were ordered in May 1965 for the new Navy frigates, serving when ashore with No.3 Squadron at Hobsonville. The first two were delivered in October and December 1966 for operations from HMSNZ *Waikato*. A third was ordered in 1970 for HMNZS *Canterbury*. The Wasp fulfilled a number of roles for the Navy, including casualty evacuation, vertical replenishment, training and reconnaissance. Its primary task was actually as a light all-weather anti-submarine platform. In this role it carried a variety of weapons including torpedoes, though it relied on the ship for targeting data and range was restricted when carrying the weapons. Special capabilities included an instant 'cold start' feature — the Rolls Royce Nimbus 710 gas turbine needed no warmup — and tail folding.

Six more Wasps — four flyable airframes and two spares — were purchased in October 1981 for two second-hand frigates purchased from Britain, and Wasps were also operated from the survey vessel HMNZS *Monowai* and supply ship HMNZS *Endeavour.* There were two losses; NZ3901 crashed into the Hauraki gulf. Another, NZ3904, crashed near Taupo during landing when it became entangled in an inadequately secured tarpaulin. However, at least six helicopters were needed by the navy, and a British attrition airframe, XT782, was acquired in 1993 for rebuilding to New Zealand standards using parts of the crashed NZ3901 and NZ3904. The process was not straight forward. Extensive corrosion was found in the fuel tank bays, evidently from a twenty five minute salt-water deluge it had received from fire fighting sprinklers while in Royal Navy service. This took some time to put right, but the Wasp, re-serialled NZ3909, entered service in July 1994.

Re-equipment: strike fighters

A new strike aircraft had yet to be selected when Morrison retired in 1966. His successor, Air Vice-Marshal Cameron Turner, made this one of his main priorities, in part because a military sales arrangement with the United States was due to expire by June 1968. In many ways the service was spoiled for choice. Although British fighter production was axed by the 1957 White Paper, United States industry produced half a dozen aircraft that could fit the bill, and types considered by the RNZAF during 1967 included the Northrop F-5E Tiger, McDonnell Douglas F-4E Phantom, McDonnell Douglas A-4E Skyhawk and the massive General Dynamics F-111.

Evaluation was complicated by pressure from across the Tasman to buy Dassault Mirage IIIO's. The RAAF was about to take delivery of 116 locally assembled examples modified to Australian standards, and the prospect of adding to the Government Aircraft Factory production run carried a significant potential reduction in unit costs, quite apart from the lure of inter-operability, unified maintenance and training facilities. However, the front runner as far as the RNZAF was concerned remained the General Dynamics F-111 swing-wing supersonic bomber. This type had first flown in late 1964 and had been purchased by the RAAF, though deliveries had yet to be made when the RNZAF examined the type — obtaining detailed information from the Australians to supplement their study. Although called a 'fighter', the F-111 was actually a swing-wing all-weather supersonic bomber with significant range, able to make precision first-pass attacks under any conditions.[12] The down side was that its complex avionics, air inlets and wing-pivot systems were all problematic in 1967 — largely because all three 'pushed the envelope' of available technology. All these problems were solved over time, and in mature form the F-111 was a formidable aircraft. Perhaps seeing this potential, the Chiefs of Staff recommended the type, but their proposal was squashed for cost reasons.

The service then turned to the McDonnell-Douglas A-4E Skyhawk. The 'bantam bomber', designed by Ed Heinemann, had been in production since the 1950s and offered a good combination of range, speed, and striking power. The type was smaller and less capable than the F-111, but combat experience in South East Asia revealed a reliability which the F-111 had yet to demonstrate in 1968. The Skyhawk was extremely capable for its size, able to carry relatively heavy ordinance loads over tactically useful ranges. Although not a fighter, its manoeuverability had proven useful during combat in South East Asia — and the capabilities of this aircraft also reflected the expected role of the RNZAF as an alliance partner.

An evaluation team under Air Commodore T Frank Gill went to the United States in April 1968 to investigate the Skyhawk more closely. They found the type would do the job, and moved on to Washington, where they negotiated to buy fourteen new-build aircraft for $NZ24.65 million. The following year, Squadron Leader W R Donaldson went to the United States to train on the type and set up a training programme. Unfortunately a multiple bird strike left him in hospital. Squadron Leader Colin Calvert was appointed Training Liaison Officer in June, arriving by commercial airline at NAS Cecil Field in Florida and discovering that the shift from New Zealand winter to southern American summer was difficult to handle. Like the Hercules training crews, he found that US base accommodation was of much lower standards than the men were accustomed to in New Zealand. Food was a contentious issue; prices in the base messes were higher than anticipated and, to add insult to injury, the New Zealanders found American tastes strange. A week after arriving Calvert reported:

> *In response to numerous uncoordinated and tedious directions an investigation is proceeding to confirm or amend the recommendations of previous teams in the matter of meal allowances. This involves a sampling of meals, assessing the acceptability to the New Zealand palate... it may be generalised at this time by saying that the quantity of food is adequate, the cooking methods are unusual but capable of gradual acceptance by New Zealand personnel, but the habit of eating a three course meal at mid-day in tropical conditions in unconditioned mess halls is unlikely to receive approval.*[13]

The Hercules conversion crews had found RNZAF training to be of much higher standard than that of US services, and this experience was matched by the Skyhawk detachment. Some 450 hours had been scheduled for training on the Skyhawks, which had been temporarily attached to VA-44 at Cecil Field, but the programmes were accomplished in less than half the time and on 10 October the US Navy asked Calvert to bring the completion dates forward. Calvert formally asked for the men to be returned to New Zealand in time for Christmas, assuring Air Staff that the programme would be well finished. Later, in January 1970, ten pilots arrived in the United States for a conversion training programme.

Plans to fly the aircraft out came to nothing, and the ten A-4K's and four TA-4K's were brought to New Zealand in early 1970 on board the USS *Okinawa*. They were landed in Auckland by crane and towed to Whenuapai by road. The aircraft were essentially the A-4E, re-designated K-for-Kiwi to reflect minor changes to meet RNZAF specifications, and were officially taken into the service in June, re-equipping No. 75 Squadron. The new aircraft transformed the striking power of the RNZAF, completely out-performing the Vampires and giving the service a front-line attack aircraft that could hold its own in most operational situations of the day.

The RNZAF also used the type for aerobatic displays. Kiwi Red, drawn from No.75 Squadron, briefly flew Skyhawks from 1970 to 1973, when the team was disbanded to save fuel after the first oil crisis. Reformed in 1981, they remained the only aerobatic team to use front-line aircraft in the normal combat paint scheme — at the time they actually comprised about half the active Skyhawk force. They were also the only aerobatic team to feature a refuelling hook-up. Demonstrated at Whenuapai in 1983, this world first featured a barrel roll by two Skyhawks linked by a refuelling line. Overseas performances included an appearance at the October 1988 bicentennial air show staged by the RAAF at Richmond, near Sydney. The team was disbanded in 1991 for cost reasons.

A new jet conversion trainer was needed to lead in to the Skyhawks, and ten British Aerospace Mk 88 Strikemasters were ordered in 1970. The first two were shown at the 1972 Farnborough air show and arrived in New Zealand later that year. Six further examples of the Viper-engined trainer were ordered in the early 1970s, and the type served with No. 14 Squadron at Ohakea in the conversion training role, much loved by the service and nicknamed 'Blunty'.

By the 1970s the Bristol Freighters were also in need of replacement. It happened that the British had a number of surplus Hawker Siddeley Andovers. Thirty had been built in the mid-1960s. The type was a military derivative of the HS 748 airliner — the main external difference was a rear loading ramp. Evaluation and negotiation to buy the type was facilitated by the British Chief of Air Staff, Air Chief Marshal Sir Andrew Humphrey, and in July 1976, a deal was finalised for ten Andovers at $13 million. Their delivery brought significant changes to Air Force structure. Four were given to No.42 Squadron and refitted for VIP transport duties, and the remaining six stayed in utility configuration with No.1 Squadron. The Bristol Freighters were withdrawn and No. 41 Squadron was disbanded. Three Cessna 421C Golden Eagles were procured in 1980 to replace the de Havilland Devons in the communications role. They were purchased for $2.1 million and arrived in early 1981, initially serving with No. 42 Squadron.

A 1978 defence review recommended dedicated VIP transports. Until that time the RNZAF had used the Hercules for the task, but passenger amenities were basic; a special container loaded into the cargo bay provided rudimentary facilities. After considering buying second-hand Boeing 737-200s from Air New Zealand, the RNZAF bought three 1968-vintage 727-100C's from United Airlines. The aircraft were delivered in mid-1981 and refurbished by Air New Zealand. Two entered service with No. 40 Squadron to supplement the Hercules in the long-range transport role. The third had been bought for spare parts and never entered service — it was scrapped in 1984. However, to fly it out to New Zealand meant it had to be legally registered, and so even authoritative reference works sometimes claimed that the RNZAF operated three Boeing 727's. The two operational aircraft filled the VIP passenger role, but by the mid-1990s serviceability had become an issue. They also retained their old-model P&W JT8D-7 turbofans, which posed problems in the face of new and very stringent airport noise regulations in some areas. A defence review at the end of 1997 confirmed that they would be replaced.

Pilot training and 'streaming'

The long-serving Harvards were replaced as the RNZAF's basic trainer in the late 1970s by the indigenous Aerospace CT/4B Airtrainer. The type was derived from a 1953 design by Australian engineer Henry Millicer. This was purchased by Hamilton-based Aero Engine Services Ltd and developed into the AESL Airtourer T6, which the RNZAF evaluated in 1968. Four were purchased for $80,000 and delivered in May 1970 for pilot conversion of Army personnel before they moved on to the Sioux. From this type, AESL — renamed Aerospace Industries — derived the CT-4 Airtrainer. Military modifications included re-stressing the airframe to tolerances of +6/-3g, and the type first flew in February 1972. Extensive trials followed at Wigram during April, and the type received a glowing report from Squadron Leader R T R Gilbert:

> *The Airtrainer is very suitable for ab-initio training of Service pilots. It is simple to operate and easy to fly. The aircraft is considerably superior to the Airtourer. For its class, the aircraft is a delight to fly through all manoeuvers.*[14]

The RNZAF ordered thirteen in July 1975, and the first was delivered a year later. Six more airframes were purchased as attrition replacements in 1977. The RNZAF was not the only customer; thirty one were also sold to Australia and twenty four to Thailand. The first students soloed on the type in August 1977. A defence review in 1983 suggested replacing the Airtrainers with a single 'all-through' training type, but this was never done. As delivered the Airtrainer was finished in a red-and-grey arrangement inherited from the Harvards, a scheme they retained for more than twenty years. A variety of new paint schemes were trialled in 1996, including an all-black finish that proved popular with aircrews. In the end, the practical requirement to be visible won out and the Airtrainers were given high-gloss yellow with black control surfaces.

The RNZAF's Pilot Training School with its Airtrainers was located for many years at RNZAF Wigram, but in 1993 the unit relocated to RNZAF Ohakea. Problems here included bad weather and air traffic congestion — Ohakea was by this time one of only three operational military airfields in the country. Manawatu weather was so bad at times that 'groundings' of several weeks were not unknown. During these periods pilots were able to concentrate on schoolroom work. Traffic congestion was simply coped with; each type was given a strictly defined region.

Until 1997, students did their basic training on the Airtrainer, then moved on to advanced training on the Strikemaster and later MB-339CB Aermacchi. That year, however, the 'basic pilots course' was renamed the Wings Course and — following overseas trends — streamed. The RNZAF was one of the last services in the world to introduce this approach. Under this system, many 'advanced' aspects previously conducted on Macchis returned to the Airtrainer. Pilots were given an initial 140 hours on the Airtrainer, then either the 'Jet Basic Course' (JBC) on the Aermacchi, Helicopter Basic Course (HBS) on the Sioux, or Multi Engine Basic Course (MBC) on the Andover or its replacement in the multi-engine training role, the King Air B200. Each course included 65 flying hours over seventeen weeks.

CHAPTER EIGHT

Reform and retrenchment

We have the world's largest moat

— The Defence of New Zealand 1991, policy paper.

New Zealand went through its worst recession for sixty years in the early 1990s. Coupled with a political philosophy of reduced state intervention across all government sectors this meant major constraints for the New Zealand defence forces. But by contrast with health, welfare and education, there were few strident voices to protest defence cuts. This was not surprising; the cold war ended in the early 1990s and at public level there seemed little reason to continue even the modest levels that had characterised New Zealand defence spending for many years. Yet in reality, the end of the old bipolar system actually enhanced the value and importance of defence forces as a means of implementing peacetime foreign policy. Old arguments submerged by the Cold War resurfaced in half a dozen places around the globe. Yugoslavia fragmented and civil war erupted. Somalia collapsed almost entirely into anarchy. There was trouble in Cambodia, genocide in Rwanda, and a new world conflict in the Gulf. Flexing its muscles for a new role in wake of the Cold War, the United Nations embarked on a number of peace-making interventions which the New Zealand government — pursuing a role as responsible international citizen — decided to join. This meant more work for the RNZAF than ever — just when capabilities were being lost and the aircraft actually doing the work needed urgent replacement.

The ANZUS dispute and new defence thinking

What became a period of sustained change for the RNZAF began with the 'ANZUS row' in the mid-1980s. This had its origins in widespread and long-standing public opposition to anything nuclear, a sentiment turned into policy by the Labour government elected in 1984. It became a hot issue in February 1985 when the United States offered to send the elderly destroyer USS *Buchanan* into New Zealand waters. The visit was refused. At the ANZUS council meeting a few weeks later in San Francisco, US Secretary of State George Schultz announced that the United States was withdrawing the military co-operation outlined in Article 4 of the treaty. At policy level it was a relatively abrupt shift for New Zealand, whose forces were geared towards a co-operative alliance role. For the RNZAF there were no more joint exercises with US forces — no chance to compare operational notes — an alteration in the way spares were procured, and a new range of duties for which existing aircraft were not well matched.

Further changes for the RNZAF during the period were driven by government reform, as the government of the day attempted to impose its economic theories on the defence sector. A major defence review during the late 1980s was the first attempt to come to grips with the post-ANZUS defence environment. The review came down in favour of regional defence, calling for closer ties with Australia, more work with the Five Power Defence Arrangement, and other activities through the United Nations. Australia was particularly important because of shared interests in the Pacific and South East Asia. However, there was also administrative change. A Defence Resource Management project was set up to review and rationalise defence assets. However, the report also imposed economy measures that were essentially inconsistent with the regional focus, pulling back New Zealand forces from Singapore, including a New Zealand battalion and RNZAF Iroquois.

A further review in 1990-91 for the incoming National administration, *The Defence of New Zealand*, updated this concept to reflect the ending Cold War and the Defence Act of 1990. Strategic issues had not changed, but the paper admitted that as a relatively poor nation, New Zealand could not afford the defence forces needed to protect its far-flung trading interests. The solution was a policy officially called 'self-reliance in partnership.' Australia remained the primary focus not only because of traditional ties, but also because Australia shared the same defence perceptions.

Close co-operation with Australia, however, brought pressures which were inconsistent with the 'lean and mean' image that successive New Zealand governments imposed on the whole state sector. The rising power of Asian economies coupled with political instability in that region turned Australian attention northwards. As far as the RAAF was concerned this meant funding new air bases across the Northern Territories to operate the relatively short-legged F/A-18; developing indigenous over-the-horizon radar; and procuring more F-111 fighter-bombers. Defence absorbed a higher percentage of Australian gross domestic product than New Zealand's government was prepared to commit, quite apart from the disparate scales of the two economies. And the question — which re-surfaced repeatedly at political level during the whole of the 1990s — was whether New Zealand could fairly contribute to the partnership.

The 1991 White Paper also identified a 'mismatch' between the capability of New Zealand's defence forces, and what was needed for the new policy in any event. One option seriously proposed was a single aircraft type to replace the ageing Hercules and Orions; in a throwback to Morrison's concept of 1962, multi-role C-130s using quick-change pallets were mooted. 'The question... will be whether a loss of surveillance capability is an acceptable price for a larger transport capability in an emergency.'[1] Five specific reviews got under way in May 1991 to identify the exact nature of the air, sea and land forces New Zealand needed beyond the two Anzac frigates already under construction.

In the event, fiscal issues meant the RNZAF had to make do with its existing aircraft, and the service limped on into the 1990s. The next defence White Paper, released in November 1997, warned again of the 'significant capability gap' emerging between New Zealand's abilities and 'those of our partners.'[2]

Project Kahu: strike upgrade

Despite the broader fiscal issues of the period, the RNZAF's strike aircraft entered the 1990s well equipped for work into the 21st century. Project Kahu, arguably the world's most comprehensive modernisation programme for any A-4 sub-type, originated in the early 1980s. By this time the original avionics fit of the A-4K Skyhawks had been left behind by technology, and as the airframes were expected to last only to the end of the decade, the RNZAF began casting around for a new combat aircraft. In many ways the service was spoiled for choice; types considered by the RNZAF included the Vought A-7E Corsair, SEPECAT Jaguar, General Dynamics F-16 Falcon, Northrop F-20 and Dassault Mirage 2000. The situation was given particular momentum by the fact that the RAAF was replacing its Mirages. When the Australians selected the McDonnell Douglas F/A-18 Hornet, there was serious consideration of a complementary order by New Zealand which could be added to the Australian production run, reducing unit cost and providing inter-operability. However, in 1983 the RNZAF evaluation group came down in favour of the F-16 at a program cost — including spares and equipment — of around $900 million. This was unaffordable, which left rebuilding the Skyhawks the only realistic option. It happened that the Australians had ten surplus Skyhawks, orphaned after their light fleet carrier was scrapped in 1982, and the RNZAF decided to enlarge and modernise its existing fleet, purchasing eight A-4G's and two TA-4G's from Australia, along with spares, equipment and jigs, including wing spars which could extend the flying life of each aircraft by 4000 hours.

These aircraft were the survivors of twenty purchased in 1967 and 1970, essentially A-4F's altered for RAN service with the deletion of drag chute, fuselage 'hump' and associated avionics. Curiously, four of the 1970 batch had flown for the United States Navy before being purchased by Australia and had seen action in the Gulf of Tonkin during the Vietnam War. The oldest — which became NZ 6215 — first flew in October 1967. The package deal ran to $40 million and included spares, engines and miscellaneous equipment. No.2 Squadron was re-formed to accomodate the new aircraft, based at Ohakea.

The $140 million modernisation phase that followed for the whole RNZAF Skyhawk fleet was intended to give the aircraft about ninety percent the capability of an F-16C. 'Project Kahu' involved a total avionics rebuild and re-sparring to zero-life the wings for service into the twenty first century. Government gave its approval in May 1985, and the United States Congress approved the technology transfer that December. Only minor changes were made to the ex-Australian aircraft in the interim. In March 1986, a contract for detail design and development was signed with Lear Siegler International. Local input was important; Fisher and Paykel of Auckland and Pacific Aerospace of Hamilton were sub-contracted to fabricate and assemble the upgrade kits. The first two 'Kahu Skyhawks' were assembled by the RNZAF and Smith's Industries at RNZAF Base Woodbourne. The job was then handed over to Blenheim based Safe Air, another indigenous New Zealand company. All the work was done at RNZAF Woodbourne.

Attrition of the Skyhawk force remained low relative to the number of hours flown. In March 1981 NZ6207 was lost in the circuit at RNZAF Ohakea due to an oil pump failure. The pilot ejected safely. One TA-4K, NZ6253, was lost in October 1984 when it flew into the ground in the Mangaweka ranges. The cause was never established. The following March, one of the newly delivered A-4G's, NZ 6218, aquaplaned on rollout after landing at RAAF Townsville in Australia, burst both mainwheel tyres and overturned, extensively damaging the canopy and tail. Curiously, this was that particular Skyhawk's second accident. It was one of the four ex-US Navy A-4F's, and in July 1969, while flying with VA 155, the aircraft had flown into power lines and suffered extensive damage. A post-repair report recommended realigning the fuselage, but this was never done and the aircraft was sold to Australia. After the accident at Townsville the aircraft was flown back to New Zealand in a Hercules, and returned to service in 1988 with a new tail section from an ex- 'Blue Angels' A-4F, which the RNZAF purchased for the repair in 1986.

Another loss came during a practise by Kiwi Red, the Skyhawk aerobatic team. In October 1989 two aircraft collided during a roll under break manoeuver at the end of a practise over Ohakea. One of the Skyhawks survived with wing damage; the other, A-4K NZ 6210, plunged into the ground, killing the pilot. Another Skyhawk was lost due to engine failure over the Manawatu in the early 1990s, and NZ 6203 crashed into a paddock five miles north of Ohakea in June 1996 after an oil pressure line failed due to corrosion. The pilot, Flight Lieutenant Anthony Fraser, ejected safely.

UNIMOG and the Gulf War, 1988–91

Until the end of the Cold War, international peace-keeping efforts were relatively infrequent by comparison with the number that were organised in the 1990s. The New Zealand government nevertheless became involved in a number of the initiatives that were undertaken, particularly in the Middle East. In late 1988 the United Nations established an observer group to enforce a peace settlement negotiated between Iran and Iraq to end their eight-year war of attrition. Ten New Zealand military personnel were asked to join, and the Ministry of Defence then raised the possibility of sending an Andover to contribute to the transport tasks. This was confirmed by Cabinet, and an Andover — painted white in UN colours — was despatched in October. Two Andovers were eventually painted for this service, though only one was ever in theatre at any one time, flying regularly between UNIMOG headquarters in Teheran and four sector headquarters in Iran, and providing the observer force with a very substantial transport facility. This continued for three years, with aircrews rotating every six months, until Saddam Hussein's invasion of Kuwait in August 1990 changed the situation. UNIMOG was disbanded in February 1991.

New Zealand involvement in the Gulf War of early 1991 was relatively low key; the Skyhawks could have conducted strike operations, but were not requested. Indeed, the RNZAF was not asked to participate until December 1990, when the RAF requested two Hercules to join an RAF transport squadron at Riyadh. The two aircraft, NZ 7001 and 7002, left Whenuapai on 20 December and arrived in Saudi Arabia four days later. They began work in theatre on 27 December, ferrying supplies and equipment to ground forces deployed against Iraqi troops along the border of Kuwait and Saudi Arabia, including bombs and spare parts. The New Zealanders did not have it easy even in Riyadh; there were fears of chemical attacks by Scud missile and protective clothing had to be ready at all times.

In early January, Hercules NZ 7002 was relieved by NZ 7003, flown by Wing Commander Henderson. By the time the ground war began on 24 February, the First New Zealand Army Medical team had joined the US Navy 6th Naval Fleet Hospital at Bahrain, and a second medical unit comprising personnel from all three services was working at an RAF hospital at Muharraq. At the beginning of March, Hercules NZ 7001 was relieved by

NZ 7004. Work included casualty evacuation and on one occasion, the off-duty crew were ordered up to evacuate an Iraqi prisoner who had a serious head injury. The Hercules was airborne within an hour. Both New Zealand Hercules returned to Whenuapai at the beginning of April 1991.

Australian co-operation 1991–98

Long-term deployment of RNZAF Skyhawks to the Australian continent was mooted during 1990; both nations saw advantages to the development, which was a first concrete step to underline the new defence relationship between both nations. An agreement was signed in January 1991, and in February six A-4K Skyhawks of No.2 Squadron flew to NAS Nowra in New South Wales. Initially the arrangement covered up to 400 hours flying per year for the Australian Defence Force, paid for by the Australians, and mainly involving maritime strike exercises — although the brief under which the Skyhawks operated included other work as necessary. No.2 squadron aircraft and crews came under the operational control of the Maritime Defence Commander of the Royal Australian Navy, but overall command was retained by the RNZAF, and squadron personnel remained subject to New Zealand military law.

Although arrangements were politically non-controversial, there was some media protest in Australia on the basis that the Australian Defence Force was hiring back the aircraft it had sold only six years earlier. Channel Nine's *Sixty Minutes* programme launched a stinging attack on the basis that Australia sold the aircraft 'for a song' and had been forced to hire them back at further cost to the Australian taxpayer. Both military services responded by highlighting the mutual benefits they expected from the relationship. Kiwi pilots regarded it as an opportunity for gaining experience and combat training that was not available in New Zealand. Work began in earnest soon after the Skyhawks arrived at Nowra. The first deployment was to Darwin — at four days notice. In mid-June 1991 the Skyhawks went to RAAF Williamtown, north of Sydney for 'dissimilar combat training' with F/A-18 Hornet fighter-bombers of the RAAF's No.81 Wing.

Three of the Skyhawks sent initially to Nowra were the two-seat 'T-Bird', and of the five pilots despatched, three were qualified flying instructors —

the squadron continued its usual duties as a training conversion unit within the RNZAF. The only down-side was that the base was geared for helicopters. The Skyhawks shared a hangar with some of the RAN's new SH-70B-2 Seahawks. Consequently, the base had minimal maintenance facilities for the jets, and major work had to be done back in New Zealand. For safety reasons, the cross-Tasman flight was an involved process. The aircraft had to fly in pairs, accompanied by a P-3 Orion for SAR support. To keep costs down, transfers were timed to coincide with major exercises. No.75 Squadron would fly from Ohakea to Australia for their exercise as usual, but on their return flight pick up No.2 Squadron aircraft from Nowra.

Despite media criticism, the Nowra deployment proved so successful that the five-year arrangement was renewed in 1996. This was only the beginning of what became a close association between trans-Tasman defence forces, formally known as Close Defence Relations (CDR). The policy provided a blanket agreement to work together; the nuts and bolts were defined by individual arrangement. More than a dozen specific agreements were made in the early part of the decade, including a scheme to combine air navigation and air electronic training at RAAF Base East Sale. The first six RNZAF navigation students arrived at East Sale in early 1993 and graduated the following year.

New Zealand aircraft also participated for the first time in what had been purely Australian exercises. Skyhawks of No. 75 Squadron joined Australian F/A-18s of 77 Squadron and F-111s of 1 Squadron at Townsville in early 1994 for the first New Zealand contribution to Exercise Iron Thunder. Co-operative work was extended later that year to include aerial refuelling, three years after the RAAF began operating Boeing KB-707 tankers out of RAAF Base Richmond. Air refuelling became a major theme of Exercise Willoh 95-1, held at RNZAF Base Ohakea in February 1995 for the first time in five years; until then it had generally been staged at RAAF Williamtown. Ten Hornets and a single KB-707 tanker crossed the Tasman to attend.

Commander of the Australian detachment at Willoh 95-1, Wing Commander John Blackburn, explained at the time that joint training was part of the Close Defence Relations (CDR) policy. 'If we get involved in any combat together, we must train together,' he told journalists. His Kiwi opposite number, Wing Commander Gavin Howse, agreed. Howse was very enthusiastic about air refuelling, explaining that it opened up combat tactics and strategies previously unavailable to the Skyhawks, which were otherwise limited to 'buddy pack' refuelling — reducing the number that could actually carry weapons. No longer would they have to attack from predictable directions — they could circle around a target, refuel, and come in from behind, for instance. Or they could carry more weapons instead of external fuel tanks. There were also peacetime benefits. Skyhawks routinely deployed as far afield as Singapore. Normally that took three days with up to five stops on the way to refuel, requiring massive logistics support. With access to the Australian tankers, some Australian stops would be cut, saving taxpayer money on both sides of the Tasman.

The exercises during Willoh 95-1 saw a mixed F/A-18 and A-4K strike force circle around East Cape and head south to make simulated attack runs against two mock airfields bulldozed out of the Central Plateau. They were supported by the KB-707 tanker. Defending forces, flying directly from Ohakea, were supported by TA-4K's equipped with external tanks and fuel hoses. Although the Skyhawk was slower than the Hornet — 420-450 knot cruise versus 470-540 knot — the difference was not significant. Typically, the Hornets flew air defence — either sweeping ahead to 'sanitise' the skies, or running in direct support of the Skyhawk strike force. Because both types were expected to fulfil attack and air-superiority roles, the Skyhawks also carried Sidewinder air-to-air missiles and were available for air combat, while the Hornets were involved in some of the strike activities.

Links between New Zealand and Australian defence forces were extended through the decade. By 1997–98, 19 routine high-level meetings were scheduled, and co-operative activities had been sanctioned under 19 different agreements. Twenty one personnel from the Australian Defence Force and the New Zealand Defence Force or Ministry of Defence were on exchanges for more than a year, and up to 100 were on shorter exchanges. There were also over 100 different training courses in both countries attended by personnel from both countries, and 23 major joint exercises.

Exercises and deployments

Traditional exercises and deployments during the 1990s included the 'Bullseye' and 'Fincastle' trophy contests. Bullseye started life in 1975 as an extension of joint exercises between the RNZAF and Canadian Air Force. The Royal Australian Air Force joined in 1979, and by the 1990s it had become a hotly anticipated event — though one with a vital training component. The opportunity to compare technique with foreign air forces was not to be missed. In 1991, the RNZAF went to great lengths to make life difficult for the competing crews. A two hour round-trip course from Whenuapai was plotted in detail by non-competing members of the RNZAF's No.40 Squadron. The planners flew the course themselves several times to photograph turning points and calculate times for each leg.

Every aspect was designed to make the competition as realistic as possible. Crews were supplied with maps, a list of 24 turning points, and a list of times when the points had to be reached. Markers included gravestones, a water tank, a derelict hut, a pond, and even a school tennis court. To keep pilots on their toes, aircraft were also forbidden to exceed certain air speeds, and had to pass through 'gates' at exact times and speeds.

Cargo drops by parachute were made more complex by instructions to gather 'intelligence'. Briefed that 'civil unrest' had broken out along a fictional border, aircrews had to note details such as the number and state of cars abandoned in a field — right at the instant when they really needed to concentrate on the cargo drop. Pilots were also expected to simulate flying in a combat zone; they could gain points by using terrain to conceal their aircraft within the limits of peacetime rules. That year, all competitors were disadvantaged by the weather. Aircraft arriving at Whenuapai were greeted with rain, and blustery winds blew the descending loads of all three competitors into trees at one stage.

One of the largest annual overseas deployments was into Singapore for the 'Vanguard' and 'Starfish' exercise programme. In September 1992 the opportunity was also taken to engage in dissimilar air combat training (DACT), which gave a first chance to demonstrate the modernised Skyhawks. Pitted against Singaporean and Thai F-16's, British Sea Harriers from No.800 Squadron, and Malaysian F-5's, the Kiwis demonstrated that the 'Kahu' avionics update had paid off. Toting AIM-9L Sidewinders, the Skyhawks could simulate 'kills' even during head-on passes. Opponents had the same missiles but less well integrated weapons systems. The Skyhawks also worked that year with Royal Navy Falcon-20 EW aircraft in simulated maritime strikes against HMS *Invincible*.

The RNZAF contributed to several international relief operations during the 1990s, and there was regular work in the Pacific to support typhoon-struck islands. The first major deployment outside the Pacific came in 1993. Somalia had collapsed into a state of anarchy; a United Nations effort to intervene had failed, and the United States organised a thirteen-nation coalition known as the United Task Force (UNITAF) to stabilise the situation. Three Andovers of No. 42 Squadron flew into Mogadishu in early January. Deployment required very significant employment of RNZAF resources; the Andovers represented a third of the entire inventory. Three out of five Hercules flew support, along with one of the two Boeing 727's. Law and order had broken down in Mogadishu by this time and RNZAF crews were based behind barbed wire and sandbags. Outside the base, even off-duty personnel carried Steyr rifles. The RNZAF impressed UNITAF forces with its ability to set up rapidly. Used to regular deployments into the South Pacific on relief work, the RNZAF arrived in Mogadishu with a complete 'instant camp' — including collapsible showers — packed into a Hercules. They were operating within 24 hours of arrival.

Under US control the Andovers operated up to ten hours a day, flying a regular morning run between Mogadishu, Baledogal, Baidoa and Bardera, a regular afternoon run between Mogadishu and Kismayu, and weekly flights to Nairobi. For the first time in nearly three decades the RNZAF also did a regular leaflet drop. Lessons were learned after the first attempt when leaflets released at 1000 feet remained suspended on thermal updrafts from the deserts below. Sheer chaos in Somalia made flying hazardous; Andover crews faced what were in effect combat missions on a daily basis, carrying full survival gear in case accident problem forced them down. Collision with illegally operated aircraft was another real risk. Warring Somalian gangs relied on imported drugs and guns, and upwards of fifty un-announced flights were made daily. Without a legal flight plan, and usually observing radio silence, these smugglers could appear out of nowhere. However, there were no incidents and the Andovers conducted 233 sorties, carrying a total of 7,620 people and 171 tonnes of freight. Eight million dollars were budgeted for the six month deployment. Of this, the New Zealand Defence Force provided just over five million — cribbed from other planned spending. A joint forces exercise was one casualty, releasing nearly $3 million for the Somalia deployment. The rest was found by cuts across the whole of the NZDF.

The RNZAF returned to Africa the following year to join another peace-keeping effort, this time for the United Nations. In April 1994, the Hutu-dominated government of Rwanda began a genocidal attack on their principal opponents, the Tutsis. The Tutsi-dominated Rwandan Patriotic Front responded with a major military campaign which toppled the Hutu government. Some two million Rwandans fled the escalating violence, including many Hutus who feared reprisal after their defeat. The result was a refugee crisis in Zaire to which the United Nations responded with an extensive relief effort. The RNZAF contributed a Hercules, NZ7002, which flew to Entebbe airport in late July with thirty six personnel under Wing Commander Graham Lintott.

Based in a camp adjacent to the hulk of the 'Entebbe raid' Boeing 707, the New Zealanders ferried supplies from Entebbe to the main refugee camp at Goma. Although the Hercules was scheduled to stay only a month in Africa, operations were extended to six weeks at the request of the United Nations. In that time the aircraft carried some 3,501,700 lbs of freight, primarily milk powder, beans, other food, shelter, and utensils. They also carried 257 passengers. Mission availability was very high, and the New Zealanders achieved up to three flights a day, adopting combat-style unloading — keeping the aircraft rolling down the runway while pushing cargo out the rear door — to reduce ground time. Lintott later said that his crews wanted to carry at least one pound of freight for every New Zealander, and by their last flight on September 15th had exceeded their goal. The Hercules carried more freight than any other single aircraft during the deployment.

There was work in Bougainville at the end of 1997, where a nine-year civil war had been resolved through New Zealand intervention. Operation Belisi — taken from pidgin for peace — despatched Kiwi military forces to the island to oversee the truce negotiated in November, supported in part by Hercules NZ7005. First flight on 20 November from Whenuapai took the reconnaissance teams to Buka; the Hercules returned overnight to New Zealand and with a new crew the next day carried personnel from the 2nd Engineer Regiment and their equipment, destined for Bougainville island itself to restore Aropa runway and enable flights directly to the island. A Wasp and three Iroquois, painted bright orange, deployed in support of regular army units. The New Zealanders were unarmed — and had arrived to monitor a truce rather than a peace treaty.

Search and Rescue: Queen's Birthday 1994

The most public post-war role of the RNZAF — though secondary to its primary function — was search and rescue. Helicopters transformed the ability of the service to pluck stranded trampers from isolated mountains or lift injured people from remote areas. The distinctive sound of an approaching Iroquois or sight of the white-and-grey Orion over storm-tossed waters became familiar to many stranded New Zealanders through the 1970s and 1980s. The service even rescued livestock during the harsh southern winter of 1992.

Nothing during those years could compare to the massive effort of Queen's Birthday weekend 1994, when storms overwhelmed a yacht race to Tonga. The RNZAF deployed all available resources to assist, working with navy and civil services for five exhausting days. What began as a simple search for one yacht, the *Destiny*, turned into a hunt for ten. Two sailed to safety; twenty one people were rescued from seven vessels. One boat, tragically, was lost with all hands. The search was co-ordinated in the National Rescue Co-ordination Centre (NRCC), on the ground floor of Aviation House in Lower Hutt.

For the Orion crews, it was an exhausting and moving experience, the ultimate test of training and equipment. Their only direct contact with the boats was by radio, and the sound of frightened voices brought home just how serious the situation was on the tossing seas below. A 5-Squadron Orion TACCO interviewed in 1996 said then that the five-day ordeal remained sharp in her memory; a legend among the crews.

Nobody could have anticipated the intensity of the storm that brewed up northeast of New Zealand during 4-8 June 1994. Winds of 70-80 knots whipped the sea into 15 metre swells, difficult even for large vessels to handle. The yachts were overwhelmed. In the early hours of 4 June the *Destiny* activated her emergency beacon, and within half an hour of the alert, the crew of the duty Orion at Whenuapai had been assembled. Pre-flighting took a further ninety minutes, and the aircraft took off into the storm. With a good fix from the emergency locator beacon (ELB) there was no problem locating the stricken yacht. However, wind and seas had dismasted the vessel. Aircraft captain Flight Lieutenant Bruce Craies, talking to *RNZAF News*, said it was 'a quantum leap worse than we had expected.' One of the crew were injured. Craies signalled a nearby merchant and circled the damaged vessel, calling every thirty minutes to reassure the sailors. After fourteen hours in the air, much of it cruising on two engines, the Orion recovered safely to Fiji. Meanwhile, a second aircraft was prepared at Whenuapai under Wing Commander Craig Inch to monitor the *Destiny* until seaborne help arrived. By this time a further distress call had been received from the *Heartlight*, and Inch took the Orion to look for her. He found the yacht and again directed assistance before returning to Whenuapai after 13 hours in the air.

All this stretched the resources of No.5 Squadron, and No. 40 Squadron were called into help. Hercules NZ 7001 took off at 0630 into the search zone — a massive area of storm-tossed ocean encompassing nine million square miles — to relieve Inch's P-3. But other priorities intervened; the Hercules was diverted instead to the aid of another yacht, the *Sofia*. Her locator beacon was operating and the RNZAF required only ten minutes to locate her. The Hercules loitered for 35 minutes while rescue was co-ordinated. Then an ELB signal was received from the *Quartermaster*, and the Hercules diverted to look for her. They found only the empty liferaft.

Craies and his crew re-entered the search on 5 June from Fiji. During a twelve hour flight they were able to assist four boats and relocated the liferaft of the *Quartermaster*. One of the boats, the *Pilot*, was not equipped with an emergency locator beacon, but was picked up during the night when the crew spotted the beam of a hand-held torch. Behind the scenes, No.5 Squadron Maintenance spent more than 25 hours working on Orions between 1000 hours Saturday and 0800 hours on Monday.

A fifth flight of more than 15 hours helped keep in touch with four boats. The sixth sortie began on 6 June, again under the command of Inch. The seventh sortie was by Flight Lieutenant Craie's crew; they had spent 42 of the past 71 hours in the air and were very tired. Tasked with keeping in contact with the dismasted *Waikiwi II*, they also searched without success for the *Quartermaster*; and an eighth sortie was launched under Flight Lieutenant Andrew Ward to look for survivors. Unfortunately it was to no avail.

Night Submarine Hunt

Anti-submarine warfare remained the prime rationale of the RNZAF's Orion fleet. Submarine hunting is an arcane science, a game of blind man's buff where technology and physics are backed with a keen understanding of how people think — the old adage of destroyer captain versus the U-boat commander still holds true. Radar, infra-red cameras and droppable sonobuoys only give a partial picture which has to be completed with skill, thought and experience. In May 1996, I joined 5 Squadron No.3 crew on board No.5 Squadron Orion 01 for a six hour night practise against HMAS *Otama*, a conventional *Oberon*-class boat cruising in the Bay of Plenty.

As night descends over Auckland we file on board the waiting Orion. A usual crew is twelve; today we have fifteen on board, including myself. We spend over an hour pre-flighting the aircraft, delayed slightly by two unexpected power-outages, and I'm on the flight deck for takeoff at 1700 hours.

The submarine lurks in a pre-determined square east of the Coromandel coast, twenty miles by thirty. It's been ordered to intermittently poke an exhaust pipe above the surface and run its diesel. That will make radar discovery easier, but if the sub captain detects the Orion's radar he'll dive deep.

We descend early to 500 feet and reconnoitre. The aircraft captain warns the crew to put on life-jackets, a regulation requirement below 1000 feet. Still called a 'Mae West', the jackets are kept on wooden hangars near the aft bulkhead and have CO2 inflation as well as an emergency radio. Other safety gear on board includes two dinghies and half a dozen neoprene dry-suits, lifesavers if the aircraft ditches into cold water. These precautions are sensible but the risks are low; the RNZAF has built up nearly 100,000 hours Orion time since 1966 without accident.

We bring the radar up for a quick look. The sea is alive with shipping; merchants, a few fishing boats — the radar even picks up a pod of dolphins. Flares to the north cause alarm. For a moment I wonder if the exercise might turn into a real search-and-rescue, but we realise the flares are coming from a naval exercise. There is another alarm when radar reports a target advancing towards us at 200 knots. It has no lights, but we know the Australians have an HS-748 (airliner version of the Andover) on an electronic warfare (EW) mission near our search square. 'We've got to think about flight safety here,' mutters the pilot. After a few minutes we realise we've found a pod of dolphins. The 'wave' as the pod undulates has fooled the radar. Tracking 'bio' is one of the little-known tasks performed by No.5 Squadron for scientific purposes.

We get down to business. Six aircrew work search equipment down the port side of the Orion's fuselage. Known as the 'tac rail', this is the nerve centre of the entire operation, combining data from sonar, radar, infra-red detection system (IRDS) and magnetic anomaly detector (MAD). The search is directed by the Tactical Co-ordinator, (TACCO) at the fourth console; he can also issue directions to the pilot.

On this particular aircraft, Acoustics 2 station has an experimental PC-based display system able to handle frequencies up to 2000 hz. The Acoustics 1 station retains its Second World War vintage AQ/A5 processor — an archaic device that burns a real-time printout of sonar data on to sensitive paper. It is only good for sonar frequencies up to 300hz, and will be replaced if the computer trials prove successful.

Around 2000 hours we enter the search area and drop an X-shaped pattern of sonobuoys. These cylinders are stowed aft; the ordnanceman, Sgt AOM Karsten, loads them into an ejector unit, ready for firing from the TACCO's console. The Air Force use various sonobuoys, all obsolescent — the ageing electronics fit on the Orion prevents them adopting the new ones. Tonight we are using passive AN/SSQ-41B LOFAR buoys — Low Frequency Analysis and Recording. These float in the water and listen, but most foreign navies have gone on to the more capable DIFAR and DICASS systems.

Some sonobuoys fail — not too surprising, as they are flung out of an aircraft cruising at 200 knots. The rest begin reporting, their messages appearing as vertical lines on a computer display. The operator points out propellor noises from a merchant we've already picked up by radar, outside the search area. Lights on the top of each buoy are visible from the flight deck as we fly past.

An hour passes. We fly a square spiral search pattern. The pilot, Flight Lieutenant van Klei, reports 'wings level' as we complete each manoeuver — it's hard to tell inside the fuselage just what the aircraft is doing after a while, but the quality of data can be affected. The TACCO pages between the sensor inputs of his crewmates, dropping sonobuoys and keeping his finger on the pulse of the hunt. There is no sign of the Otama.

Tension rises. Yardley says the search is the most important part of the operation. 'To make things happen for us... the thing we practise the most is the search... if we have not got an attack in within the first fifteen minutes of him detecting us, then the chances of success have decreased.' Radar is brought up intermittently — a constant scan would alert the submarine. About 2100 hours we spot a suspicious radar contact to the north — and as we line up to have a look the infra-red cameraman calls that he's found the sub, much closer, snorkelling to the west. In fact, Otama has been following the merchant outside the planned search area. There are murmurs about the Aussies not playing fair. The TACCO calls for the searchlight, a 60,000 candlepower lamp on the starboard wing. From the flight deck I see the periscope and snort masts of the Otama in the beam.

We eject a smoke canister and run back, dropping sonobuoys. This time the radar operator shouts 'MAD, MAD, MAD.' We have flown directly over the submarine. A temperamental device in the 'sting' at the tail picks up magnetic anomalies caused by the hull of a submarine. It only works at very short ranges. Sometimes the RNZAF's elderly example doesn't work at all — I hear the comment 'MAD u/s' over the intercom several times during the evening.

Interpreting MAD data is another arcane task. The device produces a rolling paper printout similar to a seismograph. In theory, deflections indicate an anomaly in the Earth's magnetic field — perhaps a submarine. But this only works when the Orion is flying wings-level. Manoeuvering also creates deflections. So the graph includes a readout of manoeuvers, allowing the operator to eliminate 'false alarms'.

Armed with MAD and sonar data, we make a simulated attack run. The Otama has gone deep, but we've got the boat pinpointed. The Australian captain doesn't realise he's been "sunk" several times when he's finally called up on radio. We have three hours to go and arrange a series of cat-and-mouse exercises, flying out twenty miles before coming back to pick him up again.

Disappointingly, the Australian boat doesn't manoeuver much. The Orion poles around in tight circles, five hundred feet above the water. For several hours we make attack runs, drop sonobuoys, and track the boat with the MAD. Around 0010 hours, it's all over; we turn for home, tired but elated.

Back on the ground, Van Klei taxies Orion 01 to the end of the runway into the water-spray system. We sit for a minute with engines running; the propellers help sluice fresh water across the aircraft, an essential anti-corrosion measure after prolonged operations low over the sea.

The Macchi saga

In 1991 the RNZAF took delivery of its first new aircraft for twenty years. Three Aermacchi MB-339CB advanced trainers were handed over on 19 April in a ceremony attended by the Minister of Defence and officials from Aermacchi and Rolls Royce at Ohakea. Fifteen more aircraft followed in groups of three at six monthly intervals. The type was intended to replace the Strikemasters, but early service life proved troublesome — an awkward issue at a time of political sensitivity about military purchases. The type received a good deal of unjustified criticism as a result. In perspective, these difficulties were no worse than those likely to be found on any new and complex aircraft, but the political context exaggerated the situation.

Selecting the Macchi was not easy. By the late 1980s the Strikemasters were approaching their airframe fatigue limits and needed rplacing, but the pressure was on to keep the cost down. The RNZAF required a proven design with stress data to make sure they would get twenty years' airframe life. At the same time the aircraft had to have up-to-date avionics. The RNZAF also wanted something 'off the shelf', avoiding a repeat of British experience with the Short Tucano. Eleven aircraft types from ten manufacturers were examined; the list included the Pilatus PC-9 and the Alpha Jet. Some types, like the Siai-Marchetti 211A, were cheap but not ready to fly. Meanwhile, plans were laid to extend the life of the Strikemasters until the new aircraft arrived. Complete new wings were fitted to six aircraft, coupled with a careful inspection regimen. Manoeuvering restrictions were applied to seven Strikemasters, including rolling and spinning limitations and strict G-limits. Counting strain-gauges were fitted to all aircraft. Despite these efforts, airframe hours remained limited and one Strikemaster was retired in 1990 for fatigue reasons. Only six remained in unrestricted flying condition by early 1991. Pilot intake had already been reduced in 1989 in anticipation of shortages.

By then the list of replacements had boiled down to the capable but expensive British Aerospace Hawk, or the Aermacchi MB-339C. Pilots liked the Hawk but apart from the cost it was a major jump from the Airtrainer. That left the Aermacchi, also the cheapest of the types on offer which still met Air Force requirements. The Macchi MB-339 was derived from the earlier MB-326. Customers of MB-339 A- and B- models included the Malaysians — who had purchased a number of Viper 632 powered MB-339A's — and Argentina, Peru, Dubhai and Nigeria. By the late 1980s, Aermacchi had built over 160 and switched production to the C model, which incorporated new avionics and an upgraded Rolls Royce Viper engine. The particular advantage of the C-model over its predecessors was the advanced avionics. From the RNZAF's perspective the Viper engine also offered advantages; it was a well proven design with which the service was already highly experienced, though the Viper 680-43 offered with the Aermacchi MB-339CB was a higher powered model than the units fitted to the Strikemasters.

Fiscal constraint was a key issue. The decision passed through eight committees, culminating in a contract signed in March 1990. The purchase included eighteen aircraft with 9500 hours guaranteed flight time, equating to service well into the 21st century. It also provided full engineering support, pilot training — including a simulator — spares backup, technical advice, and foreign exchange cover.

The Macchis turned out to be a delight to fly, and their advanced avionics were a useful lead-in to systems on the Skyhawks. However, there were problems. First hint of difficulty came during early operations when wet runway operations resulted in a number of flame-outs. After analysing video recordings the RNZAF discovered that water thrown up from the nose-wheel was being sucked down the engine intakes. New nosewheel chines cured this difficulty.

More serious trouble came in September 1991 when the first of four compressor-stall incidents occurred during slam acceleration. These were not consistently repeatable on any particular engine, so until a full cure could be found restrictions were placed on the flight envelope. This had a service implication because the primary restriction, requiring the aircraft to maintain greater than 240 knots indicated airspeed (KIAS) below 5000 feet, prevented *ab initio* student pilots from completing solo training. Acceleration stalls were eventually traced to the Air Fuel Ratio Control Unit, which was in effect flooding the engine as it accelerated through an area with a narrow operating stall margin. The root cause was that the unit was not well matched to the Viper 680-43. Rolls Royce advised raising engine idling speed and developed a modified fuel unit. Compressor stalls during rapid engine deceleration were traced by Rolls Royce to the Pressure Ratio Switch, which was also modified.

Then in mid-1992 an engine was stripped after a pilot reported vibration, and the centre engine bearing was found to be close to collapse. Another engine stripped in early 1992 after only 300 hours service revealed corrosion within the casing and what were euphemistically called 'minor build discrepancies including some fitting damage'. The discovery was surprising; the engines had been delivered with a specified 1000 hour time between overhaul.[3] Modifications were devised by Rolls Royce and applied incrementally over the next two years during scheduled maintenance periods at RNZAF Base Woodbourne.

Then in October 1993 an Aermacchi was lost; NZ 6465 crashed into a Northland swamp after engine failure. The aircrew ejected safely. Coming in the wake of the type's engine problems, this could have spelled a serious blow to the programme, but when the wreck was examined it was found the failure was caused by foreign object ingestion — a known operating hazard. Another Macchi, NZ 6460, suffered moderate damage in a night crash at RNZAF Base Ohakea after another engine failure induced by foreign object ingestion, and was sent back to Italy for rebuild in the factory jigs, returning to service in early 1997.

Other possible problems were identified in the location of crucial wiring looms. These had been laid across flexing parts of the airframe and were considered by RNZAF engineers to be a potential long-term maintenance headache. As the aircraft aged, the RNZAF concluded, insulation would become worn and short circuits would occur. It was an assembly issue that could have been picked up during construction had resources been available — the service had been unable to send enough personnel to Italy to inspect every aircraft during every step of the assembly process. Negotiations followed with Aermacchi, and a preventative fix was developed under warranty. More engine problems surfaced in early 1995, when cracks were found during routine maintenance in zero and first stage compressor blades of several engines. A 300 hour restriction was imposed on engine life until the problem could be cured. The Defence Scientific Establishment (DSE) and Rolls Royce discovered the cracks were the result of high crushing stresses in the blade/disk interface. As an interim solution, Rolls Royce removed a SERMETAL coating from the base of the blades to reduce crushing stresses and provide a 200-hour life 'Improved Standard' compressor blade.

All these problems affected serviceability, but the RNZAF's own maintenance expertise helped make good the problems, and by early 1996, eight to ten of the seventeen trainers were flying. Of this number, six or seven were typically available for daily operations — more than for many months previously. The RNZAF also conducted a spares and support exercise to improve the availability of critical parts. More aircraft were brought back into service during the year and by mid-1997, when the oldest Macchis were approaching their first major service point, virtually the whole fleet was operational. However, further cracks in the first-stage compressor blades were discovered during routine inspection at the end of the year, and a 220-hour life restriction had to be imposed.

Retrenchment and a new century

The last decade of the twentieth century was difficult for the New Zealand armed services. The run-down of the defence sector matched the deliberate run-down of New Zealand government services and in many ways was similar to the experience of sixty years before. However, history did not quite repeat. In the post-Vietnam, post-Cold War generation, neo-liberalism reigned supreme and the military were popularly viewed as an out-dated dinosaur absorbing scarce money that could be spent on health, education and social welfare. In practise, as was clear by the early twenty-first century, the policies that followed merely transferred the results of production to those already wealthy, at the cost of fiscal spending on every level, and then at the expense of low-to-middle income earners. But that took a generation to become obvious.

In 1980s New Zealand, public defence perceptions still focussed on invasion — a remote scenario. The New Zealand Defence Force did not attempt to counter this view; nor was this possible from within the service. There was little media effort to encourage an informed public debate of the defence issues that New Zealand actually faced, still less to discuss the position, role and function of the military in the post-Cold War world. The RNZAF was caught up in this malestrom.

With hindsight, the reality was that the end of the Cold War had not changed the fundamental *modus operandi* of the international political system. By the middle of the 1990s there was official international condemnation of any nation testing nuclear weapons, and the arsenals amassed by the Cold War combatants were dwindling. However, the end of the Cold War did not resolve world problems. Conflicts masked by the overwhelming influence of the super powers re-emerged, and regional wars suddenly became possible. In this circumstance, New Zealand's defence credibility remained entwined with its foreign policy and, with that, its trading opportunities. Under these circumstances, military spending needed to take due place, however modest, alongside continued state spending on health, welfare and education.

The defence issue was particularly important in terms of New Zealand's relationship with South East Asia. By this time some forty percent of New Zealand's trade was with East Asian nations. Ethnically complex, subject to competing interests of outside powers, and rich in resources, South East Asia contained some of the world's fastest growing markets and economies during the early part of the decade. The area was also one of the world's most rapidly militarising regions. All the so-called 'Asian Tigers' improved their defences during the 1990s, re-orienting from counter-insurgent to more conventional forces. The number of submarines in the region rose from 89 to 400 between 1991 and 1997. Asia was responsible for a quarter of the world's entire defence budget by the end of the decade, and the only part of the world where defence spending grew faster than inflation. Although there was no arms race, the possibility of serious tension following an economic recession could not be ignored — and the feared downturn was under way as the 1990s came to a close. New Zealand's ties with the Five Power Defence Arrangement were important under these circumstances. The FPDA was the strongest alliance within the area and a powerful diplomatic instrument.

The threat for New Zealand was not invasion, but damage to trade routes and trading interests. War did not have to break out for this to have an effect, as the late 1980s experiences in the Persian Gulf demonstrated. There were certainly plenty of potential flash-points in the Asian region. One of the most serious arguments was over the Spratly Islands. The archipelago was claimed by six nations — China, Vietnam, the Phillipines, Malaysia, Brunei and Taiwan — each wanting oil reserves thought to lie beneath. The Straits of Malacca, between Singapore and Indonesia, suffered from piracy. To be a credible voice in this region, New Zealand had to be seen to be able to contribute to any international effort to keep the peace.

This was recognised at political level in Australia, where there was continued commitment to an effective military as a vital part of national identity, presence and credibility. Australia embarked on steady military development during the 1990s, introducing airborne tankers, over-the-horizon radar, new frigates, and investigating AWACS aircraft — capabilities that enabled the Australians to fight an effective war unsupported. New Zealand's dwindling defence spending was a significant worry in Canberra, where there was repeated criticism that New Zealand was not pulling its weight in the special defence relationship. Actual numbers underlined the situation. As the 1990s came to a close Australia fielded six submarines against New Zealand's none, ten major surface ships against New Zealand's three, 174 aircraft against New Zealand's 32, and 108 utility helicopters against New Zealand's fourteen.[4]

These realities were understood within New Zealand government circles — and even outlined in a 1997 White Paper on defence — but did not override the fiscal issues. Fiscal policy and the general reform of the state sector during the decade had fundamental effect on the RNZAF, which was entirely subject to government policy and funding. Some changes were dictated by the 1989 State Sector Act and reflected general government sector reforms. Corporate plans were adopted in 1993, though the military were not a corporate organisation. An RNZAF 'Mission Statement' was issued at the end of 1997, redolent with 'corporate-speak' but including a list of values that upheld the history and tradition of the service.

This emphasis on history, tradition, service and allegiance to New Zealand highlighted a philosophical paradox of the day. Private sector concepts derived from the need to maximise return to shareholders by minimising expenses and maximising output; there was a mentality that devolved all activities to cost-quantifiable levels. Despite the profusion of terms such as 'empowerment' and 'teamwork', people were often regarded as merely another cost to be quantified and minimised. The military, by contrast, had a historical role as one of the more important defining elements of national identity. People were the life-blood of the military, and the kind of commitment required was absolutely unique; they had to risk their lives, and the human values associated with this activity could not be described by numbers on a neo-liberal balance sheet. History had already demonstrated this in action; the real value and cost of Jimmy Ward's selfless climb on to the burning wing of his Wellington or Lloyd Trigg's determined attack on a U-boat after all hope was gone could not be quantified in dollar terms.

In this sense most private sector euphemisms sat poorly in the military context. Defence forces were by nature consumers of taxpayer funds, not producers; and the 'output' as a contribution to national identity and credibility could not easily be quantified in monetary terms. The 1991 White Paper, wrapped as it was in an environment of neo-liberal zeal, cautiously admitted that when considered 'simply as a business', defence had 'some complex features'[5] — meaning issues with asset valuation and erratic large capital purchases. Nevertheless, government during the 1990s continued to impose a variety of private-sector jargon terms and private-sector concepts on the military services. Defence activities were described as 'national security outcomes' and there was a 'purchase agreement' by which the New Zealand government contracted its Defence Forces to supply a variety of 'services' and 'outputs'.

The moral gulf between such corporate-style terminologies and the fact that, implicitly and in practise, military service required those in it to die for their country, was clear. However, the state dismissal of human worth and endeavour in anything other than dollar terms underscored the nature of the government-driven change imposed across New Zealand from the mid-1980s. A brief boom gave way to a catastrophic stock market crash in 1987, followed in the early 1990s by the deepest economic downturn since the Great Depression of the 1930s. For the military, financial constraint was predictable in the wake of the Cold War; but it was intensified by New Zealand's difficult economic position, a downturn caused in large part by the neo-liberal revolution itself, whose architects continued to flog their ideological horse long after it was clearly dead. The drive to reduce the scale of government services presented as punitive and invalidating for all New Zealand's public services, including the military, made more severe by the fact that responsibility for reform at operational level devolved to the departments targeted by the ideological juggernaut.

For the RNZAF this meant significant creativity and adaptability on the part of virtually everybody within the service. Even maintenance came in for attention. Locally fabricated parts were found able to do the job of foreign imports at a fraction of the cost. Practical savings included expedients such as fitting civilian rather than military Global Positioning System (GPS) units in some aircraft. The Defence Scientific Establishment (DSE) discovered that indigenously developed training software — and the ordinary office computers that went with it — could be flown in the Orions, a rock-bottom cost approach that revolutionised the ability of the old aircraft to hunt submarines.

Nevertheless, there was also an absolute decline. The Cessnas and Friendships were taken out of service in the early part of the decade; navigation training was transferred to RAAF East Sale in New South Wales in 1993. Base closures and rationalisation followed. RNZAF Te Rapa and RNZAF Shelly Bay closed their doors. There was speculation that either Wigram or Woodbourne would also be shut down, but the decision to close Wigram in March 1993 was a shock because of the position the base held in service tradition. From June 1993, Wigram's personnel services were steadily relocated under the aegis of Project Recast. Command facilities moved to Auckland; the flight training to Ohakea, and ground and command training went to Woodbourne.

Wigram formally closed on 14 September 1995. By this time the base, widely considered the birthplace of the RNZAF, had been in constant use by the Air Force for more than 75 years. Events to mark the closure included a fly-past by CT/4B Airtrainers, and a graduation ceremony for pilots of No 1/94 Pilots' Course. The Queen's Colour was paraded and the base ensign lowered for the last time. Air Vice-Marshal John Hosie observed in a booklet marking the event that the decision was 'one of the most difficult to make during my term of office.' A few personnel remained until the doors finally shut on 31 December.

Further retractions were imposed during 1996 and 1997. An ongoing drive to find efficiencies continued — even extending to paint schemes. Reducing camoflague to one shade of green for the Skyhawks was estimated to save $30,000 per annum. The Andover fleet was reduced to four in 1996. Three King Air B200's were leased as a multi-engine trainer and to provide limited VIP transport; maintenance was contracted to Pacific Aerospace

Corporation Ltd (PACL). CT/4B maintenance had already been contracted to PACL during 1997 as part of a general move towards shedding all but the 'core' functions. An extension to this arrangement came in November when the RNZAF announced that it would be leasing thirteen new-model Airtrainers from PACL to replace the fifteen older B-model aircraft on inventory. The CT/4E Airtrainer had more modern instrumentation and a more powerful engine with improved performance, and was also quieter than the CT/4B. Catering was privatised as well, and the maintenance functions at the No.1 Repair Depot in Woodbourne were offered for commercial management at the end of the year.

The Wasps were replaced after a contest that came down to a choice between the Kaman SH-2F/G Sea Sprite and Westland Super Lynx. The Sea Sprite was selected in March 1997 and purchased in a two-step deal expected to cost $274 million. This was a direct outcome of the age of the Wasps — aircraft had to be available for the first ANZAC class frigate *Te Kaha*. Under arrangements finalised in March, the RNZAF took delivery later that year of four refurbished SH-2F Sea Sprites, enough to provide helicopters for two frigates, as an interim measure while four new-build SH-2G Sea Sprites were built for delivery in the year 2000. A fifth was confirmed in late 1997 to equip a third navy frigate, but at that stage no more were envisaged because of the political decision to run the navy down to a three-frigate fleet. The Sea Sprite itself derived from a 1950s design, but had been progressively updated to reflect changing technology. The Australian Defence Force ordered eleven Sea Sprites at the same time.

Work also got under way on an Orion airframe upgrade. The Orions were built with 'fail safe' structure utilising 7075T6 alloy, but hard work at low altitude made the RNZAF's aircraft world leaders in airframe fatigue, and by 1996 the aircraft were under a hundred-hour inspection regime, with flight restrictions. Part of the problem was that while the behaviour of the original airframe could be anticipated, nobody could predict the fatigue characteristics of repairs. Four fixes were explored, ranging from new aircraft to refurbishing second-hand examples. Lockheed studies confirmed that the most cost-effective option was a structural replacement programme. From this emerged Project Kestrel, designed to extend the life of the Orions for 20 years. Components that needed replacement included outer wing assemblies, horizontal stabiliser, centre section lower skin planks, and nacelle longerons.

A $71 million contract was signed in May 1995 with Lockheed Martin Aeronautical systems, which sub-contracted the wing manufacture to Daewoo of South Korea and the horizontal stabilisers to Jetstream of Britain. Phase II contracts to fit these components were signed in May 1997 with Australian company Hawker Pacific, a month ahead of schedule. Assembly was not a simple task. The wings were an integral part of the airframe, and removing them weakened the fuselage to the point where distortion was a very real risk. The first set of wings were shipped to Sydney in June that year, and the first Orion was delivered to Australia in November for the six month reconstruction. The RNZAF hoped to have all six aircraft rebuilt by the end of 2000. The flip side of the structural work was a much needed avionics upgrade. This was long-planned, but final political commitment did not come until late 1997. A White Paper issued at the end of the year admitted that there were 'serious deficiencies in the Orions' sensor suite that impair its ability to carry out both surface and sub-surface surveillance tasks.'[6] The cure was Project Sirius, designed to bring the aircraft's reconnaissance and anti-submarine capabilities up to late twentieth century standards.

The same White Paper confirmed the three-pronged service structure favoured by Morrison nearly forty years earlier, including the air attack force. This had seemed under threat earlier in the year, prompting semi-public debate between Air Force and Navy over the distribution of defence dollars. A sign of the straits the RNZAF perceived itself to be in was the release in April of a booklet entitled *Have you ever had to justify your existence?* However, all that was apparently put behind. Writing in *RNZAF News*, Air Vice Marshal Carey Adamson explained that the RNZAF now had a 'solid foundation to go ahead'.[7]

The review proposed an 'investment plan' amounting to $435 million by 2002, and an increase in the RNZAF's annual budget from $352 to $417 million. It confirmed that the Skyhawks would receive further updates — principally airborne laser designators and better weapons — and the Orions would get modernised avionics. It proposed that the Hercules would be replaced one-for-one with new C-130J models; options had been taken out for aircraft, attached to an Australian order. Warning of 'risks where speed of deployment or withdrawal is important', the report also confirmed 'fast jet transport capability'[8] — which meant replacing the Boeing 727's. No specific new type was suggested, although late-model Boeing 737's had been mooted.

Maintaining capabilities in the three essential arms of the service — maritime, transport and attack — were seen as vital, because as the experience of World War Two had shown, it was quicker to expand existing capabilities to meet an emergency than to generate them from scratch. However, the increases did not compensate for the steady erosion of the prior ten years. While the White Paper admitted that increases were needed to 'sustain a credible defence effort in the future', the review it was derived from was operating under fiscal restrictions deriving from short-term political focus. At policy level, the White Paper looked forwards twenty years and noted that international developments usually happen more quickly than military capability can be gained or expanded. But its recommendations were constrained by a coalition agreement signed barely twelve months previously, and by government policy intended to run state spending down to less than thirty percent of GDP.

These points underscored the fact that the government reforms of the late twentieth century, primarily driven by narrow ideological conviction rather than practical need, continued to constrain New Zealand's longer-term prospects at many levels, well after the reform period itself had been dismissed as a failed experiment. However, for the RNZAF the initiatives to renovate existing airframes, exploit Kiwi ingenuity, and find new operational efficiencies seemed likely to hold the service in good stead into the new millennium. There was an enthusiastic determination to remain a viable arm of the New Zealand military; and with the winds of the new millenium dancing around it, the service looked to its sixty year tradition as inspiration for the future.

EPILOGUE
Into the new millennium

I wrote *Kiwi Air Power* during the mid-1990s, a period when New Zealand's military — and, indeed, New Zealand as a whole — was undergoing a period of significant change. That change did not stop. Between the time that the manuscript for *Kiwi Air Power* was delivered to the publisher in late 1997, and the moment when the book was ready for release to trade in October 1998, the Royal New Zealand Air Force had undergone a further review. Just *six weeks* after *Kiwi Air Power* was published, the government announced that the Skyhawks were going to be scrapped, replaced by 28 General Dynamics F-16A Block 15OCU and F-16B two-seat trainers on a ten-year $200 million lease-to-buy arrangement.

These aircraft had been originally ordered by Pakistan in 1990 but had fallen victim to a Congressional arms export ban, and had been sitting at Davis-Monthan Air Force Base, semi-mothballed in 'flyable hold' status with about six hours on the airframes. They were close to brand new, the F-16 was still being built as current front-line military technology, and it seemed that New Zealand was about to enter the supersonic jet fighter age. More than one reviewer lamented the fact that I had 'missed' the news by just a few weeks — though in fact, publishing process being what they are, my text had actually been completed a year earlier. Such is the nature of writing a history book that is also required to be 'up to date', meaning it must finish with an endlessly moving 'present'.

But the point was moot, because the F-16's never arrived. The Labour government that came to power in late 1999 initiated a significant defence review that led, in 2001, to the decision to not only cancel the F-16 purchase but to scrap the combat wing altogether. The news was greeted with howls of protest both from the service and from very enthusiastic air-minded aviation fans across the country. Enthusiast-focussed books with titles such as *Topped Gun* followed, lamenting the end of nearly sixty years' worth of air combat operations.

None of this stopped the withdrawal of the combat wing over the next year or so. And in the widest strategic sense it reflected the way government had analysed the situation. Apart from estimated savings over a decade of around $870 million, the shift reflected a fundamental reorientation of New Zealand's defences away from the needs of a twentieth century with its world wars and global power blocs, towards the more fragmented and complex world of the early twenty-first, towards a world in which New Zealand was not an appendage of Britain but a small nation standing on its own merits on the world stage. In this new world, the government saw New Zealand's best contribution, as a small nation seeking to take the lead as a responsible citizen, better oriented towards peace-keeping duties and humanitarian support.

So the Skyhawks and their jet-trainer brethren, the Aermacchis, ended up in storage in Blenheim — and remained there, shrink-wrapped against the weather, for over a decade until a buyer could be found for some of them.

This reorientation was a new step both for the RNZAF, and for New Zealand generally. And that suggested to me, as I contemplated re-publishing *Kiwi Air Power* some 20 years after I had first mooted it, that to simply update the book with the 'latest' developments — the tragic Iroquois crash of Anzac Day 2010 (which unfolded before and during a radio interview I was giving to promote another of my books), the final retirement of the Iroquois, the introduction of Boeing B-757's as VIP transports, the overseas deployments, the ongoing Antarctic work, and so forth — would not work. The themes and ideas of my original text had been oriented around a clear and discrete period in New Zealand's history, an era of great world wars and of large-scale international threats and alliances. This characteristic twentieth century cycle had come to an end in the 1990s, overlapping the rise of a new focus on international peace-keeping and humanitarian work — and pre-dating the emergence of a very different dynamic to the twenty-first century.

All these issues, it seemed to me, would need a new book with its own themes. A book that could not be written instantly, not least because the themes of the early twenty-first century were far from fully emerged or played out. Kiwi Air Power, meanwhile, could take its place as the tale of the service during decades when New Zealand's priorities were framed by its colonial history, decades when world politics revolved around great wars and huge alliances. That time had quietly come to an end in the 1990s, overlapped by the new world of brush-fire conflicts and wars that were not overtly fought by professional military — but where, tragically, the front line was the cities of the developed nations. The potential for future large-scale wars was, of course, always present; but in the first decades of the twenty-first century, at least, the notion of air forces deploying vast bomber wings, backed by fighters that pitted hero-pilot against hero-pilot, seemed somehow out of place

Endnotes

Chapter One

1 Matthew Wright 'Sir Joseph Ward and New Zealand's Naval Defence Policy, 1907-1912', Political Science, Vol 41 No.1, July 1989; see also Matthew Wright 'Australia, New Zealand and Imperial Defence Policy 1909-13', MA Thesis, Massey University 1986 pp 72-93.

2 *Ibid* pp 96-101.

3 NA AIR 118/18 Information concerning the New Zealand Air Effort during the Second World War p 3, citing *Defence Department Annual Report 1914* p 11 Sect. 24.

4 For general analysis of this colonial society see Matthew Wright *Hawke's Bay — The History of a Province* esp. chs 3-5.

Quoted in Paul Harrison *RNZAF Base Wigram 1916-1995*, p 4.

6 *Ibid* pp 4-6.

7 WTu MS Papers 2183 , 'Royal New Zealand Air Force: Brief History of Development up to the Outbreak of War'.

8 NA AIR 102/3/3, Flight Lieutenant A T de Nevill 'Treatise' 3 May 1933,

9 See Wright *Hawke's Bay* p 26.

10 WTu MS Papers 1912, Martin Coll., J Martin 6 July 1918.

11 NA AIR 102/3/1 Report: Air Defence of New Zealand: Colonel Bettington (1919), hereafter cited as Bettington (1919).

12 NA G2/16 Despatch No. 696/09 'Proceedings' p 47.

13 NA N10/4, Admiral Lord Jellicoe, 'New Zealand Report' III p 4.

14 See Wright 'Australia, New Zealand and Imperial Defence Policy'

15 Jellicoe to Admiralty, 24 October 1919, in Reginald Bacon *Life of John Rushworth, Earl Jellicoe*, Cassell, London 1936.

16 Bettington (1919).

17 Bettington (1919), Bettington to Allen, 5 June 1919.

18 Quoted in Harrison *Wigram* p 6.

19 Bettington to Allen, 5 June 1919.

20 NZPD Vol 137, 6 August 1920 pp 14-15.

21 WTu MS Papers 2183-8, 'Royal New Zealand Air Force'

22 NZPD Vol 195 p 640.

23 Quoted in Harrison *Wigram* p9.

24 AJHR 1927 B-1.

Chapter Two

1 NA AIR 102/3/3

2 See e.g. Tony Simpson *The Sugarbag Years* p 13.

3 Quoted by Harrison *Wigram* p 13.
4 Quoted in *ibid.*
5 AIR 102/1/1 Report: Defence of New Zealand, Major-General Sinclair-Burgess (1933).
6 NZPD Vol 248 p 1170.
7 *Ibid* p 1171.
8 NA AIR 102/3/3 A Nevill, Treatise.
9 Cited in *ibid* p 262.
10 See *ibid* p 264-66.
11 NZPD Vol 246 p 539.
12 NA AIR 102/3/3 Report: Defence of New Zealand, Wing Commander T M Wilkes (1936)
13 *Ibid.*
14 *Ibid.*
15 *Ibid*, appendix 'The case for a Japanese invasion of New Zealand'.
16 *Loc cit.* Flight Lieutenant Arthur Nevill 'Notes on Air Defence Policy — New Zealand'; also attached papers.
17 NZPD Vol 246 p 546.
18 NA G5/111, SSDA to Governor General, 5 August 1937.
19 NA AIR 118/8 Information concerning New Zealand Air Effort during the Second World War, History of the RNZAF to the outbreak of war pp 34-35.
20 NA AIR 1 102/4/1 R A Cochrane 'Report on the Air Aspect of the Defence Problems of New Zealand, Including the suggested Duties, Strength, and Organisation of the New Zealand Air Force'.
21 *Ibid.*
22 *Ibid.*
23 *Ibid.*
24 *Ibid.*
25 Ross p 1 indicated that the Air Force Act 1937 was passed that day, but it did not go through the House until November, see 'Air Force Act 1937', NZ Statues 1 + 2 Geo VI, Session II.
26 NA AIR 102/3/3 Report: Defence of New Zealand, Wing Commander T M Wilkes (1936)
27 NA AIR 118/18 Information concerning New Zealand's Air Effort during the Second World War, Flying Training in New Zealand.
28 *Ibid.*
29 NA AIR 102/4/1 Cochrane to Saunders, 20 December 1938.
30 NZPD Vol 248 p 1160.
31 *Ibid*, pp 1175-76.
32 'Air Force Act 1937', NZ Statues 1 + 2 Geo VI, Session II.
33 NA AIR 102/4/1, Cochrane to Saunders, 20 December 1938.
34 See NA AIR 118/18 Information concerning New Zealand's Air Effort during the Second World War, Flying Training in New Zealand pp 1-2.
35 NA AIR 102/4/1, Cochrane to Saunders, 20 December 1938.
36 WTu MS Papers 2183 'Secret: Royal New Zealand Air Force' (1943 report)

Chapter Three

1 NA AIR 118/18 Information concerning New Zealand's Air Effort during the Second World War, Section A: Statistics Relating to New Zealand's Air Effort.
2 For more details see Paul Harrison, Brian Lockstone, and Andy Anderson *The Golden Age of New Zealand Flying Boats*, Random House, Auckland 1997 pp 66-72.
3 For more details see *ibid* pp 80-93.
4 A more detailed description is in *ibid* pp 188-196.
5 From interview by author with Piet van Asch, February 1991.
6 *Ibid.*
7 *Ibid.*

8 For further details see NA AIR 118/18 Information concerning New Zealand's Air Effort during the Second World War, Flying Training in New Zealand
9 WTu MS Papers 2183 'Secret: Royal New Zealand Air Force' (1943 report)
10 NA AIR 118/18 Information concerning New Zealand's Air Effort during the Second World War, Flying Training in New Zealand p 7
11 Von Dadelszen private papers, 403615 Pilot Officer Michael von Dadelszen.
12 Desmond Scott *Typhoon Pilot* p xvi.
13 WTu Neal Papers MS 1494, A McLeod to Mrs Neal
14 *Loc. cit.*, E Fancy to Mrs Neal & Ellen
15 *Ibid.*
16 N Wynn private memoir
17 WTu MS Papers 3900, A J Bradshaw Memoir
18 *Ibid.*
19 WTu MS 1390 Martin Papers , J L Martin to parents, 18 August 1942
20 NA AIR 12/15/8 RNZAF Archives Ottawa, Secret Minute, September 1943
21 WTu MS 1390 Martin Papers , J L Martin to parents, 7 September 1942
22 *Loc. cit.*, William Vesey to 'everybody', n.d.
23 *Loc. cit.*, A M McLeod to Mrs Neil & Eileen, 26 December 1941
24 *Loc. cit.*, A M McLeod to Mrs Neil & Eileen, 16 March 1942
25 *Loc. cit.*, A P Wedding to Mrs Neil, 22 September 1942
26 *Loc. cit.*, William Vesey to 'everybody', n.d.
27 *Loc. cit.*, A P Wedding to Mrs Neal, 22 September 1942
28 *Loc. cit.*, A M McLeod to Mrs Neil & Eileen, 26 December 1941
29 *Loc. cit.*, A M McLeod to Mrs Neil & Eileen, 26 October 1941
30 NA AIR 12/15/8 RNZAF Archives Ottawa, Monthly Survey No. 1, 1 June 1943.
31 *Loc. cit.*, Monthly Survey 12, 1 June 1944.
32 WTu Martin Papers MS 1390, J L Martin to parents, 6 December 1942
33 WTu MS 1591 Boot Papers, L M Boot 1944 diary
34 Recounted by Bill Houlton to author, 20 October 1997.
35 WTu MS 1494 Neal Papers, Alan McLeod to Eileen and Mrs Neal, 27 June 1942
36 *Ibid*
37 WTu MS 1390 Martin Papers, J L Martin to parents, 17 February 1943
38 NA AIR 12/15/8 RNZAF Archives Ottawa, Monthly Survey 5, October 1943.
39 *Loc. Cit.*, Monthly Survey 20, 7 March 1945.
40 AIR 100/8 Air Vice Marshall Isitt Correspondence, 4 September 1944
41 *Ibid.*
42 Wtu MS Papers 2446, H G Miller letters to his family,.
43 *Ibid.*
44 Bradshaw memoir
45 For detail on the formation of these squadrons, see NA AIR 118/18 Information concerning New Zealand's Air Effort during the Second World War, Section F: Notes on the New Zealand Squadrons in Europe.
46 Recounted by Bill Houghton to author, 20 October 1997
47 *Ibid.*
48 Von Dadelszen private papers, extract from letter from Pilot Officer Michael von Dadelszen, 21/22/1941.
49 Von Dadelszen private papers, 403615 Pilot Officer Michael von Dadelszen, also J H von Dadelszen, p 23-24.
50 Recounted by Bill Houghton to author, 20 October 1997
51 General Sir William G F Jackson *"Overlord" Normandy 1944*, Davis Poynter, London 1978 provides analysis.
52 NA AIR 118/18 Information concerning New Zealand's Air Effort during the Second World

War, Section A: Statistics relating to New Zealand's Air Effort. Figures were: 348 casualties in te Pacific, 3190 casualties in Europe, Asia and Middle East, 1680 of these with Bomber Command.

53 NA AIR 100/8 Air Vice Marshal Isitt correspondence, extracts from letter by Group Captain T W White. White could not remember whether it was Feltwell or Stradishall.

54 NA AIR 167/9 Account by Wing Commander H A Williamson of ops with 75 Squadron, two letters 3 July 1947.

55 For full details see Errol Brathwaite *Pilot on the Run* Hutchison, Auckland 1986.

56 WTu MS Martin Papers MS 1390, J L Martin to parents, 22 March 1944.

57 WTu MS Papers 2183 'Secret: Royal New Zealand Air Force' (1943 report).

58 His nickname was a corruption of 'Maori', a nickname he had gained in the RAF because he was a New Zealander.

59 NA AIR 167/9 Account by Wing Commander H A Williamson of ops with 75 Squadron, two letters 3 July 1947.

60 *Ibid.*

61 NA AIR 100/8 Air Vice Marshall Isitt correspondence, extracts from letter by Group Captain T W White, 14 November 1944.

62 *Ibid.*

63 NA AIR 118/18 Information concerning New Zealand's Air Effort during the Second World War, Flying Training in New Zealand p 20.

64 WTu MS Papers 1390, James Martin to parents, 2 February 1945.

65 *Loc. cit.*, James Martin to parents, 7 May 1945.

66 *Loc. cit.*, James Martin to parents, 29 September 1945.

Chapter Four

1 W S Churchill *The Second World War* III pp 157-58

2 Hughes private collection, E C Glanville to his wife 3 August 1941

3 *Loc. cit.*, E C Glanville to his wife 19 September 1941

4 *Loc. cit.*, E C Glanville to his wife 6 October 1941

5 McCarthy p 10

6 Hughes private collection, E C Glanville to his wife 12 October 1941

7 *Loc. cit.*, E C Glanville to his wife, 9 October 1941

8 NA AIR 102/5/1 Misc. Malayan Campaign notes by RNZAF officers, Flight Lieutenant C W Frank 'Report on squadron equipment activities overseas'

9 *Ibid*

10 Hughes private collection, E C Glanville to his wife 12 November 1941

11 *Loc. cit.*, E C Glanville to his wife 20 November 1941

12 *Loc. cit.* E C Glanville to his wife 30 November 1941

13 *Loc. cit.*, E C Glanville to his wife 3 December 1941

14 Described by McCarthy p 18.

15 The Walrus incident is more fully described in Harrison *et al The Golden Age of New Zealand Flying Boats* p 91

16 W S Churchill *The Second World War* III p 531.

17 Hughes private collection, E C Glanville to his wife, 11 December 1941

18 *Loc. cit.*, E C Glanville to his wife, 5 January 1942

19 *Loc. cit.*, E C Glanville to his wife, 10 January 1942

20 NA AIR 102/5/1 Misc. Malayan Campaign notes by RNZAF officers, Captain N H North Memo forwarded to Minister of Defence 14 May 1942.

21 *Loc. cit.*, Flight Lieutenant C W Frank 'Report on squadron equipment activities overseas'

22 Hughes private collection, E C Glanville to his wife, 14 January 1942

23 *Loc. cit.*, E C Glanville to his wife, 20 January 1942

24 *Loc. cit.*, E C Glanville to his wife, 26 January 1942

25 *Loc. cit.*, E C Glanville to his wife, 29 January 1942

26 *Loc. cit.*, E C Glanville to his wife, 2 February 1942
27 Pamphlet in Hughes private collection.
28 Hughes private collection, E C Glanville to his wife 26 January 1942
29 NA AIR 102/5/1 Misc. Malayan Campaign notes by RNZAF officers, Captain N H North Memo forwarded to Minister of Defence 14 May 1942.
30 NA AIR 102/5/1 Misc. Malayan Campaign notes by RNZAF officers, memo by P L Laing, 1 April 1942.
31 *Loc. cit.*, Flight Lieutenant C W Frank 'Report on squadron equipment activities overseas'
32 Described by R Tyers, memoir in McCarthy p 32.
33 Listed in NA AIR 102/5/1 Misc. Malayan Campaign notes by RNZAF officers
34 F A McCarthy 'Running the Gauntlet out from Singapore', *Contact* Vol 1 No. 12, March 1942.
35 Hughes private collection, E C Glanville to his wife 15 February 1942
36 NA AIR 102/5/1 Misc. Malayan Campaign notes by RNZAF officers, Report from OC C & A Flight to CO No.1 NZ ACU, 13 February 1942.
37 Described by M T B Harris, memoir in McCarthy p 38
38 Hughes private collection, E C Glanville to his wife, 26 February 1942
39 NA AIR 102/5/1 Misc. Malayan Campaign notes by RNZAF officers, Flight Lieutenant C W Frank 'Report on squadron equipment activities overseas'
40 NA AIR 102/5/1 Misc. Malayan Campaign notes by RNZAF officers, Memo by Flight Lieutenant P L Laing, 1 April 1942.
41 NA AIR 149/1 No.14 Squadron Ops Record Book April '42 — Sep '45, introductory.
42 WTu MS Papers 3900, A J Bradshaw Memoir
43 *Ibid*
44 WTu MS Papers 4598, Patricia Cole Coll., R Neal to his parents, 18 February 1942
45 Poster in *Contact* Vol 1 No. 12, March 1942.
46 Poster in *ibid.*
47 Frances Ida Kain, 1908-1997.

Chapter Five

1 'Secret: Royal New Zealand Air Force' (1943 report), WTu MS Papers 2183
2 See also NA AIR 118/18 Information concerning New Zealand's Air Effort during the Second World War, Section D: Pacific Operations p7
3 Matthew Wright 'The Royal Australian Air Force', *Air International*, Vol 47, No.2, August 1994
4 NA AIR 118/52 War History Narrative of life in Santo, Base Report, Appendix B-1 RNZAF Station Espiritu Santo. Extract from minutes of conference 5 September 1942.
5 NA AIR 131/24/3 DCAS to AMS, Minute 17 Oct 1942
6 NA AIR 118/52 War History Narrative of life in Santo, Base Report, Appendix B-1 RNZAF Station Espiritu Santo.
7 *Ibid*
8 WTu Micro MS 0842, J E Morgan Diary, 22 September 1942
9 *Ibid*, 26 September 1942
10 NA AIR 118/52 War History Narrative of life in Santo, Base Report, Appendix B-1 RNZAF Station Espiritu Santo.
11 *Loc. cit.*, Interview with W/O M Harris 18-5-48.
12 WTu MS 0842, Morgan Papers, J Morgan diary, 13 October 1942.
13 *Ibid*, 14 October 1942.
14 *Ibid*, 15 October 1942.
15 *Ibid*, 27-28 October 1942.
16 *Ibid*, 10 December 1942.
17 NA AIR 150/12 Personal Narrative of Experiences with 15 Squadron 1942-43, Basil A Berry
18 *Ibid.*
19 NA AIR 150/13 Diary and Narrative of J J Mackie, 15 Squadron in Tonga and Santo, 18

Squadron in Solomons.

20 Berry narrative.

21 *Ibid.*

22 Mackie diary.

23 Berry narrative.

24 Noted in David Duxbury, Ross Ewing, Ross Macpherson *Aircraft of the RNZAF* p 12. The Americans included a 2.5 percent per month depreciation rate and assured the New Zealand government they were getting the aircraft for 25 percent off.

25 Bradshaw memoir.

26 Morgan, 24 & 25 December 1942.

27 *Ibid*, 25 December 1942.

28 *Ibid*, 3 January 1943.

29 Morgan, 11 January 1943.

30 *Ibid*, 15 January 1943.

31 NA AIR 118/18 Information concerning New Zealand's Air Effort during the Second World War, Section D: Pacific Operations p 3.

32 Morgan, 1 April 1943.

33 NA AIR 100/8 Air Vice Marshall Isitt correspondence, 1 October 1943.

34 NA AIR 118/78 Survival Hints for Aircrew.

35 Morgan, 22 April 1943.

36 *Ibid*, 26 April, 1943.

37 NA AIR 149/1 No. 14 Squadron Operations Record Book April 1942- September 1945.

38 Berry narrative

39 NA AIR 149/1 No. 14 Squadron Operations Record Book April 1942- September 1945, 18 June 1943.

40 *Ibid*, 30 June 1943.

41 *Ibid*, 1 July 1943.

42 *Ibid.*

43 *Ibid*, 4 July 1943.

44 Bradshaw memoir.

45 *Ibid*

46 *Ibid.*

47 AIR 100/8, 1 December 1943.

48 AIR 150/13 Diary and narrative of J J Mackie 15 Squadron in Tonga and Santo, 18 Squadron in Solomons.

49 AIR 118/52 War History narrative of life in Santo, Base Report, Appendix B-1.

50 *Ibid.*

51 Mackie diary, 27 October 1943.

52 *Ibid*, 1 November 1943.

53 AIR 149/1 No. 14 Sqn Ops Record Book 8 November 1943.

54 NA AIR 149/1 No. 14 Squadron Operations Record Book April 1942- September 1945, 13 November 1943.

55 *Ibid*, 15 November 1943.

56 Mackie diary, 24 November 1943.

57 *Ibid*, 26 November 1943.

58 AIR 118/52 War History narrative of life in Santo, Base Report, Appendix B-1.

59 AIR 100/8 Air Vice Marshall Isitt Correspondence, 3 March 1944.

60 NA AIR 149/1 No. 14 Squadron Operations Record Book April 1942- September 1945, March 1944.

61 AIR 100/8 Air Vice Marshall Isitt Correspondence, 3 March 1944.

62 *Ibid.*

63 NA AIR 149/1 No. 14 Squadron Operations Record Book April 1942- September 1945, 24 March 1944.
64 *Ibid*, 14 July 1944.
65 Cited in M P Lissington *New Zealand and the United States* p 83.
66 Cited in Robin Kay (ed) *The Australian New Zealand Agreement*, p 206 n. 3.
67 *Ibid*, p 206 n. 4.
68 *Loc. cit.*, Doc. 84, p 206.
69 *Loc. cit.*, Doc 86 p 208.
70 *Loc. cit.*, Doc 87, pp 208-09.
71 *Loc. cit.*, Doc 90 p 211.
72 NA AIR 100/8 Air Vice Marshall Isitt Correspondence, 2 June 1944.
73 *Loc. cit.*, 10 August 1944.
74 *Loc. cit.*, 4 September 1944.
75 For further details see Harrison *et al The Golden Age of New Zealand Flying Boats* pp 160-70.
76 Lissington p 83.
77 *Ibid.*
78 NA AIR 149/1 No. 14 Squadron Operations Record Book April 1942- September 1945.
79 *Ibid*, 31 December 1944.
80 AIR 100/8 Air Vice Marshall Isitt Correspondence, 5 March 1945.
81 NA AIR 149/1 No. 14 Squadron Operations Record Book April 1942- September 1945, 5 April 1945.
82 *Ibid*, 26 April 1945.
83 AIR 100/8 Air Vice Marshall Isitt Correspondence, 3 March 1944
84 NA AIR 149/1 No. 14 Squadron Operations Record Book April 1942- September 1945, 1 August 1945.
85 *Ibid*, 3 August 1945.
86 *Ibid*, 7 August 1945.

Chapter Six
1 N Wynn Memoir
2 *Ibid*
3 *Ibid.*
4 *Ibid.*
5 *Ibid.*
6 *Ibid.*
7 *Ibid.*
8 *Ibid.*
9 *Ibid.*
10 WTu Phillips Papers fMS 3967, Radio log.
11 *Ibid* p 154.
12 *NZ Foreign Policy Statements and Documents 1943-57*, Document 65 pp 293-94.
13 NA AIR 149/2 No.14 Sqn Ops Book January 1955 — December 1960, 3 January 1955.
14 *Ibid*, 29 January 1955.
15 *Ibid*, 25 February 1955.
16 *NZ Foreign Policy Statements and Documents 1943-57*, Doc 106, p 391.
17 *Loc. cit.*. Doc 86, pp336-37.
18 *Loc. cit.*, Doc 102, p 382.
19 *Loc. cit.*, Doc 103a, p 383
20 *Loc. cit.*, Doc 103b, p 384.
21 NA AIR 149/2 No.14 Sqn Ops Book January 1955 — December 1960, March summary 1955.
22 *NZ Foreign Policy Statements and Documents 1943-57*, Doc 106 p 392.
23 NA AIR 149/2 No.14 Sqn Ops Book January 1955 — December 1960, 1 April 1955.

24 *Ibid*, 24 April 1955.
25 *Ibid*, 30 April 1955.
26 *Ibid*, 1 May 1955.
27 *Ibid*, 6 May 1955.
28 *Ibid*, 20 Jan 1956.
29 *Ibid*, 18 June 1956.
30 *Ibid*, 5 November 1955.
31 Cited in Paul Harrison, *Charles 130H*, RNZAF News Special, July 1994, p 4.

Chapter Seven

1 The Canberra in the RNZAF museum is an Australian Mk 20, A84-240.
2 NA AIR 149/2 No.14 Sqn Ops Book January 1955 — December 1960, 8 April 1960.
3 *Ibid*, 6 December 1960.
4 Group Captain Ian Brunton 'Service in South East Asia' in *RNZAF News* November 1997 Vol II.
5 Morrison died in September 1997.
6 Harrison, *Charles 130H*, p 2.
7 NA AIR 23/152/1 Training: ground trades: C-130 aircraft: policy.
8 *Ibid*.
9 *Ibid*.
10 Cited in Harrison,*Charles-130H* p 3.
11 NA AIR 23/156/1 P-3A Technical Services Team Report Appendix C.
12 When the type was developed, US Secretary of Defence Robert S MacNamara favoured equipment 'commonality' between services.
13 NA AIR 23/158/1 Training: ground trades; Skyhawk A4 aircraft: policy. TLO Report for Month Ending 30 June 1969.
14 Cited in Harrison *Wigram* pp 41-42.

Chapter Eight

1 *The Defence of New Zealand*, 1991 White Paper
2 *The Shape of New Zealand's Defence: A White Paper* (November 1997) p 27
3 Reportedly the same engine had also been advertised with a 1200 hour TBO, *Australian Aviation* Jan/Feb 1996 p 24.
4 Figures noted in *White Paper* (1997) p 18
5 *The Defence of New Zealand 1991* p 88
6 *The Shape of New Zealand's Defence* p 49
7 *RNZAF News* December 1997 p 3.
8 *The Shape of New Zealand's Defence* p 51.

Glossary

ADF	Australian Defence Force
AGM	Air to Ground Missile — US designation.
AIM	Air Intercept Missile — US designation for air-to-air missiles.
ANZAC	Australia and New Zealand Army Corps.
ANZUS	Australia, New Zealand and United States — popular name of the alliance signed in 1951 and suspended by the US in 1984.
ASEAN	Association of South East Asian Nations — this grouping dates to the late 1960s and essentially replaced SEATO.
ASPAC	Asian and Pacific Council — formed in the mid-1960s with membership including Australia and New Zealand.
Buttons	Second World War code name for Espiritu Santo.
Cactus	Second World War code name for Guadalcanal.
CDR	Close Defence Relations — specific policy for Australia and New Zealand
CRT	A computer-driven TV display (cathode ray tube) that replaces analog dials in aircraft cockpits.
DACT	Dissimilar Air Combat Training — pitting one pilot and aircraft against a pilot flying a different kind of aircraft.
DFC	Distinguished Flying Cross
DLOC	Directed Level of Capability — acronym to describe peacetime capability levels of the 1990s RNZAF
Doodlebug	Popular name of the Fieseler Fi-103 V-1 flying bombs employed by Germany in the Second World War.

EFTS	Elementary flying training schools
ELB	Emergency Locator Beacon.
FEAF	Far Eastern Air Force, a joint Commonwealth structure of the 1950s.
FPDA	Five Power Defence Arrangement, a defence alliance between Australia, New Zealand, Britain, Malaysia and Singapore.
Gee	Popular name of a radio direction system deployed by Bomber Command during World War Two.
H2S	British airborne radar of World War Two.
HOTAS	Hands on Throttle and Stick — a means for pilots to operate all main aircraft combat systems without taking their hands from the controls.
HUD	Head Up Display — a device for projecting important flight details into the pilot's field of view on some combat aircraft.
KIAS	Knots Indicated Air Speed.
Link Trainer	A mechanical instrument flight simulator used during World War Two.
Maverick	Common name for the AGM-84 guided air-to-ground missile.
MDGT	Mission Data Ground Terminal — a computer for setting up RNZAF Skyhawk missions before flight.
NRCC	National Rescue Coordination Centre — an office operated in Lower Hutt to co-ordinate search and rescue.
NZDF	New Zealand Defence Force
NZPAF	New Zealand Permanent Air Force
NZTAF	New Zealand Territorial Air Force
Oboe	British radio-direction system of World War Two.
OLOC	Operational Level of Capability — acronym to describe operational capability requirement of 1990s RNZAF, a generally higher level than DLOC.
PGM	Precision Guided Munition — any guided weapon, including free-fall bombs and guided missiles.
PTS	Pilot Training School
PX	Post Exchange — supply canteen operated by US forces in the Second World War
RAF	Royal Air Force
RNZAF	Royal New Zealand Air Force

SAM	Surface to Air Missile
SAR	Search and Rescue
Schrage Musik	High-angle fixed guns adopted by Luftwaffe to enable attacks from beneath.
SEATO	South East Asian Treaty Organisation — loose alliance grouping of the early 1950s.
SLAT	Special Logistics Aid to Thailand — aid programme of the early 1960s.
VC	Victoria Cross
WAAF	Women's Auxiliary Air Force
Wimpy	Service nickname for the Vickers Wellington.
WRNZAF	Women's Royal New Zealand Air Force — the name given to the WAAF by Queen Elizabeth II in 1954.

Bibliography

Primary Sources

Alexander Turnbull Library (WTu)

Micro MS 0842 John Edward Morgan diary Sept 1942-April 1943
MS Papers 1390 J L Martin collection
MS Papers 1437 Haldane collection
MS Papers 1494 Neal Family collection
MS Papers 1591 Leonard M Boot collection
MS Papers 1823 H Gladstone Hill collection
MS Papers 1912 John Martin collection
MS Papers 2183 Hon F. Jones collection
MS Papers 2446 H G Miller collection
MS Papers 3900 A J Bradshaw Memoirs
MS Papers ACC 91-326 Henderson collection

National Archives (NA)

AIR 12/15/1 RNZAF Official War History
AIR 12/15/2 History of New Zealand Bomber Squadrons in the UK
AIR 12/15/8 RNZAF Archives Ottawa
AIR 12/15/9 RNZAF History — information from RNZAF
AIR 12/15/11 Unofficial History of 488 Squadron
AIR 12/15/12 Official War History Material
AIR 23/152/1 C-130 Aircraft — Policy
AIR 23/156/1 Orion Aircraft — Policy (2 parts)

AIR 23/158/1 F111 Aircraft — Policy
AIR 23/161/1 Skyhawk A4 Aircraft — Policy
AIR 100/8 Air Vice Marshal Isitt Correspondence 1943-45
AIR 102/1/1 Defence of New Zealand (1933)
AIR 102/3/1 Report: Air Defence of New Zealand: Colonel Bettington (1919)
AIR 102/3/3 Defence of New Zealand (1936)
AIR 102/4/1 Report: Wing Commander R A Cochrane (1937)
AIR 102/5/1 Misc. Malayan Campaign — RNZAF Official
AIR 102/5/4 Report: New Zealand Minister Washington
AIR 102/10/5 New Zealand Preparations for Japanese War
AIR 106/2/1 Scale of Attack on New Zealand
AIR 118/52 War History narrative of life in Santo, Base Report; Appendix B1 RNZAF Station Espiritu Santo
AIR 118/57 No.1 Aerodrome Construction Unit
AIR 123/8/2 Imperial Conference 1926 Air Power and Imperial Defence
AIR 128/1 COMAIRSOLS: Strike Command War Diary Nov 1943-Mar 1944
AIR 139/9 No.3 (BR) Sqn — Operational Sorties Jan 1943-Jan 1944.
AIR 149/1 No. 14 Sqn Operations Record Book April 1942-Sept 1945
AIR 149/2 No. 14 Sqn Operations Book January 1955- December 1960
AIR 150/12 Personal narrative of experiences with 15 Squadron 1942-43 by B A Berry 1942-43
AIR 150/13 Diary and narrative of F/S J J Mackie of Waipukurau; 14 Squadron in Tonga and Santo, 18 Squadron in Solomons Oct-Nov 1943
AIR 167/9 Account by W/C H A Williamson of ops with 75 Sqn
N10/4 New Zealand Report

National Library
Appendices to the Journal of the House of Representatives
New Zealand Parliamentary Debates

Private papers, photographic collections and correspondence
Mark von Dadelszen
Nolan Wynn
S L and I C Hughes
Bill Houghton

Defence publications

RNZAF press releases 1990-97
RNZAF information pamphlets
Defence of New Zealand 1991: A Policy Paper
The Shape of New Zealand's Defence: A White Paper
Vision for the Future
RNZAF News — misc. issues 1990-97

Published Primary Sources

Kay, Robin (ed) *The Australian New Zealand Agreement 1944*, Historical Publications Branch, Government Print, Wellington 1972

New Zealand Foreign Policy Statements and Documents, 1943-1957, Foreign Affairs, Government Print, Wellington 1972

Secondary Sources

Bacon, Admiral Sir Reginald *The Life of John Rushworth, Earl Jellicoe*, Cassell, London 1936.

Ballantine, Colin *40 Squadron, RNZAF — To the Four Winds*, Lodestar Press, Auckland 1985.

Bentley, Geoffrey *RNZAF — A Short History*, A H & A W Reed, Wellington 1969.

Bentley, Geoffrey and Conly, Maurice *Portrait of an Air Force — The Royal New Zealand Air Force 1937-1987*, Grantham House, Wellington 1987

Brathwaite, Errol, *Pilot on the Run* , Hutchison, Auckland 1986.

Crawford, John New Zealand's Pacific Frontline, Guadalcanal — Solomon Islands Campaign 1942-45, NZDF, Wellington 1992.

Crawford, John *In the Field for Peace*, NZDF, Wellington 1996.

Darby, Charles, *RNZAF — The First Decade 1937–1946*, Kookaburra Technical Publications, Melbourne 1978.

Duxbury, David, Ross Dunlop, Ross Macpherson and Ross Ewing *New Zealand Military Aircraft, 1913–1977*, Aeronautical Press, Wellington 1977

Frances, Neil *A Short History of 21 Squadron Air Training Corps, 1942-1992,*

21 Squadron 50th Anniversary Committee, Masterton 1992.

Franks, Norman, *Forever Strong, the story of 75 Squadron RNZAF 1916-1990*, Random Century, Auckland 1991.

Garzke, William H. and Dulin, Robert O. *British, Soviet, French and Dutch Battleships of World War II*, Jane's Publishing Company, London 1980.

Gordon, Bernard K *New Zealand becomes a Pacific Power*, University of Chicago Press, Chicago 1970.

Harrison, Paul *Charles 130H*, RNZAF News Special, RNZAF, July 1994.

Harrison, Paul *D-Day over Normandy*, *RNZAF News Special*, RNZAF, Wellington, April 1994.

Harrison, Paul *RNZAF Base Wigram 1916 to 1995, the end of an era*, RNZAF News Special, RNZAF, Wellington, September 1995.

Harrison, Paul *Send for the Artist*, Random House, Auckland 1995.

Harrison, Paul, Lockstone, Brian and Anderson, Andy *The Golden Age of New Zealand Flying Boats*, Random House, Auckland 1997.

Kennaway, Richard and Henderson, John (eds) *Beyond New Zealand II — Foreign Policy into the 1990s*, Longman Paul, Auckland, 1991.

Larkin, T C (ed) *New Zealand's External Relations*, OUP, Pegasus Press, Christchurch 1962.

Lissington, M P *New Zealand and the United States, 1840-1944*, Government Print, Wellington 1972.

McCarthy, Frank, Singapore Harriers, Pictorial Record of the RNZAF No.1 Aerodrome Construction Squadron, Malaya 1941-42, unpub., Auckland.

Moore, John Hammond, The American Alliance — Australia, New Zealand and the United States 1940–1970, Cassell Australia, Melbourne, 1970.

Russell, Warren P *NZPAF & RNZAF Aircraft Colour Schemes*, Volume 1, New Zealand Aero Products, Invercargill 1982.

Ross, J M S *Royal New Zealand Air Force*, War History branch, Dept. Internal Affairs, Wellington 1955.

Scott, Desmond *Typhoon Pilot*, Secker & Warburg, London, 1982.

Thompson, H L *New Zealanders with the Royal Air Force* (5 Vols), War History Branch, Dept. Internal Affairs, Wellington 1953.

Tsuji, Masanobu *Singapore — The Japanese Version*, trans. Margaret E Lake, Ure Smith, Sydney 1960.

Verrier, Anthony *The Bomber Offensive*, Pan, London, 1974.

Walker, Martin *The Cold War*, Vintage, London, 1994.

Wilson, Stewart *Boeing B-17, B-29 & Lancaster*, Aerospace Publications, Canberra, 1995.

Wright, Matthew 'Sir Joseph Ward and New Zealand's Naval Defence Policy, 1907-1912', *Political Science*, Vol 41 No.1, July 1989.

— 'Aermacchi Trainers for the RNZAF' (*Aviation News*, Vol 20, No.1, June 1991).

— 'Skyhawks Return to Nowra' (*Airforces Monthly*, No. 40, July 1991)

— 'Aermacchi Acquisition to give RNZAF a timely boost' (*Australian Aviation*, July 1991).

— 'Skyhawks Break New Ground in Tasman defence' (*The Canberra Times*, 14 July 1991).

— 'RNZAF Skyhawks Deployed to Nowra' (*Aviation News*, Vol 20 No. 9, September 1991).

— 'Strikemaster troubles not surprising' (*Aviation News*, Vol 20 No. 10, September 1991).

— 'NZ Defence Review of Crucial Importance to Region' (*Australian Aviation*, September 1991).

— 'Not all black for the winged Kiwis' (*Air International*, Vol 42 No.5, May 1992).

— 'Exercises Underline Kiwi Defence Policies' (*Australian Aviation*, No.83, December 1992).

— 'Australian co-operation essential to New Zealand Defence Policy' (*Australian Aviation* No. 90, September 1993.)

— 'The Royal Australian Air Force' (*Air International*, Vol 47, No.2, August 1994)

— 'RNZAF Helicopters' (*NZ Wings*, November 1994).

— 'New Zealand Defence Under Siege' (*Australian Aviation*, December 1994).

— 'New Projects for Air Force' (*NZ Wings*, March 1995)

— 'Refuelling on High' (*Dominion*, 21 March 1995)

— 'Sealift for the Soldiers' (*New Zealand Defence Quarterly*, No. 8, Autumn 1995)

— 'Exercise Willoh — Aus/NZ Refuelling Inaugurated' (*Australian Aviation*, May 1995).

— 'Aermacchi MB-339CB in RNZAF Service' (*New Zealand Wings*, May 1995).

— 'Skytrain tests RNZAF and RSAF transport skills' (*Australian Aviation*, July 1996).
— 'Submarine hunting in the Bay of Plenty' (*New Zealand Wings*, July 1996).
— 'RNZAF P-3K Orions in Transition', (*Australian Aviation*, March 1997).

Index

About the author

Matthew Wright is a New Zealand writer with over thirty years professional experience as a published author and in publishing. His publications include over 60 books and more than 500 feature articles and academic papers. He has qualifications in writing, music and anthropology among other fields, and holds multiple post-graduate degrees in history. He is a Fellow of the Royal Historical Society at University College, London.

Matthew Wright's New Zealand Military Series

Collect the set

IB

www.ingramcontent.com/pod-product-compliance
Lightning Source LLC
LaVergne TN
LVHW050625100826
845148LV00011B/1739
* 9 7 8 0 9 0 8 3 1 8 2 6 1 *